BIKER BILLY'S

 Freeway-a-Fire
Cookbook

Other books by Bill Hufnagle, aka Biker Billy

Biker Billy Cooks with Fire

BIKER BILLY'S

 Freeway-a-Fire
Cookbook

Life's Too Short to Eat Dull Food

BILL HUFNAGLE

William Morrow and Company, Inc.
New York

Library of Congress Cataloging-in-Publication Data

Hufnagle, Bill.
Biker Billy's freeway-a-fire cookbook : life's too short to eat
dull food / by Bill Hufnagle.—1st ed.
p.   cm.
ISBN 0-688-16822-1
1. Vegetarian cookery.   2. Cookery (Hot peppers).   I. Title.
TX837.H793 2000
641.5'636—dc21   99-32426
CIP

Printed in the United States of America

First Edition

1   2   3   4   5   6   7   8   9   10

BOOK DESIGN BY JAMES SINCLAIR

www.williammorrow.com
www.bikerbilly.com

To my wonderful wife, Rachelle, her kind and generous parents, Philip and Martha Barkus, and the memory of my beloved parents, John and Gladys Hufnagle. Together and separately they paved the road that made this book possible.

CONTENTS

Mellow Yellow, a 1968 Harley-Davidson Sportster belonging to
Bobby Tramontin, one of the many fast Harleys that the Tramon-
tins raced.

ACKNOWLEDGMENTS

I have discovered an enduring truth traveling the freeways and back roads of America by motorcycle; that truth is, the people that you meet along the road make the journey a joyful adventure. This truth also applies to the journey of writing this, my second cookbook. Along the road to its completion I have benefited greatly from the help and encouragement of many people. With their help the journey has been a fun and exciting ride.

I would like to express my deep gratitude to all the wonderful people at William Morrow and Company with whom it has been my pleasure to work. To Pam Hoenig, for her vision and enthusiasm, without which this book would not be in your hands. To Jennifer Herman, Kate Heddings, and Lorie Young for their artful editing and light touch that allowed my voice to be heard clearly. To Richard Aquan and Leah Carlson-Stanisic for their fiery designs that make this book a visual delight both inside and out.

A book without images would be like touring without stopping to see the sights. I want to thank everyone who contributed the images that add to the visual fire of this book. First a fiery thanks to Brian Smale and his pyrotechnic crew for capturing the fiery images on the cover of this book (without cooking me in the process). Next a big thanks to W. Atlee Burpee & Company and their wonderful archivist, Barbara Wolverton, for sharing images from their long (124 years) and bountiful history. Then there is another big thank-you for my friends Bub Tramontin and Bobby Tramontin for sharing photos from their Harley-Davidson dealerships, 84 years' worth of history and three generations in the same family. And last but not least a special thanks to Sandy Craig, Dara Derrick, Brent Dugan, and Richard Frost for sharing images from their family photo albums.

I would also like to extend my thanks to all of the kind people who have written in response to the TV show, the first book, and the website; your letters and E-mails are greatly appreciated. And a special thanks to the people who have entered my Viewer Recipe Contest, some of whose win-

ning recipes are in this book. I would also like to thank the tens of thousands of fiery people who have attended my live performances around the country. Cooking for and with you has been a real blast.

And a bonfire-size thank you to George Ball Jr., president and CEO of W. Atlee Burpee & Company and fellow pepper fan for honoring me by naming a pepper after me. I would also like to thank Sharon Kaszan from Burpee for her advice and suggestions about growing hot peppers. My deep appreciation extends to Don Zeidler, Michele Addy, and all my friends at Burpee for their help and support in spreading the fire to gardens across this great nation.

A huge thanks goes to all my friends at Harley-Davidson for their help and support down through the years and for making the freedom machines that I love to ride. Without Harleys to ride, the fire would surely go out.

I would also like to offer a warm thank-you to all my special friends who have shared food, rides, thoughts, and excellent times with me. The road of life would be desolate without you, and although there are too many to list, you know who you are.

In closing I would like to offer my eternal thanks to a very special lady who has been my partner in both life and business for more than half my life. My wonderful wife, Rachelle, has shared the journey on this long fiery road with me and made each mile a joyful adventure.

And lest I forget, thank you for reading this book, sampling the recipes, and sharing the fire with the people you love and hold dear. Eat hot and ride safe!

INTRODUCTION

When we come to the place where the road and the sky collide
Throw me over the edge and let my spirit glide
They told me I was going to have to work for a living
But all I want to do is ride

"The Road and the Sky," Jackson Browne

Life's too short to eat dull food!

Life is a balancing act. There are the things we have to do and the things we want to do. All I want to do is ride. There is a freedom of spirit, an escape from the troubles of this world that can be found only on a motorcycle. Give me the wind in my face, the unending road in front of me, and the throbbing power of a Harley-Davidson beneath me and I am happy. Yes, all I want to do is ride. So where does cooking fiery food come into this? Well, in order to ride I must do something to keep things in balance and put gas in the tank. Thankfully there is something I like to do that runs a close second to riding, and that is to Cook with Fire. I am very blessed to be able to create and share fiery foods with you and all my friends; that is the other side of my personal balancing act. For that I am truly grateful. What a wonderful thing it is for me to be able to fully enjoy both sides of life. Thank you for allowing me to share the fire and the road with you!

I am a follower of a philosophy that can best be expressed as Ride to Eat and Eat to Ride. One look at my amply sized waist will confirm that. Would you really trust a cook who didn't like their own food? Well, it is easy to see that I like the food I cook. And I will be honored if you enjoy the foods you cook from this book. Just remember to share them with your friends or you could end up looking like me. Please don't get the impression that all the

recipes in this book are fattening (happily, though, some are). I just like to sample as much as I like to ride. The recipes are filled with healthy, fresh foods, which are infused with my own biker-style flavor and of course laced with FIRE. And all the recipes are vegetarian.

Surprised that a biker is a vegetarian? Well, if you don't know any bikers personally you would be surprised by who we actually are. Once you get beyond the myths and the stereotypes you will find that bikers come from all walks of life. We work in all professions and we represent every race, creed, and national origin. We are in fact a cross section of America. Yes, we are different from the non-motorcycle-riding public. But that difference can best be understood if you start with the knowledge that we are individuals, not a gang. As individuals we cherish our American freedoms and we place a high value on our rights and your rights, too. We have an appreciation of the beauty and power of nature. And we choose to balance the risks of riding with the joys of experiencing life and nature in a direct and personal way. Nothing ventured, nothing gained, which after all is the spirit that built America. Most of all, we are people who have discovered the incredible joy of living life with a passion. It is that passion that I bring to my food. So if you think that because my food is meat free it will be dull concoctions of twigs and berries, you are wrong. And you are also in for a very pleasant surprise. My food is as robust and exciting to eat as my Harley is to ride.

I couldn't imagine a life without my beloved motorcycles or a life sustained on dull foods. While we must eat to survive, there is no reason merely to feed the body when you can nourish the soul. Food is an edible art form. The perfect dish attracts you with heavenly aromas. Serenades you with the sounds of slicing, dicing, and sizzling ingredients. Excites you with vibrant colors and interesting shapes. Stimulates you with unique and varied textures. And satisfies you with complex flavors. It also makes you feel secure and at peace because food is an edible expression of love as well. It should be easy to prepare. Sounds like a lot to ask of food? Not to me. And if it is my food, I expect it to illuminate you with the warm glow of FIRE. My fiery food is just like riding a motorcycle; it will make you feel alive.

Speaking of rides, the best ones are those that lead to new adventures. And those rides are often better when shared with friends. I feel the same way about cooking. Food should bring you new taste adventures, and sharing those adventures with friends always increases the joy. Most of the people I know who ride motorcycles share a passion for good food. Many times we ride out in search of that special place to stop along the road and enjoy a well-prepared meal together. When you ride a motorcycle you are immersed in the wind, and all that fresh air creates a strong appetite. So when you see a restaurant with a lot of bikes parked outside, you know the food there must be good.

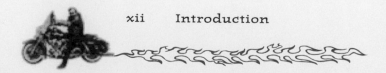

Over the many years I have ridden I have discovered one roadside eatery that caters to my tastes perfectly. There is never a wait for a table, the décor is comfortable, and the service can't be beat. Are you saying what good does that do me if I live on the other side of the country? Well, surprise—there is a location right in your neighborhood, and it happens to be your home. Only at home will you find food cooked exactly the way you like it. Made with the finest ingredients and prepared with love. Every ride, no matter how far it goes or how filled with adventure it is, begins and ends at home. Take it from a well-traveled biker, there is nothing like a good home-cooked meal to add the perfect finish to a perfect ride.

Let this cookbook be your road map to fiery food adventures. But before you run to the kitchen and begin cooking with fire, take a look at the section called Cooking Tips from Biker Billy's Garage. In it you will find lots of useful information—consider it the owner's manual for this book. Just like you would prepare your bike and riding gear before setting off on a motorcycle journey, you should prepare yourself and your kitchen before you cook with fire. I am not talking fire extinguishers and smoke detectors, although those should be in every home. Rather, I am talking about cooking style and attitude. If you have seen my television show you know that I have a tendency to get excited about cooking and make a little bit of a mess. Okay, so I make a real big mess; soon the EPA may declare me a superfund site and call in the guys in space suits to clean it up. You don't have to be as messy as me, but why worry about getting the kitchen a little dirty. Besides, cooking should be fun and this is not Home Economics; you won't be graded on neatness.

If you are new to handling and cooking with hot peppers, the Hot Pepper Rogues' Gallery will help you explore the fire while learning how to avoid getting burned. Handled properly, hot peppers will add a whole new dimension to your meals without adding fat and calories. As a bonus they are also high in vitamin C.

Every day it seems that hot peppers are becoming more common in supermarkets, and are readily available through mail order and even the Internet. However, to ensure that you have a bountiful supply of your favorite varieties of hot peppers at the peak of freshness, there is no substitute for growing your own, and it is easier than you think. In Homegrown Hots I outline the basics of growing your own hot peppers. If you want to enjoy the new Biker Billy jalapeño peppers, which the nice folks at Burpee have developed and named after me, you will have to grow them yourself. Currently they are available as seeds and starter plants only. I am looking forward to producing chipotles and bringing food products to market featuring this fiery new hybrid pepper. Watch my Internet site, www.bikerbilly.com, for developments; the seeds can be ordered from Burpee, toll free, at 1 (800) 888-1447 or on the Internet at www.burpee.com.

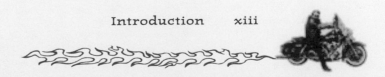

Excluding some hot peppers, almost all of the ingredients in this book are commonly available in your neighborhood grocery store. A few may require a trip to a local health food store. Some of the ingredients I thought required a few words of "Biker Wisdom," so I have provided that information in a section called The Biker's Pantry.

The Sources section at the back of the book lists places where you can acquire hot peppers if your local markets are not already part of the spreading flame of the explosion of fiery foods. And it also contains some useful information on how to get involved in the wonderful world of motorcycling. After you expand your culinary adventures, you may want to join me on the road to adventures in motorcycling.

I believe that cooking should be a fun-filled experience, approached with a carefree attitude. I also believe that anyone who can taste food can be a good cook. You don't need a Ph.D. in boiling water or a silly white chef's outfit to create incredibly good food. So tell all those fancy French gourmets to get real and go for a ride. And while they are out of the kitchen let's have some fun together. Because, after all, life is too short to eat dull food.

Cooking Tips from
Biker Billy's Garage

I've divided this chapter into five sections so you can easily find the information you want. The Hot Pepper Rogues' Gallery will tell you about the hot peppers in this book, and will teach you how to judge their firepower. With that information in hand, you can learn to adjust any recipe in this book to suit your love of fire. It is also a good reference when shopping for hot peppers. If you want to grow your own peppers, the Homegrown Hots section will help you set your garden ablaze with fresh hot peppers, even if you've never grown a thing before. Fiery Tips and Other Stuff has all sorts of useful information about handling and cooking with hot peppers and other handy kitchen tidbits. The Biker's Pantry section is full of information about some of the less common items I cook with and where to find them. And last but not least, Cooking Like a Biker will get you in the mood to start burning up your kitchen with devilish delights. So put on your best riding gear and start Cooking with Fire.

HOT PEPPER ROGUES' GALLERY

In this section I have gathered together the usual suspects. Every hot pepper that is used in the recipes is described and rated in Scoville units. I don't rate my recipes on a firepower scale because everybody has a different tolerance for fire. Instead, I expect you to learn about the peppers you choose and develop an idea about what works in your house. As a method for communicating fire levels with your family and friends, consider the jalapeño pepper as a reference point, since most people have tried jalapeños and can

tell you how they liked them. With a little knowledge and experimentation you can become a master of fire.

The reference chart here contains a list of the most commonly available hot peppers, but it is by no means complete. These varieties provide a tremendous opportunity to begin exploring the thrills of cooking with fire.

As a general guideline I use the firepower scale below. This is based on my personal tastes rather than on a hard scientific rating.

However, there *is* a scientific method used to judge how hot hot peppers are, and to rank them accordingly; this is measured in Scoville units. Scoville units are named after their inventor, Wilbur L. Scoville, who was a pharmacologist working for the Parke-Davis Company during the early twentieth century. The original testing method he developed relied on a group of human testers who assigned a Scoville unit rating to a hot pepper by a consensus of three out of five taste testers. This method has since been replaced by the use of high-pressure liquid chromatography, which measures the amount of capsaicin in parts per million. From a scientific standpoint the new high-tech method is very exact, but it represents the exact firepower of only the sample tested, not the absolute firepower of every pepper in that variety. Hot peppers grow in a vast variety and in a wide range of firepower, with some varieties being very hot and others having just a little zing. Many factors can affect how hot a pepper is, including breeding, soil condition, geography, weather, and time of harvesting. It is even possible for peppers from the same plant to vary in fire level. In the kitchen Wilbur L. Scoville's original testing method of tasting and rating them will provide the final judgment on how hot the peppers you are cooking with really are. So use the following information as a guideline and begin conducting your own hot-pepper test firings; the results are sure to thrill and delight you.

Mild	0 to 2,500 Scoville units
Medium	2,500 to 10,000 Scoville units
Hot	10,000 to 100,000 Scoville units
Atomic	100,000 to 300,000 Scoville units

Since no fire rating for the peppers is given with the recipes, you should use this chart as a guide when cooking with them. Remember that when you add several different peppers together, they combine to create a more intense fire level.

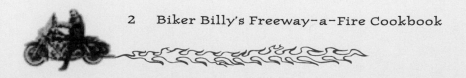

Mild	Anaheim, 500 to 2,500 Scoville units
	pasilla, 1,000 to 1,500 Scoville units
	ancho/poblano, 1,000 to 2,500 Scoville units

Medium	cherry, 0 to 3,500 Scoville units (cherries can be mild, but it is safer to expect medium)
	New Mexico, 500 to 10,000 Scoville units (New Mexico can be mild, but it is safer to expect medium)
	chipotle, 2,500 to 10,000 Scoville units
	jalapeño, 2,500 to 10,000 Scoville units
	Biker Billy jalapeño 6,000 to 10,000 Scoville units

Hot	serrano, 10,000 to 20,000 Scoville units
	guajillo, 10,000 to 30,000 Scoville units
	de árbol, 15,000 to 30,000 Scoville units
	cayenne, 30,000 to 50,000 Scoville units
	Thai, 30,00 to 50,000 Scoville units

| *Atomic* | habanero, 200,000 to 300,000 Scoville units |

The following is a quick reference chart for fresh and dried peppers:

Fresh

Anaheim

Biker Billy jalapeño

Cayenne

Cherry

Chilacas

De árbol

Guajillo

Habanero

Jalapeño

Long, slim red cayenne

New Mexico

Poblano

Serrano

Thai

Dried	Guajillo
Anaheim	Habanero
Ancho	Long, slim red cayenne
Cayenne	New Mexico
Chipotle	Pasilla
De árbol	Thai

Anaheim: Now known as a variety of the New Mexico pepper family, this was formerly the market name given to most chile peppers with this particular pod shape. Anaheims are long (6 to 8 inches), blunt-tipped peppers that can often be found in their fresh green form in supermarkets or Latin groceries. In their green state they have a fresh garden flavor similar to that of green bell peppers, and they become sweeter as they ripen to red. The firepower level ranges from mild to medium (500 to 2,500 Scoville units). You can substitute any of the New Mexico varieties, but some New Mexico varieties may be hotter.

Ancho/poblano: The ancho is the dried red form of the fresh green poblano chile. These heart-shaped peppers are 2 to 3 inches wide and 3 to 5 inches long. When dried, they have a fruity flavor with a wonderful aroma. The fresh green poblano is excellent roasted and stuffed and can be used like an Anaheim or a New Mexico chile. The firepower level is usually mild, but sometimes they achieve a medium firepower rating (1,000 to 2,500 Scoville units). Ancho peppers have a unique flavor for which there is no exact substitute; however, you can use pasilla or dried New Mexico peppers in their place. The flavor will change, but the result will still be enjoyable. Luckily, fresh green poblano peppers are becoming more readily available in large supermarkets.

Biker Billy jalapeño: I am indeed honored by this new hybrid jalapeño named after yours truly and created by W. Atlee Burpee & Company. My good friend George Ball Jr., president of Burpee and a fellow pepper fan, and the team of plant experts at Burpee developed this blazingly hot variety of jalapeño so it would be just like me—big and extra hot. The pods of this jalapeño are large, about 2 inches wide and 3½ inches long, and feature light brown veins on the skin. They are surprisingly hot for a jalapeño pepper. This new hybrid is now available to the public for the first time in seed packets and as starter plants from Burpee, so you may not find them in your supermarket produce section just yet. These peppers are easy to grow and

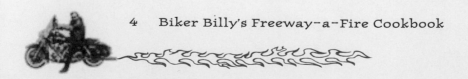

will produce plants that are about 24 inches tall and sprout pods that are ready to harvest in 66 days. The pods start as green and eventually ripen to a beautiful deep red. Use in cooking as you would other jalapeños—just remember they are hotter than you think. The firepower level is still a medium (6,000 to 10,000 Scoville units), but at the high end for jalapeños. The seeds can be ordered from Burpee, toll free, at 1 (800) 888-1447 or on the Internet at www.burpee.com.

Cayenne: This type of pepper is most commonly sold as a powder called ground red pepper or ground cayenne. There are several varieties of cayenne pepper; the primary difference is in the pod size. I have specified the long, slim variety in some of this book's recipes. The long, slim red cayenne pods range from 2 to 4 inches in length and are pencil thin, with a curved, wrinkled shape ending in a fine point. Other varieties can reach up to 1 inch in diameter and 8 to 10 inches in length. Since all sizes are equally hot, you will want to use less of the the larger peppers when substituting for the long, slim red cayenne to compensate for the size difference. They produce a clean, crisp flavor that is acidic and tart, but their heat is more pronounced than their flavor. The firepower level is hot (30,000 to 50,000 Scoville units). You can substitute de árbol chiles, but the heat level will be lower. Also, try the small red chiles found at Asian markets that are sometimes called "Korean peppers." To use ground red pepper as a substitute for whole fresh or dried cayenne, start with a level ¼ teaspoon per whole pepper used in the recipe. You will have to experiment because not all commercial ground red peppers are the same.

If you want to grow your own fresh hot peppers, the long, slim red cayennes are a good variety to start with. I have had success growing them both in the garden and in pots. They produce a good harvest, and the pods can be left on the plant until they are red, with little risk of loss due to rot. They are excellent fresh and freeze very well, giving you a source of fresh peppers all year round. They also air-dry quite nicely.

Cherry: As the name implies, these peppers look like large red cherries when fully ripe. They are most commonly found pickled whole or sliced, in both the green and red stage. You can also find them fresh in supermarkets and at farm stands. They freeze well, which preserves the fresh taste for cooking without the vinegar flavor of the pickled variety. Pickled or fresh cherry peppers are good as a garnish on salads, sandwiches, Mexican foods, and, of course, pizza. The firepower can range from mild to medium (0 to 3,500 Scoville units); rinsing the pickled varieties will slightly reduce the fire level.

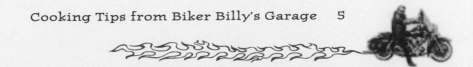

Chipotle: This is the smoked jalapeño pepper. Since jalapeños have too thick a flesh to air-dry well, they are smoke-dried instead. The smoking process produces a wonderful flavor that is quite different from that of fresh or pickled jalapeños. They have a delicious smoky taste and a hint of sweetness, which is produced by the caramelization of natural sugars that occurs during smoking. Chipotles can be purchased as dried peppers or packed in a tomato-based sauce called adobo. I use both types in this book's recipes. The dried ones (once they have been rehydrated) can always be used as a substitute for the ones packed in adobo sauce. If the recipe calls for the dried chipotles and you wish to use canned chipotles in adobo sauce, a light rinse will remove the sauce (if the adobo is undesirable). The firepower level of chipotle peppers is the same as that of jalapeños: medium (2,500 to 10,000 Scoville units); however, the ones from Mexico tend to be more potent.

De árbol: In Spanish, de árbol means "treelike," which describes the appearance of the de árbol plant. These peppers are very similar in size and appearance to the small varieties of cayenne pepper, but they tend to have a straighter pod shape. They may be related to cayenne, but there is some disagreement among the experts. The taste is similar to that of cayenne, and they work well in the recipes that call for cayenne. The firepower level is hot (15,000 to 30,000 Scoville units), so if substituting de árbol peppers for cayenne, start with the same quantity and increase only if more fire is desired.

Guajillo: These peppers are very popular in Mexico, and are frequently found in Latin markets. They are similar in shape and size to New Mexico peppers, but a careful comparison will reveal that guajillos are more tapered and have a pointier tip. Some people claim that these are also related to cayenne peppers. They can be used in place of New Mexico peppers, especially when you want more fire, as they are more potent. The firepower level is hot (10,000 to 30,000 Scoville units), somewhere between the New Mexico and de árbol peppers.

Habanero: The hottest pepper in the world. There are attempts under way to breed a hotter pepper, but the habanero is still the king of fire. These peppers should be handled with care and respect, or you'll get burned. I don't want to scare you away, but it is a warning worth observing. I love these little devils and use them in several of the recipes in this book, because their fire is a real treat. Habanero peppers ripen to a variety of colors from yellow to orange to red and even to brown, and their shape can be described as bonnet-, bell-, or lantern-like. Their size ranges

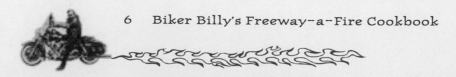

from as small as a dime to the size of a half-dollar. They have a fruity flavor to them, and for me, the fire seems to bloom on the palate as opposed to bursting. There is no substitute for habaneros, but many related varieties of this pepper are marketed under different names, such as Scotch bonnet, rica red, chocolate habanero, and goat pepper. They are most commonly available dried or pickled, but are becoming more readily available fresh at supermarkets, Latin groceries, and farm stands. They freeze very well, and I find that the frozen ones are easier to core without getting the burning juice on my hands (although I always wash my hands thoroughly after handling them, and so should you). These are the definition of hot (200,000 to 300,000 Scoville units), but keep in mind that not every batch has the same firepower. Some will seem mellow and the next batch could be atomic. I have had good results with growing habaneros—even one plant can produce a good harvest—but the peppers may be milder than those grown in a more tropical environment, like Belize or Mexico. When using habaneros in a recipe, be sure to chop the habanero as finely as possible (unless the recipe specifies using it whole or in large pieces and later discarding). This helps to spread the habanero's heat throughout the dish.

Jalapeño: The jalapeño may be the best-known hot pepper in America. The peppers are a staple in salsas, hot sauces, nachos, Tex-Mex, and Mexican foods. You will find them almost everywhere as a pickled condiment (whole, sliced, or chopped), and they can now be purchased fresh, year round, at many supermarkets and Latin groceries. America is in love with jalapeño peppers. The smoke-dried version of the jalapeño is called chipotle (see page 6). Green jalapeños have a crispy, green pepper flavor; when they are allowed to ripen to red, the flavor becomes sweeter. They freeze well and maintain much of their fresh quality after being defrosted. Rinsing the pickled ones will slightly reduce their heat. I have observed that the range of fire in jalapeños can vary from mellow to surprisingly hot; the ones that come from Mexico tend to be hotter. There is even a variety of jalapeños called the Burpee False Alarm hybrid jalapeño that is bred to be milder. At the hotter extreme, there is the Biker Billy jalapeño (see page 4), bred by Burpee, and it is the hottest jalapeño variety I have ever sampled. The firepower of jalapeños is medium (2,500 to 10,000 Scoville units). They make a good reference point for most people when comparing the perceived fire of other hot peppers.

New Mexico: The New Mexico pepper comes in many varieties and was formerly called Anaheim. For a period of time, this pod type was predominately grown in California, hence the name Anaheim. Now that New Mexico is the major producer of these chiles, the name has been changed. And the names are still often confused outside the Southwest. These peppers can be enjoyed in their fresh green state in salsas and salads or roasted, stuffed, and breaded as Relentless Chiles, a tasty recipe from *Biker Billy Cooks with Fire*. They are most commonly recognized as the beautiful dried red peppers strung into ristras, the edible, pepper decoration synonymous with the Southwest. Most varieties of New Mexico peppers ripen to red, but there are others that ripen to vibrant yellow or orange or even brown. These peppers add a full-bodied, earthy flavor that most people will recognize as an essential part of the taste of Mexican foods. The firepower ranges from mild to medium-hot (500 to 10,000 Scoville units).

Pasilla: In Spanish, pasilla means "little raisin," and is the name given to the dried form of chilacas chiles, but you will rarely find them fresh outside Mexico and the Southwest. I occasionally find them at farm stands or hot pepper festivals. In Mexico the pasilla is a part of the trio of peppers used to create their famous mole sauces. The dried pods are about 1 inch wide and 4 to 8 inches long, dark brown to almost black in color, and somewhat wrinkled in complexion. They add a rich flavor with hints of fruit, smoke, and an earthiness that is a welcome addition to foods cooked with anchos or New Mexico chiles. The firepower level is mild (1,000 to 1,500 Scoville units).

Serrano: These bullet-shaped chiles range from 1 to 3 inches in length and about ½ inch in diameter. Very popular in Mexico, they can also be found in the United States, fresh or pickled, in Latin groceries and some supermarkets. They are more common in their green state and produce a clean, sharp fire; when red they become a little sweeter. The red and green can be freely interchanged. Excellent in salsas and sauces, these chiles can replace jalapeños when you want to add more fire to a dish. The firepower level is hot (10,000 to 20,000 Scoville units).

Thai: These are sometimes called Thai Dragon. They are small, thin peppers about ¼ inch in diameter and 1 to 2 inches long. They can be found fresh or dried in Asian markets, where the fresh peppers are most often green, with red ones occasionally available. In terms of firepower, they range from equal to that of jalapeños to up to six times as hot (30,000 to 50,000 Scoville units). I have also seen identical peppers marketed as Korean peppers or bird peppers. You can also substitute cayenne or de árbol peppers for Thai peppers.

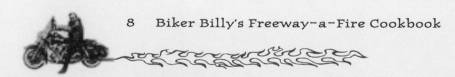

HOMEGROWN HOTS

Why should you grow your own hot peppers when they are becoming more available in supermarkets? There are many good reasons. Freshness, quality, selection, and pride are four undeniable ones. The peppers that you pick only moments before you cook with them (or freeze them) will be days, if not weeks, fresher than store-bought. From your garden, you can pick peppers at peak harvest time for the best flavor, color, and texture. Store-bought peppers are picked earlier so they will still be of acceptable quality after the time spent in transport and distribution to your local market. You can grow those peppers you desire the most, including varieties that are rare, if not unobtainable, in many markets. And last, but not least, there is pride. If you have not yet grown food from seed, cooked it, and shared it with friends and family, you are depriving yourself of a great joy.

Let me share some of my own homegrown biker philosophy. In many ways, the act of growing your own food is a vital part of the history of the American experience. Consider that the people who settled here in America cherished a direct connection with the land and the bounties it could bring forth. Stories like John Steinbeck's *Grapes of Wrath* speak of Americans and their connection with farming and the land. You can participate in that pride and connect with that experience in a small way by growing your own hot peppers. I believe that you can gain a lot of personal satisfaction by growing even a small part of the food you eat. In the past few decades, we have become so detached from the sources of our food and, as a result, we have lost some intangible connection with life's deeper meaning. It may sound like a lot to expect from so simple an act as growing hot peppers, but the seed is there.

I have a whole book's worth of information on growing hot peppers and gardening that I will one day soon share with you. In the space I have available here, I want to share the basics, which should help get you started on the road to growing your own hot peppers. Hot peppers are, in general, very easy to grow—much more so than, say, tomatoes. You can successfully reap a good harvest in almost any part of the continental United States. If you have a growing season of as little as 66 to 95 days, good seeds, and a small amount of sunny space, you're well on the way to hot pepper paradise.

Let's begin with planning. The first thing to consider is the length of your local growing season. This should be defined by the average number of days between the date of the last possible frost in spring and the first possible frost in the fall. The United States Department of Agriculture divides the country into "hardiness zones" (as shown in the diagram on page 10) that will give you a rough guide to your growing season. But the most accurate information can be acquired from your local garden supplier or university

Find Your
Hardiness Zone

This USDA map divides the country into Plant Hardiness Zones based on average lowest winter temperatures (see chart below). To determine the correct time for seed starting and transplanting for your garden. Find your location on the map, determine your Zone and follow the recommendations for your Zone on the seed package.

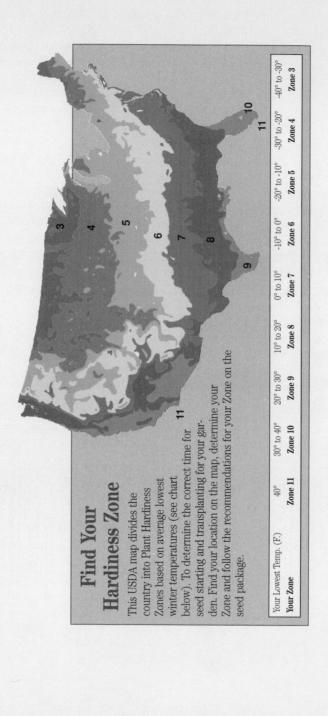

Your Lowest Temp. (F)	40°	30° to 40°	20° to 30°	10° to 20°	0° to 10°	-10° to 0°	-20° to -10°	-30° to -20°	-40° to -30°
Your Zone	Zone 11	Zone 10	Zone 9	Zone 8	Zone 7	Zone 6	Zone 5	Zone 4	Zone 3

farm extension program. With this information, you can select the varieties of peppers that will successfully bear mature pods (fruits) in your area.

Most seed and plant sources will provide an indication of the average number of days a particular variety needs to produce mature pods. This is the time from when baby plants are transplanted into the garden (often referred to as "set in the garden"), and does not include the time from when the seeds are started until they are ready for transplanting. When you are starting plants from seeds, planning becomes very important, since the time from starting seeds to transplanting averages between 8 to 10 weeks. As an example, if the last frost in spring occurs in mid-April, you should be starting seeds in the beginning of February. (There are ways to shorten this time that will be covered later.)

Companies such as Burpee now can deliver baby plants (including the Biker Billy jalapeño) right to your home at the right time for transplanting, with the shipping timed to arrive for weekend gardening. Whether you are starting your peppers from seeds or ordering baby plants, try to order early. Baby plants are becoming more popular and can sell out, and if your schedule is busy, having the seeds a little early helps ensure a timely start.

Now that you have selected the pepper varieties that will successfully grow in your area, let's consider the quality of seeds. Although pepper plants are usually very hardy and grow almost as easily as weeds, their seeds are very sensitive to damage by exposure to moisture. So the storage and handling of them is important. One reason I recommend using Burpee hot pepper seeds is that they store and package them in a climate-controlled environment. Their patented "Life Lock" packaging protects the seeds from moisture until you open them. Plus, Burpee's standard for viability exceeds government standards; this means that you receive seeds that will actually grow. It is important to consider that when pepper plants of different varieties are grown near each other, they may cross-pollinate. Although this will not affect that year's pods, the seeds from those pods may not deliver plants the following year with the same fire levels. So it is well worth buying fresh seeds each season.

To start seeds successfully does not require a green thumb or years of experience. All you need are good containers, good soil, water, and lots of sunlight. I like to use containers that have individual cells as opposed to one large planting area. This allows you to separate the baby plants easily without damaging the roots. I also like containers that allow for watering from the bottom (these have small holes in their bottoms). This is good for several reasons: First, bottom watering won't wash away the seeds before they germinate; second, the plants are encouraged to develop strong root structures that will reach deep for the water (top watering can have the opposite effect); and last, bottom watering, with good drainage, helps to prevent drowning the seeds and reduces the occurrence of root rot. Another feature

that is desirable to seed growth is a clear dome that covers the container, which will help prevent the soil from drying out too rapidly (most homes have dry air due to heating during the time of year that you will be starting seeds).

In terms of soil, I have used everything from just plain dirt from the garden to all kinds of special packaged soil mixes. I have achieved the best results from using specially blended mixtures for seed starting, and I believe that the use of a soilless seed starting mixture is critical to achieving the best results. The reason is simple: Soilless seed starting mixtures don't have the harmful soil organisms that will kill young seedlings regardless of how well you are raising them. Also they provide a perfect balance between drainage, water retention, and aeration, which creates the optimum environment for germinating seeds. As a bonus, the seeds have enough nutrients to support healthy growth during this critical stage. Seed starting mixes are available in compressed pellets, which are perfectly sized to fit into small seed starting cells. There are even ones that, once rehydrated, become their own biodegradable pot filled with starting mix. With all these special-purpose products, success is not only easy but also downright convenient.

Before you start your seeds, you will have to choose a location in your home that has a stable temperature between 65° and 75°F, and is not exposed to direct sunlight. Direct sunlight at this stage can dry out the soil and can cause surprising increases in temperature. It is also a good idea to look ahead and make sure you will have enough space available in sunny windows (at cooler room temperature) when the seedlings emerge. As a rule, seeds need a warm temperature (closer to 75°F) to germinate, and a cool temperature (closer to 65°F) with plenty of light to grow into strong, stocky seedlings. I once got so ambitious starting seeds that I had to turn our sunny enclosed porch into an emergency greenhouse with plant trays and electric heaters everywhere.

To start the seeds, gather your chosen containers, soil, and a watering can filled with warm water, leaving the seeds in their packages at this point. Fill all the containers with soil (don't pack them solid) and add enough warm water to completely moisten the soil. Allow the containers to drain so the soil is moist, not soaking wet. The soil should be at room temperature. Now is the time to label your containers, especially if you are growing several varieties (most pepper plants look alike until they bear fruit). Place about three or four seeds into each container and cover with about ¼ inch of moistened soil (or according to package directions). This is critical, since some seeds do not require covering. Gently pat down the soil and, if your container comes with a dome, cover it. If your container does not have a dome, you can use small pieces of wood dowels (or even plastic forks) to support a tent of clear plastic wrap over the container. Covering the soil like this will help retain moisture and stabilize soil temperature. Check the seed

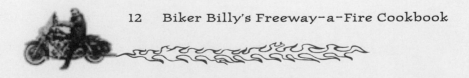

containers every 2 to 3 days. If they appear to be drying out, water or mist them to maintain moist (not wet) soil. On average, seedlings should emerge in 10 to 21 days (consult the seed package for more exact timing). You can shorten this amount of time by using a device called a seed propagation mat. This is an electric heating unit that you set the seed trays on; it is designed to raise the temperature by a few degrees and uses a special thermostat to frequently vary the temperature so as to, in effect, simulate nature, albeit a warmer climate. The plant trays are not in direct contact with the waterproof heating element, and air is allowed to flow freely around the tray to prevent cooking the seeds. Don't try to use a regular heating pad (for obvious safety consideration) to save time.

As soon as the first seedlings emerge, remove the dome (or tent) and move the containers to a sunny window in a room with cooler temperature (and remove them from the heating pad if you used one). Continue to check the soil for moistness as before, and water as needed. Rotate the containers in relation to the window to keep the seedlings growing straight, since they will grow toward the sun. After the seedlings are about 1½ to 2 inches tall, thin out all but the healthiest seedling in each (cell) container. Do this by pinching off the weak seedlings at the soil level; do not pull them out, as this may damage the one you want to keep. The reason for thinning the seedlings is to allow the strongest plant to grow uncrowded and with no competition for nutrients, water, or sunlight. Two plants in one cell does not get you more—it just gets you two weak plants in one cell.

During the last 2 weeks before transplanting, you will need to "harden off" the little plants. Placing them outside, weather permitting, for a little while each day will do this. Start with about 1 hour a day and increase until they move outside completely, again weather permitting. This process will help reduce the shock of transplanting. The exposure to gentle breezes will strengthen the plant stems and they will also receive stronger sunlight, which is not filtered by the glass of your windows. During this period, you can start to feed the plants with a weak fertilizer, using care to avoid too strong a fertilizer, which can burn the delicate little plants. When the danger of frost and cold weather has safely passed and the plants are hardened, it will be time to transplant them.

Meanwhile, as the plants are hardening, prepare the soil in your garden. Preparation of a garden and its soil is a large topic unto itself, much too large to cover completely here. As a general guideline, however, your soil should provide a balance of good drainage, water retention, and aeration, plus an ample supply of nutrients and the correct pH (acid level). Your local garden supplier can provide valuable information about soil conditions in your area as well as being a source of supplies to improve your soil.

In a garden, most pepper plants should be planted about 2 feet apart in

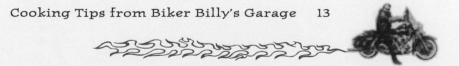

rows that are 2 to 3 feet apart (consult the seed package for more exact spacing). I have also used pots. With pots, I tend to transplant them to a small pot first, then retransplant them into larger pots as they grow. Most pepper plants will do well in pots that are about 18 inches in diameter. It is best to have the plants in their final pot before they start to flower so as to avoid disturbing them at this phase. In most cases, they should be in their final pot about halfway through the period of time they are expected to produce pods.

Transplanting is rather simple (just remember to label the plants as you transplant them). Dig a small hole about 2 inches deeper and wider than the root ball of the plant. Add enough seed starting or potting soil to the bottom of the hole so that the top of the root ball will be about ½ inch below the surrounding ground level. Gently remove the small plant and its block of soil from the container and place it in the hole. Fill in with more seed starting or potting soil, firmly pat down the soil, and water thoroughly. I like to use seed starting or potting soil when transplanting because I believe it gives the roots an easier time when they are spreading into the surrounding soil. I also like to gently loosen the root ball before placing it in the hole, especially if the roots seem to be wound around the block of soil. Another little trick is to pour a small amount of the weakly fertilized water into the bottom of the hole before placing the plant in it.

From this point on, the plants do most of the work. All you need to do is water them and remove weeds on a regular basis, then wait for the peppers to arrive. In 1½ to 3 months, depending on the type of pepper, the plants will develop little white (in most cases) flowers that will shortly transform into peppers. You can begin to harvest the peppers in their green stage as soon as they are full-sized (consult the seed package for size information) or let them ripen to red (or to orange, yellow, purple, or even brown). When you pick the peppers, use scissors or a sharp knife to cut the stems—this will prevent damaging the plants. I have noticed that the more peppers you pick, the more the plants will tend to produce. Then the real fun begins in the kitchen. Alright!

FIERY TIPS AND OTHER HOT STUFF

Learn not to burn: Although adding the fire from hot peppers to your food is very desirable (and if you don't think so, drop this book now and run away), you don't want to get burned by handling hot peppers. I suggest wearing disposable latex or rubber gloves while handling hot peppers. If your skin is sensitive, this is advice well heeded. Even if you're not sensitive, wear gloves if you are handling large quantities of hot peppers, especially the habanero varieties. I suggest using disposable gloves, since poorly

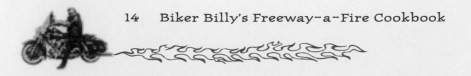

washed gloves can harbor dangerous bacteria. Even better, use disposable, sterile, powder-free gloves. However, if you are like me, wearing gloves in the kitchen is not something you like to do. In that case, if you are diligent about washing your hands with warm, soapy water (at least twice) after handling small amounts of peppers, you should be okay. You should wash your hands thoroughly even if you do use gloves. While your hands (or gloves) have the juices from hot peppers on them, touching sensitive parts of your body like your eyes, nose, mucous membranes, and "private parts" will give you an experience that is close to torture. Take my word for it, I have been there, felt the burn, and don't want to go back. If you find yourself there, try to remember the old adage "This too shall pass"—you will surely begin subscribing to the saying "Once burned, twice shy." And if you are grinding hot peppers into powders, wear a good-quality dust mask and goggles. Even the vapors from pureeing hot peppers will clear your sinuses and bring tears to your eyes. With all that said, don't be afraid, just show hot peppers some respect and enjoy Cooking with Fire!

Grinding custom pepper powders: If you enjoy sprinkling crushed hot pepper on your pizza, then you will find true happiness grinding your own dried hot pepper powder. You will become familiar with the flavors of the different peppers used in this book. When you find the ones that really hit the spot, try grinding them in a food processor, mortar and pestle, or spice mill (don't use the coffee grinder unless you can thoroughly wash it—talk about hot coffee!). Combine different peppers and, if you like, add spices, too. Remember to wear a dust mask and gloves (goggles could also help), work in a well-ventilated place, and wash up with plenty of warm water and soap. Store the powders in airtight containers, and you are ready to shake up a little fire.

Using dried peppers in place of fresh: Dried peppers must be rehydrated before you use them. In recipes that call for using dried peppers, you will find boiling water specified in the ingredients and a reference to this "fiery tip." To begin rehydrating, remove the stems (and seeds, if the recipe says so) from the dried peppers. Place the peppers in a small, heatproof bowl and cover with water that has just reached a full boil but is not still bubbling, allowing the water to cool for 2 to 3 minutes before you pour it over the peppers. If you use water at a full rolling boil, the peppers may develop a bitter taste. If you are substituting dried peppers in a recipe that call for fresh peppers, use only enough water to cover the peppers; using too much water may affect the recipe. Cutting the dried peppers into pieces (unless the recipe specifies a whole pepper) will allow you to use less water. Set the peppers aside to soak until they are fully rehydrated (this usually happens in the time it takes for them to reach room temperature, but in a cold room it could take longer). If you are in a hurry and want to use a microwave oven to speed the rehydration process by reheating the soaking peppers, just be careful not to boil them.

Using pickled peppers in place of fresh: The main concern here is whether the addition of the vinegar from the pickling process will affect the recipe (for example, by curdling cream or changing flavors). To reduce the effects of the pickling liquids, thoroughly rinse the pepper off with cool water. Since oftentimes a pepper will become filled with the pickling liquid, examine the pepper before rinsing it to determine if it is filled. If it is, cut it open and rinse it again. The rinsing may reduce the pepper's firepower, so you will have to adjust the recipe according to your taste. Pickled peppers can be substituted, as directed, for fresh in the recipe.

Using fresh peppers in place of dried or pickled: If you are replacing dried peppers with fresh peppers, it is not necessary to rehydrate them with boiling water. Therefore, omit the boiling water from the recipe unless it is needed to rehydrate other ingredients (for example, spices or sun-dried tomatoes). When substituting fresh peppers for dried peppers in dough recipes, you may have to add a bit more water to the dough to adjust the balance of dry ingredients versus liquids. Fresh peppers can be freely substituted for pickled peppers.

Blanching hot peppers: Blanching is a useful technique for preparing hot peppers for stuffing or for use as a condiment or garnish where a raw flavor is not desirable. To blanch fresh hot peppers, bring a pot of water to a boil over high heat. Add a few peppers at a time (don't add so many that the boiling stops), using a slotted spoon or strainer to keep them submerged. Boil for 1 to 3 minutes, or until they begin to change color. Remove the peppers and submerge them in cold water to stop the cooking process. Use as directed in the recipe.

Roasting peppers: The best way to roast peppers is to find a comfortable chair, a barbecue grill, and a perfect early fall afternoon. With that setup, you can roast the peppers slowly on the grill while you admire the fall sunlight sparkling on your bike's chrome. But since that may not always be possible, there are other techniques that you can apply to roasting peppers. If you have an indoor grill (lucky you), use that, or follow the technique below, which substitutes a heavy frying pan and hot oil for the grill. Use fresh Anaheim, New Mexico, or poblano peppers if you are planning to stuff them after you roast them.

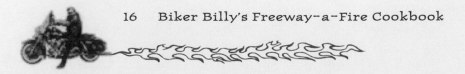

Using the tip of a sharp knife, pierce the peppers near the stem (if you don't put a hole in the pepper it will explode). In a heavy frying pan, heat ¼ inch of olive oil over high heat. Place the peppers in the hot oil and turn often. When the skins have turned brown all over (don't let them get blackened), remove from the pan and wrap in wet paper towels. Put the wrapped peppers into a plastic bag. This will steam the peppers and, as they cool to room temperature, their skins will loosen and slip right off. When the peppers have cooled, remove them from the plastic bag, unwrap the paper towels, and peel off the blistered skin. Cut a slit into one side of each pepper and remove the seeds and the core. If you are stuffing the peppers, leave the stems attached for easier handling. The roasted peppers are now ready to be used.

Hot pepper purees: Several of my recipes use pepper purees; some are made from rehydrated dried peppers (for rehydration information, see page 15), others are made from fresh or pickled peppers. In general, I use one or more whole peppers in the puree to produce the fire level I enjoy. Your enjoyment of fire is different from other people's, so your hot could be my mild or vice versa. Since peppers are a natural product, their size and firepower vary, even among those picked from one plant, and they vary to some degree depending on what part of the pepper you use. Therefore, it is difficult to control the fire of a dish by merely using fewer whole peppers in the puree. What I find works best is to puree the suggested number of peppers and add the puree to the dish a little at a time until the fire is right. If you find that the dish is not fiery enough for you, next time increase the number of peppers you puree and continue adding the puree until you are happy with the fire.

If you have puree left over, divide it into teaspoon-size mounds (or the size of your choice) on a plate and place in the freezer overnight. Transfer the frozen puree mounds into a sealable plastic bag and use whenever you want to add a little fire to a recipe. This is also an excellent way to store roasted or excess fresh peppers. The key is to select a measurement that works with your taste in fire, since frozen puree is hard to divide.

Freezing fire: Frozen hot peppers retain many of the virtues of fresh ones, and some companies market frozen whole or processed hot peppers. Hot peppers are easy to freeze at home, so if you grow them or buy them fresh, try freezing them to prolong their life. To freeze whole fresh peppers, wash and remove any excess moisture. Place them in a single layer on a cookie sheet and put in your freezer overnight. Once they are frozen solid, pack them in dated, zippered plastic bags. They will keep for up to 1 year in the freezer without any noticeable loss of flavor. If you are constantly in and out of the freezer, or the freezer temperature is set to keep ice cream soft, the storage life of the peppers will be reduced. You can also freeze excess canned hot peppers, like chipotles packed in adobo sauce. Just arrange them on a plate with a small separation between the peppers to prevent them from becoming one frozen solid mass, and proceed as you would for fresh whole peppers. Extra adobo sauce adds a nice kick to canned soups, stews, or chili, and can be frozen like pepper purees (see page 17).

Controlling the fire: Besides using fewer peppers, there is something you can do to reduce the fire you get from each hot pepper. The part that produces the fire is most concentrated in the fleshy center of the pepper, which holds the seeds, and the seeds, by contact, also contain a lot of fire. Simply removing the seeds and the fleshy core will reduce the firepower of that pepper.

Fire extinguishers: Of course you should have a few "fire extinguishers" around, and I am talking about pepper fire. The chemical that makes hot peppers burn is called capsaicin and it is fat-soluble. So when your mouth is on fire, you want to reach for something with fat in it—ice cream, sour cream, whole milk, cheese, you get the idea. The fat will basically wash away the capsaicin. Some people find that bread or starchy foods (rice, potatoes, etc.) also help them find relief. Beer's ability to put the fire out is only a legend; all it does is impair your ability to drive a car or ride a motorcycle. Milk will serve you better.

Peeling fresh tomatoes: While tomato skins add fiber when the tomatoes are eaten raw, they can be less desirable when the tomatoes are cooked or pureed into a dish. Peeling tomatoes, however, can be a real chore due to their thin skins, which are strongly attached to the flesh. I use a simple trick that literally makes the tomatoes jump out of their skins; it's called blanching. To blanch fresh tomatoes, bring a pot of water to a boil over high heat. Add a few tomatoes at a time (don't add so many that the water stops boiling), using a slotted spoon or strainer to keep them submerged. Boil for 30 to 90 seconds, or until they begin to change color (if the skins begin to crack open they are done). Remove and submerge in cold water to stop the cooking process. Cut the stem end off and peel away the skin. I will sometimes hold them over a bowl with the cut end pointed down and give them a gentle squeeze; if they are blanched enough, they will jump out, leaving you holding the whole skin. Use as directed in the recipe.

Kitchen thermometer: Before I bought one, I never knew how useful this kitchen tool is. Several recipes in the book require you to know the tem-

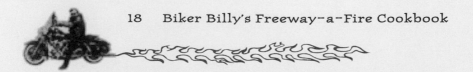

perature of various ingredients. This knowledge is critical in deep-frying and baking with yeast. Consider the cost of one ruined meal and the thermometer has paid for itself. I use one that reads from 100° to 400°F, and will cover the range of temperatures called for in this book. A thermometer with a removable clip will allow you to leave it attached to a pot while cooking; this is especially convenient when deep-frying.

Slicing, dicing, chopping, mincing, etc.: I highly recommend using a food processor—it saves a lot of work and I don't think I could live without one. It won't totally replace using a knife, but much of the cutting up required in this book can be done with a food processor. When you are using a chopping blade, I suggest you choose the pulse function to control how finely you chop things. Please read the manual that comes with your machine and follow all the safety instructions (this applies to any power tool). When using a food processor to make dough, be sure your machine is designed to handle the heavy load this creates; I have burned out a machine doing this.

Learning to Ride

Take an MSF (Motorcycle Safety Foundation)–approved rider education course. Even if you have been riding for years, you will learn something. If you have already taken a course, take an intermediate or experienced course about every 2 years to keep your knowledge current and your skills sharp. Along with learning new things, you can also unlearn bad riding habits. Safety is a state of mind that starts with knowledge and builds with practice and self-discipline. Always maintain your riding skills, motorcycle, and equipment. This includes maintaining yourself—alcohol and drugs (including prescription and over-the-counter) don't mix with riding a motorcycle. Even lack of sleep will reduce your abilities—be smart, ride straight. Get involved; join the AMA (American Motorcyclist Association), the MRF (Motorcycle Riders Foundation), and your local state MRO (Motorcycle Rights Organization), such as ABATE (American Bikers Aimed Toward Education). For more information, see page 245. Of course, have fun as you find adventure by riding and consider sharing that adventure with someone. And remember to Eat Hot and Ride Safe.

THE BIKER'S PANTRY

Most of the ingredients in this book are items that are always lurking in my pantry (and probably yours, too). I like to have a good supply of ingredients on hand so I can cook almost anything I want when the mood strikes. As a rule,

I don't like to run to the store any more than I have to. First off, it is because I am lazy. Second, since so many people drive as if traffic laws are suspended in parking lots, it is no fun going to the store when you're riding a motorcycle. And last, I have been known to spend way too much time and money in supermarkets (I also have this problem in bike shops). The benefit of this book is that most of the recipes can be cooked without having to make a special shopping expedition for ingredients. The exceptions to that rule are items like dairy products, eggs, and produce, which are best purchased as fresh as possible.

In general, the ingredients for the recipes are commonly available in supermarkets around the country. Since I have traveled throughout the United States doing cooking shows, I have personally tested this fact. There are a few items that are not 100 percent mainstream, but can be found in health food stores, Latin or Asian grocery stores, or are available through mail-order merchants and the Internet.

Bean curd: Unless otherwise specified, I find that extra-firm bean curd produces the best texture for most recipes in this book. You can, of course, use firm or soft bean curd, if that is all that you can find. Also note that bean curd and tofu are the same product. The major difference between soft, firm, and extra-firm bean curd is in the water content. As the water content is reduced, the bean curd becomes more firm. As a result, the amount of calories and protein for a given measured weight of bean curd increases as the texture (density) increases. This is not based on scientific study, just on a careful reading of package labels.

Dried bean curd is a special variety of bean curd that has a very low moisture content and an extra-chewy texture, making it a satisfying alternative to traditional bean curd. It is most often found in Asian groceries and is frequently labeled "flavored bean curd." Usually the flavoring is soy sauce–based, which works well with many of the recipes in this book. In the past, dried bean curd was mostly manufactured by and for the Asian food industry and appeared infrequently on Asian restaurant menus outside of major American cities. Now a growing number of health food and gourmet companies produce dried bean curd in a range of flavors from Asian to Mexican. This is a product worth trying and can be substituted for extra-firm bean curd in most recipes.

Black pepper: Black pepper, although pungent, is not related to hot peppers. It comes from a completely different species of plant *(Piper nigrum)* that is indigenous to India and the surrounding region. The spicy, hot sensation from black pepper is not the same as that of hot peppers, simply because black pepper does not contain capsaicin, the chemical that creates the burn from hot peppers. Despite the difference, black pepper and its history can be thanked for the spread of hot peppers around the world.

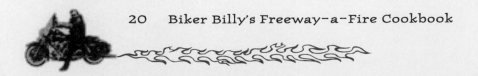

At the time of Columbus's discovery of America, black pepper was one of the more valuable trade commodities, so much so that it was sometimes used as currency. Among the things Columbus found while searching for India and its gold and spices were chile peppers (capsicums), which are indigenous to the Americas. By bringing hot peppers back to Europe, Columbus helped spread them around the globe. So next time you enjoy a fiery Chinese dish, remember that Columbus helped make it possible.

TELLICHERRY BLACK PEPPER: I don't specify this type of pepper in the book, but if you enjoy the pungent taste of black pepper, then you should search out Tellicherry peppercorns. Tellicherry pepper comes from India and is widely recognized as the most flavorful type of black pepper. It is best to buy it as whole peppercorns and grind it fresh, as you need it. The flavor is exceptional; it packs a lot of fire and the aroma is breathtaking. I buy mine at Kalustyan's, a specialty spice store in New York City that sells enough to ensure that their supply is always fresh (see Sources). Keeping the peppercorns in an airtight jar away from direct sunlight and heat will help retain their flavor for up to 1 year.

Bulgur wheat: Bulgur wheat is whole grain wheat that retains much of its germ and bran, making it high in protein and dietary fiber. It has an almost nutty flavor and a chewy texture. The variety sold in supermarkets today is precooked and only requires mixing with hot water and soaking for 15 minutes before it is ready to eat. Watch out for the "cracked wheat" that is sold in many health food stores. It is often confused with bulgur wheat, but it is not precooked and requires a much different preparation. The recipes in this book all use precooked bulgur wheat.

Butter: I love butter; it adds a wonderful richness to everything you cook with it. Some professional chefs believe you should use only unsalted (sweet) butter. The logic behind this is that the only way to control the salt in a dish is to add the salt yourself. I tested my recipes using salted butter. If you are on a low-salt diet, by all means use sweet butter. If you are a vegan or concerned with the issues of saturated fat and cholesterol, you can substitute stick margarine. Soft and squeeze margarines are not good substitutions, since they will not give the desired results, especially in baking or sautéing.

Canola oil and peanut oil: Although my favorite cooking oil is olive oil, it burns at too low a temperature for deep-frying, so I recommend using canola or peanut oil. Canola oil is made from rapeseeds; it is low in saturated fat, high in monounsaturated fat, and has a very mild taste. Peanut oil contains more saturated fat and less monounsaturated fat than canola oil and has a more robust flavor. Both oils work equally well for deep-frying, so the choice is yours. The only time I would recommend peanut oil over canola is when a recipe uses peanut butter, and this is only a small flavor consideration.

Couscous: Often mistaken for pasta and even incorrectly packaged as Moroccan pasta, couscous is in fact a grain. It is the hard heart of semolina wheat that is dried and processed into small granules. Most brands of couscous sold in supermarkets today are instant or precooked and require only mixing with hot water and soaking for 5 minutes before it is ready to eat. Just remember to check the package directions before preparing it, as not every couscous is equally precooked. It is a fast and welcome starch alternative to potatoes or rice, and it absorbs flavors fantastically.

Dried beans and dried split peas: Most recipes in this book call for canned beans or frozen peas; however, a few specify dried beans and peas. When using dried beans or peas, you must sort and rinse them first. Since these are natural products that grow in soil and are almost always packaged by machines, you will likely find small rocks or clumps of dirt among them. You should take the time to inspect and wash the beans or peas carefully before using them. If you find that they are dirt- and rock-free, consider yourself lucky.

Eggs: I use several sizes of eggs in this book. This allows me to have more accurate control of the quantity of egg used in a given recipe. If you have ever seen my show (especially live at an event), you probably can't imagine me being concerned about controlling the measurements of ingredients (I can measure by eye and things always taste delicious no matter how carefree I am with measuring). Since you may find buying different sizes of eggs bothersome, I have provided the following chart to allow for easy substitution. I have placed large eggs in the center of the chart so you can adjust up or down from this middle-of-the-road size.

Small	Medium	Large	Extra Large	Jumbo
1	1	1	1	1
3	2	2	2	2
4	3	3	3	2
5	5	4	4	3
7	6	5	4	4
8	7	6	5	5

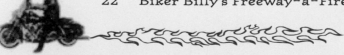

Garlic: In many recipes, I call for chopped garlic. In these cases, I have used commercial chopped garlic from a jar. I use the type packed in water, not in oil. This type of garlic is very convenient, but it is not quite as strong as fresh garlic. Take this into account when substituting it for freshly chopped garlic. Chopped garlic from a jar will have a higher moisture content than freshly chopped garlic, so it tends to tolerate longer cooking before it begins to burn. How well browned you like your garlic is a matter of personal taste. I like mine well browned, but if you prefer it lighter, just add the garlic a little later in the cooking process. If you're like me, and would rather be riding your bike than peeling garlic cloves, there is a product made just for us: prepeeled garlic cloves. This wonder of modern convenience foods tastes so much like fresh garlic that I almost never peel garlic cloves anymore.

Kasha: Roasted buckwheat (kasha) is not very popular in this country but is a staple in parts of Russia and Eastern Europe. The unique, almost smoky flavor and aroma of kasha may be an acquired taste for some. This versatile grain can be purchased whole or ground into coarse, medium, or fine granules. It provides good protein and fiber, and since the new Federal Food Guide Pyramid recommends between 6 and 11 servings from the bread, cereal, rice, and pasta group a day, this grain offers another tasty choice.

Leeks: These members of the lily family are expensive cousins of onions. They yield a wonderful earthy flavor that I have come to love, and you will, too. But for their subtle contribution to recipes you have to pay the price: extra washing. Leeks have a nasty habit of hiding sand and grit deep between their leaves. While the dirt may be easily seen where the leeks change color from white to dark green, the grit can be found down into the white section. Pay special attention to cleaning them. I like to wash them, then cut them, as called for in the recipe. Transfer them to a strainer and give them a thorough second rinse.

Masa harina: Masa harina, a flour made from corn processed with lye or wood ash, is a staple in Mexico. It is the basis for authentic corn tortillas. Processing the corn with lye or wood ash contributes to masa harina's excellent supply of vitamins and minerals, which is much higher than that of unprocessed corn. Don't substitute cornmeal or corn grits for the masa harina. You can find masa harina in Latin groceries, and don't be surprised if it appears on your supermarket shelves soon.

Molasses: Molasses is a by-product of the sugarmaking process. It is basically what is left over after sugar is extracted from sugarcane sap. You will find three types of molasses in the market (based on the order in which they are extracted). The first extraction is the lightest-tasting and is frequently sold as golden molasses. The second extraction is more robust and is called dark molasses. The last extraction (the crude oil of sugar) is blackstrap molasses and has the most pronounced flavor. I have found that the lighter grades of molasses impart more sweetness than the darker varieties. When a recipe calls for dark or blackstrap molasses you can substitute golden, while using blackstrap molasses in place of golden may really change the taste of the recipe. If you can't find golden molasses, use honey instead. It will lack the snap of molasses, but will function almost as well.

Olive oil: This is by far my favorite oil for everything except deep-frying. Olive oil burns at too low a temperature for deep-frying, but works very well for many other uses. The health benefits of olive oil are related to its high monounsaturated-fat content which some research indicates may reduce the level of bad cholesterol (LDL, or low-density lipoproteins) in the blood while increasing the level of good cholesterol (HDL, or high-density lipoproteins). Olive oil also does not contain any cholesterol. So what is the difference between extra-virgin olive oil, virgin olive oil, and olive oil? When olives are pressed to extract their natural oils (pitted olives are about 20 to 30 percent oil), the first pressing is called extra-virgin olive oil. The term "extra" means that the acid content of the oil is 1 percent or less, and it also indicates that the oil was pressed from a high quality of ripe olives. Virgin olive oil can have an acid content of 3 to 4 percent, and is more likely to be pressed from a slightly lower grade of olives. Oils simply labeled "olive oil" can be from second or later pressings, made with lower grades of olives or blends of different olive oil grades. The classification of olive oils is based on Italian law, and most manufacturers follow these guidelines when labeling their oils.

Purely from a taste standpoint, extra-virgin olive oils tend to have the strongest olive flavor. I have indicated extra virgin where I felt the added flavor was important. Simple olive oil has a less pronounced flavor, but at a lower cost. There are milder-tasting olive oils now on the market labeled "extra mild." Since all oils add fat and calories to a dish, extra-virgin olive oil is my first choice because it has the most flavor.

Onions: I often refer to onions as one of my favorite vegetables, but that description may be slightly less than accurate. Onions, like their garlic and shallot cousins, are members of the lily family, so it would be more accurate to say that they are my favorite flowers. Unless otherwise specified, I use yellow onions. They seem to add the most zip, but you can use your favorite variety of onion. Red onions can turn gray after cooking, so consider this factor if the onions will be a visible part of the finished dish.

Phyllo: Phyllo is pastry dough rolled to tissue thinness. It can be found in the frozen foods section of most supermarkets. Since it takes a lot of work and time to make from scratch, I always buy it frozen. Phyllo dough will produce a flaky golden-brown crust that is fantastic, and it is simpler to use than it appears. Phyllo must thaw before it can be used or it will crack. I allow it to thaw overnight in the refrigerator (check the package instructions).

Being so thin, uncooked phyllo dough will dry out and fall apart very rapidly if left exposed to air. Following a few simple guidelines will help you achieve delicious results: First, the filling should be cooked and ready for use before you open the phyllo package (the filling should not be too hot or it will melt the dough). Second, prepare your work area and have all the ingredients and tools ready. Third, unwrap the phyllo and cover with plastic wrap and several sheets of moist paper towels. Fourth, remove only as many sheets of phyllo dough as you will use at once and cover the rest of the dough while you work. Finally, in order to achieve a crispy, golden result, you should brush the phyllo with melted butter or margarine (you can use olive or canola oil, but butter tastes best and produces a more golden-brown color) during assembly.

It is necessary to use several layers to create a good thick crust; I use two or three sheets at a time and brush melted butter on each set before adding the next. The top or outer layer should be well covered with butter to ensure a beautiful golden appearance.

Salt: By many accounts, salt is the oldest seasoning in the world, and at times during history it has been more valuable by weight than gold. I like salt and use it liberally, but I have tried to design my recipes so that most people will not find things too salty. As is true with hot peppers, it is easier to add more salt later in the cooking process and impossible to remove it when there is too much. One seemingly eternal question is, should the water you cook pasta in be salted? I think that pasta can be cooked with or without salt in the water, so it is your choice. No stuffy rules here.

Scallions: I like to use scallions (also called green onions) to give a wonderful onion flavor to recipes. To trim the scallion, cut the tip off the root end and trim any dry leafy matter from the dark green end. These beauties add great color as well as flavor to recipes.

Shallots: These small cousins to the beloved onion are such a wonderful treat. They have a flavor that is a cross between garlic and onions. The taste and aroma are milder than those of yellow onions and add a subtle accent anywhere onions and garlic are at home. Although their addition or omis-

sion will not ruin a dish, they do contribute to the depth and complexity of flavor that make them a welcome friend in your pantry.

Sun-dried tomatoes: In this book I use both sun-dried tomatoes packed in olive oil and those that are not. In most cases, they are interchangeable. However, some recipes need the oil that comes with the sun-dried tomatoes, so you may have to add a little extra olive oil to the dish. If substituting oil-packed tomatoes for the dried variety, you may need to cut down on the amount of oil in a recipe. However, none of the recipes will be ruined because of the substitution. Although the oil that the sun-dried tomatoes are packed in may not be the very best grade, it will have been infused with great tomato flavor and will undoubtedly add some jazz to your cooking.

Texmati rice: This hybrid of long-grain American rice and Indian basmati rice has a great taste that is as delicious as its namesake (Texas) is big. Grown in America, this rice has the fast-cooking qualities of American long-grain rice and the flavor and aroma of basmati rice. The aroma and taste of this rice reminds me of popcorn. The slightly nutty flavor and excellent texture have made it a favorite around my kitchen garage. There is also a brown-rice Texmati available. You can substitute basmati or any variety of long-grain rice for Texmati. Please read the package directions regarding cooking times, since there can be a big difference from one type or brand to another.

COOKING LIKE A BIKER

What do I mean by cooking like a biker? Well, you don't have to wear black leather, but that could also be fun. And you don't have to cook in the garage like me, that is, unless the thought of a little mess (or the sight of you in black leather) terrifies your family. But you do have to say NO to the stuffy attitudes espoused by fancy French gourmets and highfalutin chefs. In fact, you may want to cop an attitude of your own that proclaims you're a free spirit and will follow your own culinary road.

I am a strong advocate of doing your own thing in your own way whether the subject is riding motorcycles or cooking. On a bike, it is critical that you ride your own ride. This means you ride within the limits of your skills, your machine, and the surrounding situations. Riders call this "riding within your envelope," and when you prudently explore the edges of that envelope, you find the greatest combination of fun and safety. By pushing the boundaries of that envelope, you will learn more about yourself and also expand your envelope. This is part of what makes motorcycling so lib-

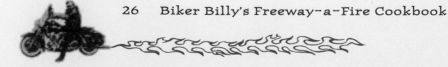

erating, because it puts you in direct contact with reality, and it demands that you be honest with yourself about your skills and abilities, and, frankly, about who you are.

Cooking is very similar in that you need to know what you like and dislike, and this is especially important when you cook with fire. Know your own limits when it comes to how fiery you like your food. The best experience you'll ever have with a fork is when you taste all the flavors in the food you have prepared, with the fire adding an extra dimension to those tastes. Remember your enjoyment of fire will be different from mine and will likely be different from that of the people you share food with, so always adjust the fire to suit your tastes. In both riding a motorcycle and cooking through education and practice, you can expand your abilities and your taste for adventure. A few forays into cooking with fire will define your personal fiery envelope. With that knowledge and the information in this book, you will be ready to blaze new trails while exploring culinary freeways and byways.

For me, recipes are like custom road maps ordered from an auto club. They are designed to get you somewhere, but they were designed by someone else. You have selected the destination and maybe chosen the scenic route, but they map out only one of many paths to your goal. Great motorcycle adventures always begin when you choose to leave the prescribed route and venture into unmarked territory. When I ride out on a motorcycle journey, I have a place I want to go and I arm myself with maps and planned routes. But I always wander from the plan and explore the things I see along the way because that is one of the joys of adventuring by bike. From the saddle you experience the world you travel through directly, with an intimacy that only a motorcycle can create. Cooking is the same for me. I start out in the kitchen with a taste I want to create, having armed myself with ingredients and an idea of how to get there. Then the fun begins. I start wandering, adding new things and discarding old ideas. I always wander from the path, whether it is a classic dish, a Viewer Recipe Contest entry, or some strange dish I dreamed up. For me, the joy is in the adventure of discovery. Sometimes things aren't perfect and so I try again, most times finding myself with a pleasant new taste destination. A nice part of these culinary adventures is when my wife, Rachelle, says, "Umm, you could cook this all the time." That's a rewarding compliment, but being the wandering soul I am, that is about the time I am dreaming of a new taste to explore.

When I find a new road or a great scenic place to stop, I love to share this with my riding buddies. I am the same when it comes to food, and you are one of my cooking buddies. This book is filled with culinary road maps. I have custom-designed them to take me to great taste destinations and I want to share them with you. I hope that you enjoy them—this would make

me proud. More than that, I hope that within these pages you will discover the desire to explore food and the many wonderful adventures of cooking with fire. When you wander from the path and use my recipes as starting points for your own process of creation, then you will be cooking like a biker. Indeed, you will discover the fun and freedom of Cooking with Fire. ALRIGHT!

The Grass Is Always Greener on the Other Side: Salads

In the hands of some cooks, salad is a diet food that has all the excitement of eating grass with the horses. Well, this biker takes an approach to salad that is more like riding a bucking bronco, and I don't mean the kind that runs on a quarter outside the drugstore. The salads in this chapter are wild, a little crazy, and even devious. Some are devious because they look so harmless, but looks in this case are definitely deceiving. For instance, Nu-Mac Salad (page 36) and Nuclear Potato Salad (page 34) have been known to sit innocently on a picnic table waiting for a victim. They look so rich and creamy, but they conceal a megaton blast of fire in each forkful. There is even an egg salad that makes the most potent deviled egg look like angel food. Yes, my egg salad is powerful enough to burn the short hairs off the Devil himself. And yes, the grass may always look greener on the other side, but on this side the salads are meaner. Once you have grazed on the hotter and wilder side of salads, you'll never go back.

To Die Thai Salad Dressing

Every time I eat at a Thai restaurant, I fall in love with the peanut sauces. At a few places, I have ordered a salad with a warm peanut dressing that was to die for. So I created this recipe to enjoy those flavors at home in my garage. It may sound weird to put a warm dressing on a cold, crisp salad, but it is wonderful. If you are having your riding buddies over for an Asian feast, the perfect way to start it off is with a salad topped with this killer dressing. The combination of coconut milk, peanut butter, and peanut oil is not a dieter's delight. But since you don't use that much on a single salad serving, it won't kill you and the taste is to die for.

This dressing can be refrigerated, but be aware that it will solidify to a consistency like peanut butter. To reheat it, combine some of the dressing with a little water in a small microwave-safe bowl, taking care not to add too much water or it will become too thin. Stir well and microwave on low power for 30 seconds. Stir well and repeat until it is tepid.

> 4 Thai peppers, stemmed and crushed
> 1 tablespoon boiling water (see page 15)
> ¼ cup peanut oil
> 7 garlic cloves, peeled
> One 1-inch piece fresh peeled ginger, minced
> 1 large shallot, minced
> ½ cup cashews
> ½ teaspoon ground coriander
> ½ teaspoon ground white pepper
> ¾ teaspoon salt
> 1 cup chunky peanut butter
> ¾ cup coconut milk
> 1 cup hot water
> ¼ cup fresh cilantro leaves, minced
> Juice of ½ lime

Place the Thai peppers in a small bowl and cover with the boiling water. Allow to cool to room temperature. Drain the peppers and reserve the soaking water.

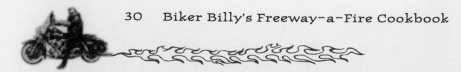

In a small saucepot, heat the peanut oil over medium heat. Add the Thai peppers, garlic, ginger, shallot, and cashews and cook, stirring often, until the cashews are golden brown, 5 to 7 minutes (using care not to burn them).

Add the reserved pepper soaking liquid, coriander, white pepper, and salt and stir well. Add the peanut butter and stir until dissolved. Add the coconut milk and hot water and stir until smooth. Reduce the heat to low and simmer for 5 to 7 minutes, stirring often. Transfer the mixture to a blender or a food processor equipped with a chopping blade. Add the cilantro and lime juice and puree until smooth and creamy, 2 to 3 minutes. Serve warm over salad greens.

MAKES ABOUT 3 CUPS

Mean Green Salad Dressing

This ain't no low-fat, low-calorie dieter's salad dressing. No sir, this is the real stuff that salad greens dream of. The avocado and buttermilk make it rich, green, and creamy while the cayenne pepper makes it mean. One taste will have you pillaging the countryside for fresh salad goodies.

There are two varieties of avocado: the large, bright green, smooth-skinned California type, and the smaller, dark green, bumpy-skinned Hass variety. I enjoy the Hass variety.

1 fresh cayenne pepper, stemmed and seeded
1 ripe avocado, skin and pit removed
1 small onion, quartered
1 medium-size ripe tomato, peeled and seeded (see page 18)
1 cup buttermilk
½ teaspoon dried cilantro
½ teaspoon ground cumin
1½ teaspoons salt
1 teaspoon ground white pepper

In a blender or a food processor equipped with a cutting blade, combine the cayenne pepper, avocado, onion, and tomato. Process until finely chopped, about 1 minute. Add the buttermilk, cilantro, cumin, salt, and white pepper and process until well blended, 1 to 2 minutes.

MAKES ABOUT 2 CUPS

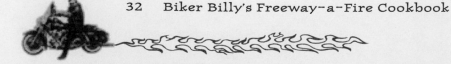

Janie Egger's Kool Hot Tomato Salad

This salad is so simple and sinfully delicious that there may be a law against eating it. I am sure you have heard people talk about bringing the fresh flavors of the garden straight to the table. Well, this salad not only talks the talk, it walks the walk, and if you add enough jalapeños, it may just run the marathon. So sharpen your favorite knife and chop up some kool salad that is as hot as an August afternoon and as fresh as a spring morning.

For a real "kool hot" thrill, try using a Biker Billy jalapeño.

2 large ripe tomatoes, diced, with their juice
1 medium-size cucumber, peeled, quartered
    lengthwise, and cut into ½-inch pieces
1 medium-size onion, diced
1 jalapeño pepper, stemmed and minced, or more to
    taste
⅓ cup packed fresh basil leaves, minced
2 to 4 garlic cloves (to your taste), minced
¼ teaspoon salt
¼ teaspoon ground black pepper
2 tablespoons extra-virgin olive oil

In a large salad bowl, toss together the tomatoes with their juice, cucumber, onion, jalapeño, basil, and garlic. Sprinkle with the salt and pepper, drizzle with the olive oil, and toss again. Cover and refrigerate for 1 hour. Toss again just before serving.

MAKES 4 TO 6 SERVINGS

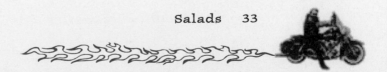

Nuclear Potato Salad

If you're looking for a way to add some excitement to your next picnic, I've got a blast for you. Here is an old-fashioned American favorite, potato salad, re-created with a Thai flair. And that Thai flair will light a flare on your taste buds: The habanero really kicks. So pack this salad into your saddlebags and ride around the countryside until you find a scenic picnic spot far from civilization. Then sit yourself down and share this with your buddies. Just remember to declare the area a nuclear test site.

When making this recipe, don't peel the red potatoes. Instead try to cut them so most pieces have some skin on them. This adds color and texture to the salad and helps to retain more nutritional value in the potatoes. Preparing this salad a day before you serve it allows the potatoes to absorb more flavor.

> 4 cups small red potatoes (about 8 potatoes),
>   cut into ½-inch cubes
> 1 fresh habanero pepper, stemmed and seeded
> ¼ cup honey
> 2 tablespoons peanut butter
> ¼ cup plain yogurt
> ½ teaspoon salt
> 4 scallions, trimmed and cut into ¼-inch-thick
>   slices

Place the potatoes in a large saucepot and cover with cool water. Place the pot over high heat and bring to a boil. Reduce the heat to medium and simmer until the potatoes are tender, 10 to 15 minutes. Drain and rinse with cool water, set aside, and cool to room temperature.

In a blender or a food processor equipped with a cutting blade, combine the habanero pepper and honey. Puree until no large pieces of habanero remain, 1 minute. Add the peanut butter and blend until smooth, 1 minute. Add the yogurt and salt and puree for until the mixture is smooth, 1 more minute.

In a large salad bowl, toss together the potatoes and scallions. Pour the dressing over the potatoes and toss until well coated. Refrigerate overnight. Serve chilled.

MAKES 8 SERVINGS

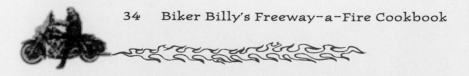

Lucifer's Angelic Egg Salad

This recipe puts the Devil in egg salad, but it is tasty enough to make the angels sing. Say good-bye to wimpy egg salad and hello to a real biker-style salad. Just make sure that the habanero is well minced or you'll need to go for a fast ride with your mouth open to cool off your tongue.

> ½ fresh habanero pepper, stemmed, seeded, and
>   minced
> 2 tablespoons spicy brown mustard
> 2 tablespoons coarsely chopped Spanish olives
> 1 scallion, trimmed and minced
> 4 hard-boiled eggs, shelled and minced
> Salt and ground black pepper to taste

If you are preparing the salad by hand, combine the habanero pepper and mustard in a small bowl. Add the olives and scallion and stir to coat. Add the eggs and mix until thoroughly blended.

If you are preparing the salad using a food processor, it is not necessary to pre-mince any of the ingredients. Equip the processor with a chopping blade and puree the habanero and mustard. With the blades still spinning, add the olives, scallions, and eggs and process until the eggs are well chopped. Scrape down the sides of the bowl and pulse once or twice, or until the texture suits your taste (I like mine with the egg whites finely minced). Refrigerate for 1 hour. Add salt and pepper and serve.

MAKES 2 TO 4 SERVINGS

Nu-Mac Salad

If you think of macaroni salad as a bland blend of elbow-shaped pasta and mayonnaise, then this salad will open your eyes. The fresh cayenne pepper will also open your sinuses, and the rich sour cream–based dressing will make your mouth open and yell for a second helping. Although it's not quite nuclear-hot, this colorful dish will melt down your boredom with ordinary macaroni salad.

> 1 fresh cayenne pepper, stemmed and seeded
> 1 small onion, quartered
> 1 cup sour cream
> ½ teaspoon ground cumin
> ½ teaspoon garlic powder
> 1 teaspoon salt
> 1 teaspoon ground white pepper
> One 12-ounce package tricolor rotelle pasta, cooked until al dente, or just tender
> 2 celery stalks, trimmed and cut into ¼-inch-thick slices
> ½ cup baby carrots, cut into ¼-inch-thick slices
> 1 red bell pepper, cored, seeded, and cut into ½-inch squares
> 1 medium-size onion, diced

In a blender or a food processor equipped with a chopping blade, combine the cayenne pepper and onion. Process until finely chopped, about 30 seconds. Add the sour cream, cumin, garlic powder, salt, and white pepper and process until well blended, about 1 minute.

In a large salad bowl, combine the cooked pasta, celery, carrots, bell pepper, and diced onion and toss well. Add the sour cream dressing and toss until well coated. (I like to combine this salad in a large, well-sealing storage container and shake it biker-style until it surrenders. You'd be surprised how mixed up the salad gets.) Refrigerate until thoroughly chilled, 30 minutes.

MAKES 12 SERVINGS

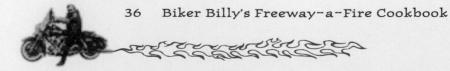

Quickie Taco Salad

This down-and-dirty salad looks real fancy with almost no work and no dishes to clean. It is a festive way to start a Mexican-style biker feast and a perfect vehicle for the Mean Green Salad Dressing. So whip them both up, chuck 'em on the table, and listen to the happy sounds of hungry bikers munching on this crunchy salad. The ingredient amounts are for one salad, so multiply according to your needs.

> 5 fresh spinach leaves, thick stems removed and leaves thinly shredded
> 3 radicchio leaves, thick stems removed and leaves thinly shredded
> 1 large taco shell bowl (see Note)
> 1 scallion, trimmed and cut into 1½-inch pieces
> 3 baby carrots, cut in half lengthwise
> Mean Green Salad Dressing (see page 32)
> Shredded cheddar cheese to taste
> One 2-inch-wide strip red or yellow bell pepper, cut into ¾-inch squares

Toss the spinach and radicchio leaves together in the taco shell bowl. Lay the scallion and carrot pieces in the flutes of the taco bowl in an alternating arrangement. Add a generous spoonful of the salad dressing to the center of the salad and sprinkle with the cheddar cheese. Arrange the bell pepper pieces around the edges of the dressing for eye-popping color and a sweet, crispy taste.

MAKES 1 SALAD

NOTE: Preprepared taco shell bowls are available in supermarkets, but if you are unable to find them, simply prepare the salad in a serving bowl and garnish with the scallion and carrot pieces.

Vulgar Bulgur Salad

Have you ever wanted a perfect one-dish meal that you could stuff into your saddlebags and hit the road with? Well, here it is. This Middle Eastern–inspired salad packs enough fuel to power you through a veritable desert. It's full of protein, fiber, and, of course, flavor; it's even low in fat. What more could you ask for? A fork?

  1 tablespoon dried mint
  2 tablespoons boiling water (see page 15)
  2 dried New Mexico peppers, stemmed and seeded
  1 cup bulgur wheat
  2 cups water
  1 medium-size onion, diced
  1 medium-size ripe tomato, diced
  1 yellow bell pepper, cored, seeded, and diced
  One 19-ounce can chickpeas, drained and rinsed
  ½ cup coarsely chopped Spanish olives
  ¼ cup packed fresh basil leaves, coarsely chopped
  1 tablespoon chopped garlic
  ½ teaspoon salt
  ½ teaspoon ground black pepper
  ¼ cup extra-virgin olive oil
  Juice of 1 lemon

Place the mint in a small bowl and cover with the boiling water. Set aside and allow to cool to room temperature.

In a medium-size saucepan over high heat, combine the New Mexico peppers, bulgur, and water and bring to boil. Reduce the heat to low and simmer, covered, until all the liquid has absorbed, about 15 minutes. Remove from the heat and allow to cool to room temperature. Remove the New Mexico peppers from the cooked bulgur and set aside.

In a large salad bowl, toss together the onion, tomato, bell pepper, chickpeas, olives, and basil. Add the bulgur and toss well.

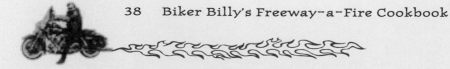

In a blender, add the reserved New Mexico peppers, garlic, salt, pepper, olive oil, lemon juice, and the rehydrated mint and puree until smooth, 1 to 2 minutes.

Drizzle the puree on the salad and toss until well mixed. Cover and refrigerate for 1 hour. Toss again just before serving.

MAKES 8 TO 10 SERVINGS

Circa early 1940s: Elizabeth "Bette" Wimmer on her husband's 1929
Harley JD model during World War II. Bette always made great
meals and snacks for the kids.

Snack Attack: Appetizers

They start as little rumblings, barely noticeable at first. Left unattended, they begin to grow slowly, as if approaching from a great distance. You can almost feel and hear them. Then, as if out of nowhere they roar full force upon you, unseen but felt, as if the ground was shaking from the combined exhaust of ten thousand Harleys. But the sound is not the roar of invaders from outside—the sound is coming from deep inside you. It is the gut-wrenching wail of the snack attack siren. Yes, the dreaded battle cry of the munchies—the ravisher of diets, the raiders of pantries, and the expanders of waistlines everywhere.

What can you do when the snack attack siren howls? Well, you could reach for some wimpy package of snack food that will leave you full but unfulfilled. Or you could ride to the rescue with a plateful of soul-satisfying biker appetizers. Yes sirrree bob, there are enough fiery taste sensations in this chapter to feed an army of hungry hounds from hell. From exotic Poblano Scallion Pancakes and Portly Portobellos to Down-Home Corn Fritters and Killer Quesadillas, there is something in here to please every munchie-crazed marauder.

FRITTER AWAY

I have been known to fritter away endless hours in my garage tinkering on the motorcycles. Doing all that work develops a tremendous appetite, and I am always looking for something to munch on. I created the following three recipes so I could have tasty finger food to enjoy while working. Prepare some of these before your next session of motorcycle maintenance. You will surely fritter your way into a state of fiery-food Zen.

41

Cheesy Italian Zucchini Fritters

Zucchini may be the perfect vegetable for making fritters, and I have used them in many fritter recipes. This one is a simple but tasty favorite of mine. The ancho pepper adds warm, earthy tones to the fresh garden flavor of the zucchini, while the Parmesan cheese rounds out this zesty combination.

> 1 ancho pepper, stemmed, seeded, and torn
>   into small pieces
> ¼ cup boiling water (see page 15)
> 1 large egg
> ½ teaspoon baking powder
> ½ teaspoon salt
> ½ teaspoon ground black pepper
> ¼ cup all-purpose flour
> ¼ cup freshly grated Parmesan cheese
> 1 medium-size zucchini, shredded
> Olive oil for frying

Place the ancho pepper in a small bowl and cover with the boiling water. Allow to cool to room temperature.

In a blender or a food processor equipped with a chopping blade, puree the rehydrated pepper and the soaking water until no large pieces of ancho remain, about 1 minute. Add the egg, baking powder, salt, and black pepper and puree for 1 minute. Add the flour and Parmesan cheese and puree until smooth, about 1 minute.

Place the zucchini in a large mixing bowl, cover with the batter, and mix well.

In a medium-size frying pan, heat ¼ inch of olive oil over medium heat. Place a heaping tablespoonful of the zucchini mixture into the oil and flatten gently with the back of a spoon. Repeat until the pan is full of fritters. Fry until the edges start to brown, 2 to 3 minutes. Turn and fry the other side for another 2 to 3 minutes. Continue until all the batter is used up. Drain on a paper towel and serve piping hot.

MAKES ABOUT 8 FRITTERS; 4 SERVINGS

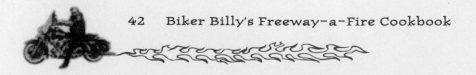

Rice Burner Fritters

What do you do with yesterday's leftover rice? Make Rice Burner Fritters, of course. These hearty fritters are so tasty and easy, you may be tempted always to cook extra rice. The smoky chipotle pepper blends so well with onion and garlic, and burns new life into old rice. Serve these as an appetizer or alongside your breakfast eggs in place of hash browns.

> 1 chipotle pepper packed in adobo sauce, minced
> 1 teaspoon chopped garlic
> 1 large egg
> ½ teaspoon baking powder
> ½ teaspoon salt
> ½ teaspoon ground black pepper
> ¼ cup all-purpose flour
> 1 medium-size onion, minced
> 1 cup cooked rice
> Olive oil or butter for frying (see Note)

In a blender or a food processor equipped with a chopping blade, combine the chipotle pepper, garlic, egg, baking powder, salt, and black pepper and puree for 1 minute. Add the flour and puree until smooth, about 1 minute.

Place the onion and rice in a large mixing bowl, cover with the batter, and mix well.

In a medium-size frying pan, heat ¼ inch of olive oil over medium heat. Place 1 heaping tablespoonful of the rice mixture into the oil and flatten gently with the back of a spoon. Repeat until the pan is full of fritters. Fry until the edges start to brown, 2 to 3 minutes. Turn and fry the other side for another 2 to 3 minutes. Continue until all the batter is used up. Drain on a paper towel and serve piping hot.

MAKES ABOUT 8 FRITTERS; 4 SERVINGS

NOTE: These fritters taste wonderful when fried in butter. This adds cholesterol, but what's life without some risk?

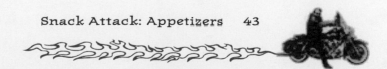

Down-Home Corn Fritters

Corn reminds me of the pleasures of childhood visits to Grandma's farm. There was always something fresh and wholesome cooking in her kitchen. These Down-Home Corn Fritters bring those memories rushing back to me. Cook them for your family and create a new generation of down-home memories. The light snap of the cherry peppers contrasts well with the sweet flavor of the corn to produce a memorable appetizer, snack, or side dish.

>   2 large eggs
>   ½ teaspoon baking powder
>   ½ teaspoon salt
>   ½ teaspoon ground white pepper
>   ½ cup all-purpose flour
>   2 cherry peppers, stemmed and minced
>   One 12-ounce can whole kernel corn, drained
>   Olive oil or butter for frying (see Note)

In a blender or a food processor equipped with a chopping blade, combine the eggs, baking powder, salt, and white pepper and puree for 1 minute. Add the flour and puree until smooth, about 1 minute.

Place the cherry peppers and corn in a large mixing bowl, cover with the batter, and mix well.

In a medium-size frying pan, heat ¼ inch of olive oil over medium heat. Place 1 heaping tablespoonful of the corn mixture into the oil and flatten gently with the back of a spoon. Repeat until the pan is full of fritters. Fry until the edges start to brown, 2 to 3 minutes. Turn and fry the other side for another 2 to 3 minutes. Continue until all the batter is used up. Drain on a paper towel and serve piping hot.

MAKES ABOUT 8 FRITTERS; 4 SERVINGS

NOTE: These fritters taste wonderful when fried in butter. This adds cholesterol, but what's life without some risk?

The Three Jalapeños

These three recipes will ride to your rescue if you're attacked by the raging jalapeño munchies. They are all Viewer Recipe Contest Winners, which proves beyond a doubt that my TV audience is munching on fiery treats while watching the show. If you have a hot night planned in your home theater, grab your sharpest fencing sword and swashbuckle your way into culinary history with The Three Jalapeños.

These recipes were designed to use average jalapeño peppers, but if you want to make them nuclear, just grow some Biker Billy jalapeños to use for stuffing.

Hal's Belly Burners

They say that the way to a biker's heart is through his or her stomach. Well, these cheesy stuffed jalapeños will burn their way right through your stomach and into your heart. After you enjoy these fiery delights with your loved ones, give Hal a big, biker-style thank-you. Alright, Hal, you and your Belly Burners are real winners!

For the stuffing:

1 cup shredded smoked Gouda cheese
½ cup shredded sharp cheddar cheese
½ cup roasted sunflower seeds, coarsely chopped
2 tablespoons Pickapeppa Sauce
½ teaspoon salt

For the breading:

1 cup cornmeal
1 cup Italian or plain dried bread crumbs
3 tablespoons chili powder
½ teaspoon salt
15 to 20 small jalapeño peppers, stemmed, cored,
   and left whole
Canola or peanut oil for deep-frying
1 jumbo egg, beaten

continued

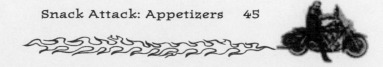

To prepare the stuffing, in a large mixing bowl, combine the Gouda cheese, cheddar cheese, and sunflower seeds and toss together well. Add the Pick-apeppa Sauce and salt and, using a fork, mix together until well blended. Cover and refrigerate for 1 hour.

To prepare the breading, in a medium-size mixing bowl, combine the cornmeal, bread crumbs, chili powder, and salt and blend thoroughly with a wire whisk. Set aside.

In a deep pot or deep-fryer, heat several inches of oil to 365°F (see page 18).

Meanwhile, to assemble, stuff the jalapeños with the cheese mixture. Dip the jalapeños, one at a time, into the beaten egg and then roll in the breading mixture. Place on a plate that is lightly dusted with some of the breading mixture. Repeat until all the jalapeños are breaded. Place a few of the breaded jalapeños in the hot oil at a time, using care not to crowd them. Fry until they are golden brown, 2 to 3 minutes. Drain on a paper towel and serve piping hot.

MAKES 15 TO 20 BELLY BURNERS

Jim and Sue's Hopping Poppers

These hopping poppers would make Oscar Madison feel right at home, since the batter is made with cornflakes and beer. Breakfast cereal with beer sounds pretty awful, but what a delicious breading it makes for these stuffed jalapeños. Go ahead, mess up your kitchen as you whip up these hopping poppers. The culinary blast from one bite will blow away any debris left strewn in the kitchen, sort of like self-cleaning food. Alright!

For the stuffing:

1 medium-size carrot, grated
½ red bell pepper, cored, seeded, and minced
2 scallions, trimmed and minced
1 tablespoon chopped garlic
¼ teaspoon salt
¼ teaspoon ground black pepper
One 8-ounce package cream cheese, softened

For the beer batter and breading:

½ cup all-purpose flour, plus extra for dusting
2½ cups cornflakes, crushed
¾ cup beer

To fry:

15 to 20 small jalapeño peppers, stemmed, cored,
    and left whole
Canola or peanut oil for deep-frying

If you are preparing the stuffing by hand, in a large mixing bowl, combine the carrot, bell pepper, scallions, garlic, salt, and black pepper and toss together well. Add the cream cheese and mix with a fork or a spoon until well blended. Cover and refrigerate for 1 hour.

If you are preparing the stuffing using a food processor, it is not neces-

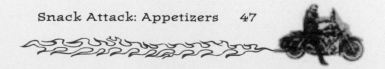

sary to pre-mince any of the ingredients. Equip the food processor with a chopping blade and add the carrot, bell pepper, and scallions, one at a time, pulsing between additions, until coarsely chopped. Add the garlic, salt, black pepper, and cream cheese and pulse until well blended. You may have to scrape down the sides of the bowl and pulse again once or twice to completely blend the mixture. Transfer to a medium bowl, cover, and refrigerate for 1 hour.

To prepare the batter, in a medium-size mixing bowl, combine the flour and ½ cup of the crushed cornflakes. Add the beer and thoroughly mix using a fork or a spoon. Set aside.

In a deep pot or deep-fryer, heat several inches of oil to 365°F (see page 18). Meanwhile, to assemble, stuff the jalapeños with the cheese mixture. Dip the jalapeños, one at a time, into the beer batter and roll in the remaining crushed cornflakes. Place on a plate that is lightly dusted with some flour. Repeat until all the jalapeños are breaded. Place a few of the breaded jalapeños in the hot oil one at a time, using care not to crowd them. Fry until they are golden brown, 2 to 3 minutes. Drain on a paper towel and serve piping hot.

MAKES 15 TO 20 POPPERS

Ormond's Jalapeño Missiles

These jalapeño missiles deliver a first strike of fiery flavor. Blanching the jalapeños mellows their heat, and the nutty cream cheese balances their fresh fire. They make a nice change from deep-fried stuffed jalapeños. You can make high-yield hors d'oeuvres with these by cutting them into slices and serving on crackers.

> 4 ounces cream cheese, softened
> 1 teaspoon onion flakes
> 1 tablespoon snipped fresh chives
> 2 tablespoons coarsely chopped pecans
> 10 jalapeño peppers, blanched (see page 16),
>   stemmed, cored, and left whole

Place the cream cheese in a small bowl. Add the onion flakes, chives, and pecans and mix together with a fork. Stuff each jalapeño with the cheese mixture. Refrigerate in a covered container for 1 hour. Serve chilled.

MAKES 10 JALAPEÑO MISSILES

The Fourth Jalapeño

Here is one more stuffed jalapeño recipe for the road. I designed it for the new Biker Billy jalapeño pepper that W. Atlee Burpee named after me. The rich filling is flavored by a wonderful combination of garlic, shallots, and garden-fresh scallions. The blending of cream cheese and cheddar cheese will help tame the blast of these scorching peppers. The breading has a south-of-the-border flair that works well with the green pepper snap of the jalapeños.

For the filling:

3 scallions, trimmed and minced
5 garlic cloves, minced
1 shallot, minced
1 tablespoon minced fresh cilantro leaves
1 teaspoon ground cumin
½ teaspoon salt
½ teaspoon ground black pepper
4 ounces cream cheese, softened
½ cup shredded mild cheddar cheese

For the breading:

1 teaspoon ground cumin
1 teaspoon ground coriander
1 teaspoon garlic powder
1 teaspoon onion powder
1 tablespoon dried parsley
1 teaspoon salt
1 teaspoon ground back pepper
½ cup plain dried bread crumbs

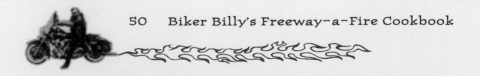

For assembly:

10 Biker Billy jalapeño peppers, blanched
   (see page 16), stemmed, seeded, and halved
   lengthwise
1 jumbo egg, beaten

If you are preparing the filling by hand, in a large mixing bowl, combine the scallions, garlic, shallot, cilantro, cumin, salt, and black pepper and toss together well. Add the cream cheese and cheddar cheese and mix with a fork until well blended. Cover and refrigerate for 1 hour.

If you are preparing the filling using a food processor, it is not necessary to pre-mince any of the ingredients. Equip the food processor with a chopping blade, add the scallions, garlic, shallot, and cilantro one at a time and pulse between additions until coarsely chopped. Add the cumin, salt, black pepper, cream cheese, and cheddar cheese and pulse until well blended. You may have to scrape down the sides of the bowl and pulse again once or twice to completely blend the mixture. Transfer to a medium-size bowl, cover, and refrigerate for 1 hour.

To prepare the breading, in a medium-size mixing bowl, combine the cumin, coriander, garlic powder, onion powder, parsley, salt, black pepper, and bread crumbs and blend thoroughly with a wire whisk. Set aside.

In a deep pot or deep-fryer, heat several inches of oil to 365°F (see page 18). Meanwhile, to assemble, stuff the jalapeño halves with the cheese mixture. Dip the jalapeños, one at a time, into the beaten egg and roll in the breading mixture. Place on a plate that is lightly dusted with some of the breading mixture. Repeat until all the jalapeños are breaded. Refrigerate for 10 minutes. Place a few of the breaded jalapeños in the hot oil at a time, using care not to crowd them. Fry until they are golden brown, 2 to 3 minutes. Drain on a paper towel and serve hot.

MAKES 20 STUFFED JALAPEÑOS

Poblano Scallion Pancakes

In my travels, I have seen some Chinese restaurants refer to scallion pancakes as "Chinese pizza." But the only thing these biker-customized delicacies have in common with pizza is their shape. Serve them as an appetizer or as bread with your favorite biker-style Asian dish. These tasty devils are so good you'll want to fill your saddlebags with them and ride to China.

1¼ cups all-purpose flour, plus extra for kneading
1 cup very hot water
2 poblano peppers, stemmed, seeded, and coarsely chopped
6 scallions, trimmed and coarsely chopped
1 teaspoon salt
Peanut oil for frying

In a large mixing bowl, combine the flour and water and mix well. Cover and let rest for 30 minutes.

Turn the dough onto a lightly floured surface, knead the dough for 1 to 2 minutes until smooth, and return to the bowl. Sprinkle the dough with the poblano peppers, scallions, and salt and knead them into the dough, adding extra flour as necessary, until the dough is not sticky and the poblanos and scallions are well integrated.

On a lightly floured surface, use your hands to roll the dough into a 1-foot-long cylinder and cut into 12 equal pieces. Use your hands to flatten one piece at a time into a pancake shape about ⅛ to ¼ inch thick. (You could use a floured rolling pin to roll the pancakes, but forming them by hand produces pancakes with more interesting shapes and texture.)

Heat a large frying pan (cast iron works best) over high heat. Lightly coat with oil and fry each pancake until golden brown, 2 to 3 minutes on each side. Drain on a paper towel. Repeat until all the pancakes are fried, adding more oil as necessary. Cut into wedges, à la pizza, and serve piping hot.

MAKES 12 PANCAKES

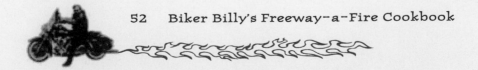

Killer Quesadillas

When you experience a snack attack, you want something that packs maximum munchie-stopping power. And these Killer Quesadillas pack true munchies-mashing might. Oozing with rich, buttery cheese and fragrant seasonings, they kill hunger on contact.

4 tablespoons (½ stick) butter
2 scallions, trimmed cut into ¼-inch-thick slices
1 to 2 chipotle peppers packed in adobo sauce (to your taste), minced
6 garlic cloves, minced
½ teaspoon ground cumin
2 tablespoons minced fresh cilantro leaves
¼ teaspoon salt
½ teaspoon ground black pepper
2 tablespoons water
Four 10-inch flour tortillas
2 cups shredded mild cheddar cheese

Melt 2 tablespoons of the butter in a small sauté pan over medium heat. Add the scallions, chipotle peppers, garlic, cumin, cilantro, salt, and black pepper. Cook until the scallions are golden brown, 7 to 10 minutes. Remove from the heat and cool to room temperature. Transfer the mixture to a blender or a food processor equipped with a chopping blade, add the 2 tablespoons of water, and puree, until smooth, about 1 minute.

Melt ½ tablespoon butter in a large frying pan over medium heat. Place 1 tortilla in the frying pan and fry until lightly browned, 1 to 2 minutes. Turn the tortilla over. Spread up to one fourth of the puree on the tortilla and cover with ½ cup of the cheese. Fry until the cheese melts and the tortilla is golden brown, 2 to 3 minutes. Fold the tortilla in half and remove from the pan. Allow to cool for 1 minute, then cut into 6 wedges. Repeat with the remaining butter, cheese, and tortillas. Serve with Firecracker Salsa (page 232).

MAKES 4 QUESADILLAS

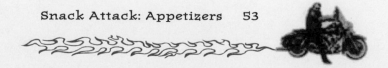

Portly Portobellos

Portly just like I am (well, not exactly), these baked stuffed mushroom caps are succulent. The earthy flavor of the portobellos are amplified by the port wine and complemented by the smoked mozzarella.

2 tablespoons extra-virgin olive oil,
plus extra for greasing and brushing
4 medium-size portobello mushrooms,
stems removed and reserved (see Note)
1 medium-size shallot, minced
1 small onion, minced
6 garlic cloves, minced
1 chipotle pepper packed in adobo sauce, minced
2 cups baby bella mushrooms (see Note), minced
½ teaspoon ground savory
1 tablespoon port wine
4 ounces smoked mozzarella cheese, cut into 4 slices

Preheat the oven to 400°F. Grease a baking dish with olive oil.

Place the mushroom caps upside down on the dish and brush with olive oil. Bake until the mushroom caps become dark and juicy, 15 minutes.

Heat the 2 tablespoons olive oil in a small sauté pan over medium heat. Add the shallot, onion, garlic, and chipotle pepper and cook until the onions are golden brown, 7 to 10 minutes. Reduce the heat to low. Add the minced baby bella mushrooms and cook until the mushrooms have darkened and have reduced in volume by half, 8 to 10 minutes. Remove from the heat and add the savory and port wine. Stir well. Spoon the mixture evenly into the portobello mushroom caps and cover with the cheese. Bake until the cheese melts, 5 to 7 minutes. Serve warm.

MAKES 4 SERVINGS

NOTE: Baby bella mushrooms are nothing more than young portobello mushrooms. They are also called cremini mushrooms. The measurement of 2 cups of minced baby bella mushrooms should include the stems of the 4 medium portobellos.

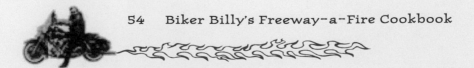

Souped-Up

A stride my souped-up Harley with a full tank of high-octane and the open road before me, I feel that all is right with the world. The freedom and power that I feel as I twist open the throttle of this big, powerful bike and rush toward the distant horizon are breathtaking. The rhythm of the motor roaring in syncopation with the sound of my heart throbbing in my ears is the surround sound of the highway. The wind whips tears of joy from my bulging eyes as I ride through the wide-screen panorama of reality. My hunger for adventure mounts, and I seek to discover what can only be found over the rise of the road or around the next bend. I could ride forever listening to the sweet sounds of my souped-up Harley-Davidson. But, alas, both the bike and I must eventually pause for nourishment. I lovingly feed my bike high-octane fuel to sustain the fire inside her. And I seek a high-octane fuel to maintain the fire within me. Soup. The flowing, fire-laced source of warmth and energy.

There are all sorts of wild soup adventures for you here. Maybe you lust for Wanton Wontons or want to Kick Asparagus Soup. Why not try on a new identity with Split Personality Pea Soup or take a mental holiday with Catatonic Carrot Soup? Launch a cruise missile with the Nuclear Navy Bean Soup or ride the Radical Red Bean Soup. Or hide out with some Chipotle Cheese Soup after committing Murderous Minestrone. The choice is yours, but let me warn you that once you are souped-up, the fire inside you will make you ride on the wild side. Alright!

Kick Asparagus Soup

This soup kicks. Well, you know what I mean. More politely put, this rich, creamy soup packs a two-fisted punch. The ancho peppers give a little warning tap and then the habanero delivers the knockout punch. Since you add the habanero-laced asparagus tips to each serving, you can adjust the impact you receive. If you think you're seeing stars, don't worry, it's the burst of color the red bell peppers create in the sea of green. So go ahead, make your day, and have a bowl of Kick Asparagus Soup.

> 8 cups water
> 6 scallions, trimmed and cut into 1-inch pieces
> 2 celery stalks, trimmed and cut into 1-inch pieces
> 1 green poblano pepper, stemmed, seeded,
>   and cut into small pieces
> 1 pound asparagus, trimmed of thick, woody ends,
>   and cut into 1-inch pieces, tips reserved
> 6 tablespoons (¾ stick) butter
> 1 fresh habanero pepper, stemmed, seeded, and cut in
>   half
> 1 red bell pepper, cored, seeded, and cut into 1-inch
>   squares
> 3 tablespoons all-purpose flour
> ¼ teaspoon ground white pepper
> 1 teaspoon salt
> ½ cup light cream

In a large soup pot over high heat, bring the water to a boil. Add the scallions, celery, poblano pepper, and asparagus stems, reduce the heat to medium, and simmer for 30 minutes.

With a slotted spoon, transfer the solids to a food processor equipped with a cutting blade. Add about 1 cup of the liquid and puree until smooth, 1 to 2 minutes. Return to the soup pot and use a wire whisk to remove any "strings" that remain from the celery. Allow to simmer for 20 to 30 minutes while you prepare the rest of the soup.

In a small sauté pan, melt 3 tablespoons of the butter over low heat. Add the habanero pepper and the reserved asparagus tips and cook for 5 min-

utes. Add the bell pepper and cook until the bell pepper is tender, about 5 minutes. Remove the habanero pieces and discard. Cover and keep warm.

Fill the bottom half of a double boiler (not quite halfway) with boiling water and place over medium heat (you don't want the top part of the double boiler to be in direct contact with the water). Every so often, check the water level to ensure that the pot does not boil dry. Keep another pot of water boiling on the stove so you can add water if necessary. Melt the remaining 3 tablespoons butter in the top of the double boiler. Add the flour, 1 tablespoon at a time, and using a wire whisk, thoroughly blend the flour into the melted butter. Add the white pepper and the salt and whisk in thoroughly. Cook for 3 to 5 minutes, stirring often with the whisk. Slowly add the cream, whisking continuously. Cook for 2 to 3 minutes, continuing to whisk until the mixture thickens.

By this time the soup should have reduced in volume by about half. Slowly add the cream mixture to the soup while stirring. Simmer until the soup thickens, 3 to 5 minutes. When you serve the soup, spoon some of the asparagus tips and bell peppers into the center of each bowl.

MAKES 6 TO 8 SERVINGS

Split Personality Pea Soup

Here is a real hearty biker-style soup. It will stick to your ribs and warm you after a long winter ride. The ancho and de árbol peppers add a flavor and fire that work well with the split peas. The only way to explain it is to say that it's "like chrome on a Harley." What more can a biker say? So rev up your soup pots with this custom soup and roar off into culinary history.

6 cups water
1 pound dried split peas, sorted and rinsed (see page 22)
½ teaspoon salt
1 bay leaf
1 ancho pepper, stemmed, seeded, and torn into small pieces
1 to 3 dried de árbol peppers (to your taste), stemmed and crushed
1 cup boiling water (see page 15)
1 teaspoon celery seeds
2 tablespoons dried parsley
2 tablespoons butter
2 medium-size onions, coarsely chopped
7 garlic cloves, minced
2 cups baby carrots, cut into ½-inch-thick slices
1 teaspoon salt
1 teaspoon ground black pepper
1 cup hot water (optional)

In a large soup pot over high heat, bring the water to a boil. Add the split peas, salt, and bay leaf and boil for 10 minutes, stirring often. Reduce the heat to medium and simmer for 30 minutes, stirring often.

While the soup simmers, place the ancho and de árbol peppers in a small bowl and cover with the boiling water. Allow to cool to room temperature. In a blender or a food processor equipped with a chopping blade, puree the rehydrated peppers and the soaking water for about 2 minutes, or until smooth.

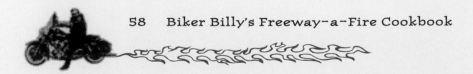

Remove the bay leaf from the soup and discard. Using a slotted spoon, transfer the solids from the soup along with 1 cup of liquid to the blender or food processor and puree until smooth, 2 minutes. Return to the soup pot and add the celery seeds and parsley. Reduce the heat to low, cover, and stir often.

In a large sauté pan, melt the butter over medium heat. Add the onions, garlic, and carrots and cook until the onions begin to brown, 5 to 7 minutes. Transfer the mixture to the soup pot and stir well. Add the salt and pepper and continue to simmer until the carrots are tender, about 30 minutes. You may wish to add some hot water to the soup if it is too thick for your taste. I like mine on the thick and hearty side. Serve piping hot.

MAKES 4 TO 6 SERVINGS

Catatonic Carrot Soup

Have you ever heard the term "food coma," the trancelike state of relaxation that is induced by a hearty meal? Well, this soup has been known to do that to people. It is so rich and creamy that one bowlful will put you in a trance. And when you awake, your eyesight may be sharper from the megadose of carrots. Well nourished, rested, and with enhanced vision, you will be ready to go for a marathon motorcycle ride. Just make sure to pack a thermos full of this soup so you can maintain a state of carrot catatonia.

4 tablespoons (½ stick) butter
1 fresh red cayenne pepper, stemmed,
   seeded and coarsely chopped (see Note)
8 garlic cloves, coarsely chopped
2 medium-size onions, coarsely chopped
4 cups thinly sliced carrots
½ teaspoon celery seeds
½ teaspoon salt
½ teaspoon ground black pepper
3 cups water
¼ teaspoon dried basil
⅛ teaspoon ground cumin
1 cup half-and-half

Melt the butter in a large sauté pan over medium heat. Add the cayenne pepper, garlic, onions, and carrots and stir well to coat with butter. Cook until the carrots are tender, 10 minutes.

Transfer the mixture to a large soup pot, add the celery seeds, salt, black pepper, and water and stir well. Place over high heat and bring to a boil. Reduce the heat to low and simmer, covered, for 30 minutes, stirring often.

Using a slotted spoon, transfer the solids from the soup along with 1 cup of liquid to a blender or a food processor equipped with a chopping blade. Puree for 2 minutes, or until smooth. Return to the soup pot and add the basil and cumin. Cover and simmer for 5 minutes, stirring often.

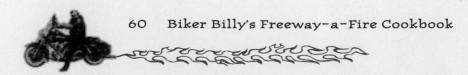

Just before serving, transfer 1 cup of the soup to the blender or food processor, add the half-and-half, and puree until smooth, 1 minute. Stir the puree into the soup until well blended and serve immediately.

MAKES 4 TO 6 SERVINGS

NOTE: I recommend using a red cayenne pepper, since the red color of the pepper will blend well with the orange of the carrots. But you can use a green cayenne, and the fire and taste will be just fine.

From the Dugan family album: an unknown rider enjoying a country lane.

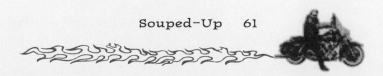

Chipotle Cheese Soup

Warm and soothing, this soup is a winter rider's best friend. The slightly smoky overtones of the chipotle peppers intermingle beautifully with the creamy cheese base. This soup will give you that warm, sitting-by-the-fireside feeling on a frosty day. It packs enough calories and hot pepper fire to fuel your body for a long afternoon of winter motorcycling. Don't be a hog, share a bowl of this cheesy delight with your riding buddies, then ride your Hogs through a winter wonderland. Alright!

1 large broccoli stalk
3 tablespoons butter
½ teaspoon celery seeds
2 cups baby carrots, quartered
1 medium-size onion, diced
1 to 2 chipotle peppers packed in adobo sauce (to
    your taste), minced, plus 1 tablespoon adobo sauce
5 cups water
2 tablespoons chopped garlic
1 tablespoon dried parsley
1 teaspoon ground savory
1 teaspoon salt
1 teaspoon ground black pepper
1 red bell pepper, cored, seeded, and diced
1 cup whole milk
1 pound Velveeta cheese, cut into ½-inch chunks
1 tablespoon all-purpose flour

Trim the broccoli, remove the florets, coarsely chop them, and set aside. Thinly slice the stalk.

Melt 2 tablespoons of the butter in a medium sauté pan over medium heat. Add the sliced broccoli stalk, celery seeds, carrots, and onion. Cook until the onion is transparent, 6 to 8 minutes.

Transfer the cooked vegetables to a large soup pot set over high heat. Add the chipotle peppers, water, garlic, parsley, savory, salt, and black pepper and bring to a boil. Reduce the heat to medium, cover, and simmer for 45 minutes, stirring often.

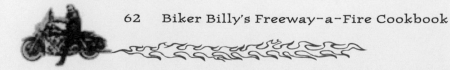

Add the broccoli florets and bell pepper and stir well. Reduce the heat to low and simmer for 15 minutes, stirring often.

Add the milk and Velveeta cheese and stir until the cheese melts. Reduce the heat to very low and simmer, stirring often, while you prepare the roux.

In a small saucepot, melt the remaining 1 tablespoon butter over low heat. Add the flour and stir well. Continue to stir until the flour is a very light brown, 2 to 3 minutes. Add the adobo sauce and 2 cups of liquid from the soup, and mix thoroughly with a wire whisk. Transfer the mixture to the soup and stir until well blended. Simmer, stirring often, until the soup thickens, 5 minutes. Serve immediately.

MAKES 6 TO 8 SERVINGS

Murderous Minestrone

This is one of those soups that is so warming that you would like to have a pot of it on the stove all winter long. It will thaw you out after a long cold ride. It will soothe your aching bones. It will even calm the spirit. No, it's not some miracle drug, but every bowl of this soup is a complete meal unto itself. I have virtually lived on it and crusty Italian bread for several days at a time. In fact, the only thing murderous is the tubettini pasta, which will slowly drink the life-giving liquids out of the soup, transforming it into a stew (and a good one at that). Your only defense is to cook the pasta until tender and add it just before serving. If your leftover soup becomes really thick, be careful not to add too much water in an effort to thin it, or you may be guilty of soupicide.

5 quarts (20 cups) water
1 cup dried garbanzo beans, sorted and rinsed (see page 22)
1 cup dried cannellini beans, sorted and rinsed (see page 22)
1 cup tubettini pasta
2 tablespoons extra-virgin olive oil
2 large onions, diced
1 cup baby carrots, cut into ½-inch pieces
2 chipotle peppers packed in adobo sauce, minced
2 shallots, minced
10 garlic cloves, minced
1 cup green beans, ends trimmed and cut into ½-inch pieces
6 ripe plum tomatoes, peeled (see page 18) and diced
1 medium-size zucchini, quartered lengthwise and cut into ¼-inch-thick slices
1 teaspoon celery seeds
3 teaspoons dried basil
2 tablespoons dried parsley
24 sun-dried tomatoes, minced

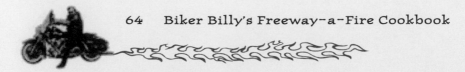

2 teaspoons salt
2 teaspoons ground black pepper

Combine 8 cups of the water and beans in a large soup pot. Place over high heat and bring to a boil. Reduce the heat to low and boil for 2 minutes. Remove from the heat, cover, and soak for 1 hour. Drain and rinse the beans (this will shorten the overall cooking time and rinse away extra starch). Return the beans to the soup pot and add the remaining 12 cups of water. Place over high heat and bring to a boil. Reduce the heat to low and simmer for 1 hour, stirring often.

Fill a large pot with water and bring to a boil, salted if you prefer. Cook the pasta until tender, according to package directions. Drain and rinse with cold water to stop the cooking process and to remove excess starch. Allow the pasta to drain thoroughly and set aside.

While the beans are simmering, heat the olive oil in a large sauté pan over medium heat. Add the onions and carrots and cook until the onions are tender, 5 to 7 minutes. Add the chipotle peppers, shallots, garlic, green beans, tomatoes, zucchini, celery seeds, basil, parsley, sun-dried tomatoes, salt, and black pepper and stir well. Cook until the vegetables are just tender, 8 to 10 minutes. Transfer the mixture to the soup pot and stir well. Simmer until the beans are tender, 20 to 30 minutes, stirring often. Five minutes before serving, add the cooked pasta. Serve piping hot.

MAKES ABOUT 4 QUARTS; 8 TO 12 SERVINGS

Nuclear Navy Bean Soup

This recently declassified recipe is the secret power source of the American Nuclear Navy. The flavor and fire provide a 10-megaton blast for your palate. Enjoying just one bowl of Nuclear Navy Bean Soup will give you enough energy to cruise around the world on your Harley. Three Mile Island never leaked anything this hot. So put on your lead apron and cook up a real melt-down.

3 tablespoons butter
1 dried habanero pepper, stemmed and crushed
1 leek, trimmed, washed well,
   cut into ¼-inch-thick slices
2 tablespoons chopped garlic
2 carrots, thinly sliced
2 celery stalks with leaves, trimmed
   and cut into ¼-inch-thick slices
One 16-ounce can navy beans or small white beans,
   drained and rinsed
3 cups water
¼ teaspoon dried thyme
⅛ teaspoon celery seeds
¼ teaspoon ground sage
½ teaspoon salt
½ teaspoon ground white pepper
1 cup whole milk
¼ teaspoon ground savory

Melt the butter in a large soup pot over medium heat. Add the habanero pepper and cook for 30 seconds. Add the leek, garlic, carrots, and celery and cook until the garlic begins to brown, 2 to 3 minutes. Add the beans and water and bring to a boil. Reduce the heat to low. Add the thyme, celery seeds, sage, salt, and white pepper and simmer, covered, for 30 minutes, stirring often.

Add the milk and savory while stirring. Simmer for 10 minutes, stirring often. Serve piping hot.

MAKES 4 TO 6 SERVINGS

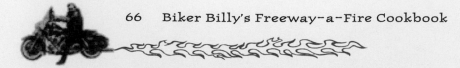

Radical Red Bean Soup

Like riding a wild radical chopper, this soup will give you a rush. The chunky texture has a solid feel, just like a rigid-framed bike. And the chipotle peppers will make you hear the sound of a hopped-up Harley motor thumping in your ears. Your soup spoon will call out to you like the throttle of that chopper, daring you to open her up and enjoy the ride.

3 tablespoons butter
2 medium-size onions, minced
2 cups baby carrots, cut into ½-inch pieces
3 celery stalks, trimmed and cut into ¼-inch-thick slices
2 tablespoons chopped garlic
2 chipotle peppers packed in adobo sauce, minced
1 dried New Mexico pepper, stemmed, seeded, and crushed
Two 16-ounce cans red kidney beans, drained and rinsed
½ teaspoon celery seeds
1 teaspoon dried cilantro
1 tablespoon dried parsley
¼ teaspoon ground cumin
1½ teaspoons salt
½ teaspoon ground black pepper
5 cups water
1 tablespoon all-purpose flour

In a large soup pot, melt 2 tablespoons of the butter over medium heat. Add the onions and carrots and stir well to coat with butter. Cook until the onions are transparent, 6 to 8 minutes. Add the celery, garlic, and chipotle and New Mexico peppers and stir well. Cook until the onions begin to brown, 2 to 3 minutes. Add the kidney beans, celery seeds, cilantro, parsley, cumin, salt, black pepper, and 4 cups of the water. Bring to a boil, then reduce the heat to low. Simmer until the soup has thickened and the vegetables are tender, 1 hour. *continued*

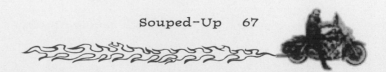

In a small saucepot, melt the remaining 1 tablespoon butter over low heat. Add the flour and stir well. Continue to stir until the flour is golden brown, 3 to 4 minutes. Add the remaining 1 cup water and mix thoroughly with a wire whisk. Transfer to the soup pot and stir until well blended. Simmer, stirring often, until the soup thickens, 5 to 10 minutes. Serve with biscuits (page 202 or 204).

MAKES 6 TO 8 SERVINGS

NEW RED HOT PEPPER

Wanton Wontons

Yes, these wontons are wanton all right; they're a-wantin' you to eat 'em. So run to the kitchen and get cooking, then fulfill those wanton wontons' wildest dreams: Eat them. Just don't be surprised if you find yourself wantin' more than one bowlful.

This recipe has two main components: the soup and the stuffed wontons. Start by preparing the soup, and while it simmers, prepare the wontons. If you are creating a multicourse Asian feast, the soup stock and wontons can be prepared a day in advance, refrigerated separately, then combined and cooked fresh the next day.

For the soup:

8 cups water

1 ancho pepper, stemmed, seeded, and torn into small pieces

1 pasilla pepper, stemmed, seeded, and torn into small pieces

1 dried long, slim red cayenne pepper, stemmed

4 tablespoons (½ stick) butter

¼ cup peeled and coarsely chopped fresh ginger

2 tablespoons chopped garlic

6 scallions, trimmed and coarsely chopped

3 shallots, coarsely chopped

½ cup sliced cremini (brown) mushrooms

½ cup sliced shiitake mushroom caps

½ cup light teriyaki sauce

For the wontons:

1 ancho pepper, stemmed, seeded, and torn into small pieces

1 pasilla pepper, stemmed, seeded, and torn into small pieces

continued

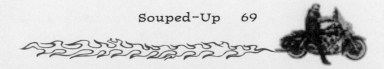

1 dried long, slim red cayenne pepper, stemmed and
   crushed

4 tablespoons (½ stick) butter

1 pound *extra-firm* bean curd, drained and
   crumbled

4 scallions, trimmed and cut into ¼-inch-thick
   slices

1 tablespoon peeled and coarsely chopped fresh
   ginger

1 tablespoon chopped garlic

1 teaspoon ground black pepper

¼ cup light teriyaki sauce

1 tablespoon Liquid Smoke

One 12-ounce package wonton wrappers (about 48)

1 large egg, beaten

All-purpose flour for dusting

For assembly:

3 large bok choy leaves, coarsely chopped

1 red bell pepper, cored, seeded, and julienned

To prepare the soup, place the 8 cups of water in a large pot over high heat. Allow the water to come to a boil, then reduce to a slow simmer.

Meanwhile, in a blender or a food processor equipped with a chopping blade, combine the ancho, pasilla, and cayenne peppers and chop for 1 minute.

In a small sauté pan, melt the butter over medium heat. Add the chopped hot peppers and cook for 2 minutes. Add the ginger, garlic, and scallions and cook until the scallions are golden brown, 3 to 5 minutes. Using a slotted spoon, transfer the mixture to the pot of hot water, leaving the butter in the sauté pan.

Place the shallots and both mushrooms into the sauté pan with the reserved butter, and place over medium heat. Cook until the mushrooms are tender, 3 to 5 minutes, and remove from the heat.

To make the soup, place a medium metal strainer across the top of the large pot of simmering water and pour the mushroom mixture into the strainer (see Note). Add the teriyaki sauce and simmer the stock over low heat for 1 hour; if necessary, add additional water to maintain the same level. Remove the strainer with the mushrooms and set aside.

To prepare the wontons, in a blender or a food processor equipped with

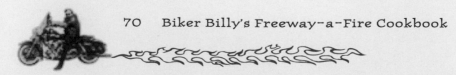

a chopping blade, combine the ancho, pasilla, and cayenne peppers and process until finely chopped, 2 minutes.

In a large sauté pan, melt the butter over medium heat. Add the chopped hot peppers and cook for 2 minutes. Add the bean curd, scallions, ginger, garlic, and black pepper, and cook until the bean curd is crispy and browned, 5 to 7 minutes. Add the teriyaki sauce and Liquid Smoke and stir well. Remove from the heat and allow to cool.

Remove the wonton wrappers from their package and carefully separate several of the wonton squares. Arrange these on your work surface and place a spoonful of bean curd mixture on the center of each square (there should be an even border of the wonton wrapper around the filling, allowing you to seal the edges easily). Brush the exposed edges of the wonton wrappers with the beaten egg. Pick up one corner of the wrapper and fold it over the filling to create a triangle. Pinch the edges closed (it is important that the filling is sealed inside the wrapper). Pick up the triangle, holding it by the two corners that are connected by the fold. Gently bring the two corners together so that they overlap and pinch them together. Place the assembled wontons on a flour-dusted plate; they should not touch each other or they will stick together. Repeat until all the wontons are assembled.

To assemble the soup, in a large pot (about 8 quarts), combine the bok choy, bell pepper, and the reserved mushrooms. Pour the mushroom stock in through a strainer and discard the strained solids. Place the pot over high heat and bring to a boil, then immediately reduce the heat to medium and simmer for 15 minutes. Add the wontons and continue to simmer until the wontons are tender, 10 to 15 minutes. Serve piping hot.

MAKES 6 TO 8 SERVINGS

NOTE: The intention is to allow the caramelized mushrooms to impart their flavor to the stock, then use them again later in the soup while removing the other solids from the soup stock. The strainer should allow the mushrooms to be covered with the soup.

The start of the Stage Coach Enduro, circa 1949; the riders are ready to roll in front of Tramontin Pontiac in Clifton, New Jersey.

High-Performance Pasta

Pasta may well be one of the most versatile food groups around. In many respects, pasta is like a motorcycle—it is made in a myriad of designs to satisfy a variety of tastes. Pasta can wear a sauce like a big-bucks custom chopper wears an exotic paint job. That same pasta can also pack its own flavor punch just as that custom bike packs a radical cam in a high-compression motor. Or pasta can be like a long-distance touring bike, stuffed with all the goodies for a ride to adventure. Some pasta resembles commuter bikes, quickly taking care of business while still delivering thrills. Then there are the purebred race bikes of the pasta world, combining brute power with cutting-edge design. And, of course, there are the vintage bike pastas—classic dishes with a sense of history and heritage. In their own way, each of the following pasta dishes is high-performance. While I can't give you a fleet of bikes, I can offer you a kitchen garage full of fiery, flavorful pasta dishes and sauces.

Ancho Fettuccine

Colored pastas look so appetizing, but often the dried stuff you buy at the supermarket is more show than go in the taste department. Well, this rich red pasta packs both robust flavor and a nice warm punch. Just the thing you need to kick some life into that old tomato sauce. Try serving this with the Primavera à la Biker sauce (page 76) and watch your family dance with delight like a prima ballerina—leather clad, of course.

Did I hear you say, "Sounds good, but I'll bet it's too much trouble"? Fresh pasta is a real treat, and it takes less work than you might think, even if you do it all by hand. If you use a food processor, it's downright easy. I have included the instructions for both methods, and you probably have most of the ingredients already. So what are you waiting for?

> 2 ancho peppers, stemmed, seeded, and torn into
>   small pieces
> 1 cup boiling water (see page 15)
> 4 tablespoons (½ stick) butter, cut into small pieces
> 1 teaspoon salt
> 2 cups all-purpose flour, plus extra for kneading
>   and dusting

Place the ancho peppers in small bowl and cover with the boiling water. Allow to cool to room temperature.

If you are preparing the pasta by hand, puree the rehydrated peppers and the soaking water in a blender until no large pieces of ancho remains, about 1 minute. Add the butter and salt and puree until smooth, 1 minute. Place the flour in a large bowl and form a well in the center. Pour the pepper puree into the well. Cut the pepper puree into the flour using a dough cutter or two knives. When a dough has formed, remove it from the bowl and knead on a lightly floured surface for 2 to 3 minutes. The dough should not be sticky, but if it is, work in a little extra flour as you knead it until it is smooth and dry to the touch. Place the dough in a covered bowl or a sealable plastic bag and let rest for 30 minutes.

If you are preparing the pasta using a food processor, puree the rehydrated peppers and the soaking water in the workbowl of the processor, equipped with a chopping blade, until no large pieces of ancho remain,

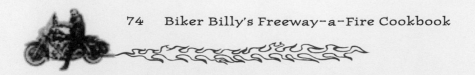

1 minute. Add the butter and salt and puree until smooth, 1 minute. Add the flour, ½ cup at a time, processing for about 1 minute after each addition, until the pepper puree is well cut into the flour. Continue to process until the dough forms a ball that revolves around the processor bowl (it may be necessary to stop processing periodically to scrape down the sides of the bowl). If the dough sticks to the processor bowl, add a little flour and process again. The dough should not be sticky and should freely separate from the food processor bowl and blade. Place the dough in a covered bowl or a sealable plastic bag and let rest for 30 minutes.

Divide the dough into 4 pieces (when rolled, these should produce manageable-sized sheets of pasta). Using a floured rolling pin on a lightly floured surface, roll 1 piece of dough into a rectangle, ⅛ inch thick. Roll from the center toward the outside and turn the dough a quarter-turn between each rolling. Always make sure there is enough flour on the rolling pin and surface to prevent sticking. When you have finished rolling out the pasta, lightly dust it with flour and fold it in half, dust the top again, and fold it once more. With a sharp knife, cut the pasta across the folds into ⅜-inch-wide pieces. Use a downward cutting action, since dragging the blade through the pasta may cause tearing. Unfold the cut pasta and place in a single layer on a flour-dusted surface or wax paper. Repeat with the remaining 3 pieces of dough.

Bring a large pot of water to a boil, salted if you prefer. (Since fresh pasta cooks very fast the sauce should be heated before the pasta goes into the water.) Place the pasta in the boiling water and stir gently with a wooden spoon to prevent sticking. The pasta will be done in 1 to 3 minutes, but doneness can be judged only by tasting. It is always better to err on the side of too firm. Drain, rinse, and cover with the sauce of your choice. Serve immediately.

MAKES 4 TO 6 SERVINGS

Primavera à la Biker

A one-dish wonder if ever there was one, combining garden-fresh flavors with the crisp snap of cherry peppers. The cheesy sauce keeps the relatively low-powered cherry peppers from overwhelming the delicate flavors of the vegetables. You will get a warm, gentle glow from this hearty but simple sauce. However, if you want more fire, you can boost the culinary horsepower by substituting serrano or cayenne peppers. Whichever hot peppers you add to this sauce, they will make your pasta simply perfect.

> 4 tablespoons (½ stick) butter
> 2 to 3 cherry peppers (to your taste),
>   stemmed and minced
> 1 cup baby carrots
> 1 medium-size onion, diced
> 1 small zucchini, halved lengthwise,
>   cut into ¼-inch-thick slices
> 1 cup sliced mushrooms
> 1 red bell pepper, cored, seeded, and julienned
> 1 yellow bell pepper, cored, seeded, and julienned
> 1 large broccoli stalk, florets only,
>   cut into bite-size pieces
> 1 tablespoon chopped garlic
> 1 pound fettuccine pasta
> 1 cup freshly grated Parmesan cheese
> 1 cup light cream
> Salt and ground black pepper to taste

Fill a large pot with water and bring to a boil. Meanwhile, melt the butter in a large sauté pan over medium heat. Add the cherry peppers, carrots, and onion and cook until the onions are tender, 3 to 5 minutes. Add the zucchini and mushrooms and cook until the mushrooms darken, 3 to 5 minutes. Add the bell peppers, broccoli florets, and garlic and cook until the broccoli florets darken, 3 to 5 minutes.

While the vegetables cook, cook the pasta in the boiling water, according to package directions until it is al dente. Rinse with hot water to remove excess starch. Allow the pasta to drain thoroughly.

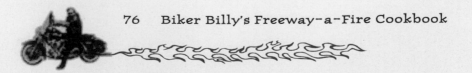

Reduce the heat under the sauté pan to low. Sprinkle the cheese over the vegetables and toss well. Add the cream and simmer for 2 minutes, stirring often to blend the sauce. Season with salt and black pepper.

Combine the pasta and vegetables in a large serving bowl, toss well, and serve immediately.

MAKES 4 TO 6 SERVINGS

Pierina Tramontin on her bike during
World War II, circa the early 1940s.

Chipotle Pasta Sauce

The chipotle peppers give this quick-and-easy sauce a wonderful smoky flavor and a surprising amount of fire. The taste reminds me of the rush I get from winning at the traffic-light drag races. Picture yourself astride a throbbing Harley sitting at a red light. In the lane next to you is a cell phone–toting, foreign car–driving member of the yup generation. The light flashes green and two motors howl, you accelerate away at maximum warp with the wind in your face, leaving behind a wannabe racer saying, "I should-a had-a V-twin!"

2 chipotle peppers, stemmed
¼ cup boiling water (see page 15)
2 tablespoons extra-virgin olive oil
2 medium-size onions, diced
1 cup sliced mushrooms
1 yellow bell pepper, cored, seeded, and diced
2 tablespoons chopped garlic
1 tablespoon minced fresh oregano leaves
1 teaspoon salt
1 teaspoon ground black pepper
One 28-ounce can whole peeled tomatoes,
    coarsely chopped, with their juice

Place the chipotle peppers in a small bowl and cover with the boiling water. Allow to cool to room temperature.

In a blender or a food processor equipped with a chopping blade, puree the rehydrated peppers and the soaking water until no large pieces of chipotle remain, 1 minute.

Heat the olive oil in a large sauté pan over medium heat. Add the onions and mushrooms and stir well to coat with oil. Cook until the onions are golden brown, 5 to 7 minutes. Add the chipotle puree, bell pepper, garlic, oregano, salt, black pepper, and tomatoes with their juice to the sauté pan. Bring to a boil, reduce the heat, and simmer until the sauce just thickens, 8 to 10 minutes.

MAKES ABOUT 4 CUPS

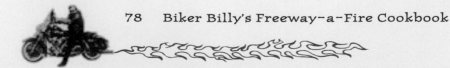

Meany Rotini

Eeny-meeny-miny-moe, which pasta in the pot will go? Why use one pasta shape instead of another? Because rotini does a good job of holding on to cooked sun-dried tomatoes, onions, and garlic. The single chipotle makes this dish spicy but not mean; add more if you want to be a real meany. I enjoy this when I want fast, zippy pasta without a heavy sauce.

1 chipotle pepper, stemmed
¼ cup boiling water (see page 15)
¼ cup extra-virgin olive oil
¼ cup sun-dried tomatoes packed in oil, minced
1 large onion, coarsely chopped
1 tablespoon chopped garlic
½ teaspoon salt
½ teaspoon ground black pepper
4 cups tricolor rotini pasta

Place the chipotle pepper in a small bowl and cover with the boiling water. Allow to cool to room temperature. Remove the chipotle from the water and mince. Discard the water.

Fill a large pot with water and bring to a boil over high heat.

In a large sauté pan, heat the olive oil over medium heat. Add the chipotle, sun-dried tomatoes, and onion and cook until the onion is tender, 3 to 5 minutes. Add the garlic, salt, and black pepper and cook until the onions are golden brown, 2 to 3 minutes. Reduce the heat to very low and keep warm while the pasta cooks.

Cook the pasta in the boiling water according to package directions until it is al dente. Rinse with hot water to remove excess starch. Allow the pasta to drain thoroughly.

Place the pasta in a large serving bowl. Cover with the sauce, toss well, and serve immediately.

MAKES 4 TO 6 SERVINGS

Pasta e Fagioli à la Biker

Oh baby, here is a biker concoction sure to satisfy. Firm pasta, cozied-up with beans, swimming around in a wonderful sauce—a rich medley of cooked onions, garlic, sun-dried tomatoes, and herbs, creamed to perfection with the warm sparkle of fresh jalapeños. Burn rubber on your way to the kitchen and cook up a big batch of Pasta e Fagioli a la Biker. Alright!

¼ cup extra-virgin olive oil

1 medium-size onion, minced

2 tablespoons chopped garlic

6 sun-dried tomatoes, minced

2 jalapeño peppers, stemmed and minced

One 16-ounce can cannellini beans, drained and rinsed

½ teaspoon dried oregano

½ teaspoon dried basil

1 teaspoon dried parsley

1 teaspoon salt

½ teaspoon ground black pepper

1 tablespoon pignoli nuts, coarsely chopped

1 cup water

½ cup half-and-half

1 pound ditalini pasta

Fill a large pot with water and bring to a boil over high heat.

Heat the olive oil in a large sauté pan over medium heat. Add the onion, garlic, sun-dried tomatoes, and jalapeños and cook until the onion is tender, 3 to 5 minutes. Add the beans and cook for 2 minutes. Add the oregano, basil, parsley, salt, black pepper, pignoli nuts, and water and stir well. Reduce the heat to low and simmer for 10 minutes, stirring often. Slowly add the half-and-half while stirring. Simmer for 5 minutes, stirring often.

Cook the pasta in the boiling water according to package directions until it is al dente. Drain and rinse with hot water to remove excess starch. Allow the pasta to drain thoroughly.

Place the pasta in a large serving bowl. Cover with the sauce, toss well, and serve immediately.

MAKES 4 TO 6 SERVINGS

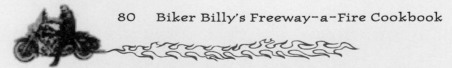

Rude Oily Pasta

You know there is only one thing that makes this pasta rude. It is so tasty you will want to hog it all for yourself. And that is rude, especially since the aroma of garlic will drive everybody within 100 yards crazy. So share this pasta with your friends; they'll love you for it. Just don't tell them they have garlic breath because that would be truly rude.

> 3 tablespoons dried parsley (see Note)
> ½ teaspoon dried oregano (see Note)
> ½ teaspoon dried basil (see Note)
> ¼ cup boiling water (see page 15)
> ½ cup extra-virgin olive oil
> 1 medium-size onion, minced
> 3 jalapeño peppers, stemmed,
>   seeded, and minced
> ¼ cup minced fresh garlic, or more to taste
> ¾ cup pignoli nuts (about 3 ounces)
> ½ teaspoon salt
> ½ teaspoon ground black pepper
> 1 pound angel hair pasta
> Freshly grated Parmesan cheese (optional)

Place the parsley, oregano, and basil in a small bowl and cover with the boiling water. Allow to cool to room temperature.

Fill a large pot with water and bring to a boil over high heat.

Heat the olive oil in a small sauté pan over medium heat. Add the onion and jalapeños and cook until the onion is tender, 3 to 5 minutes. Add the garlic and pignoli nuts and cook until the garlic just begins to brown, 2 to 3 minutes. Add the rehydrated herbs with the soaking water, salt, and black pepper, reduce the heat to low, and simmer for 2 to 3 minutes, stirring often.

Cook the pasta in the boiling water according to package directions until it is al dente. Rinse with hot water to remove excess starch. Allow the pasta to drain thoroughly

continued

Place the pasta in a large serving bowl. Cover with the sauce, add the cheese (if you like), toss well, and serve immediately.

MAKES 4 SERVINGS

NOTE: If you want to use fresh parsley, oregano, and basil, triple the amounts listed and reduce the water to 2 tablespoons. It is not necessary to soak the fresh herbs. The herbs should be coarsely chopped before measuring and then packed in the measuring spoons.

Racing at Wall Stadium in Wall Township, New Jersey, circa 1952. The racer on the left is Al Sedusky and on the right is Al Wilcox (number 5).

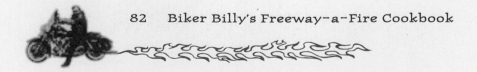

Sorta Stroganoff

Rich and creamy with the hearty flavor of mushrooms, this stuff is "sorta" delicious. The sherry lends a subtle highlight and the cayenne adds a clean fire to the dish. This recipe falls squarely in the category of luxury food and will leave you with a warm, satisfied feeling. I have used fettuccine here, but you could use wide egg noodles or your favorite pasta shape. After a plateful of Sorta Stroganoff, you may feel like restoring an old Teutonic motorcycle and heading off for a tour of the Alps.

4 tablespoons (½ stick) butter
1 fresh long, red slim cayenne pepper, stemmed and minced
1 medium-size onion, diced
4 cups mushrooms (about 10 ounces), minced
⅛ teaspoon ground nutmeg
1 teaspoon salt
½ teaspoon ground white pepper
1 tablespoon dried chives
1 tablespoon chopped garlic
2 tablespoons dry sherry
1 cup sour cream or half-and-half
¼ cup freshly grated Parmesan cheese
¼ teaspoon ground savory
One 12-ounce box spinach fettuccine pasta

In a large sauté pan, melt the butter over medium heat. Add the cayenne pepper and cook for 2 minutes. Add the onion and cook until the onion is tender, 3 to 5 minutes. Reduce the heat to low. Add the mushrooms and cook until the mushrooms darken and begin to release their juices, 5 to 7 minutes. Add the nutmeg, salt, white pepper, chives, and garlic and cook 2 to 3 minutes. Add the sherry and stir well. Cook for 2 minutes to allow the alcohol to evaporate. Slowly add the sour cream while stirring and simmer for 5 minutes. Add the cheese and savory and stir well. Reduce the heat to very low and keep warm, stirring often, while the pasta cooks.

Fill a large pot with water and bring to a boil over high heat. Cook the pasta according to package directions until it is al dente. Rinse with hot water to remove excess starch. Allow the pasta to drain thoroughly.

Place the pasta in a large serving bowl. Cover with the sauce, toss well, and serve immediately.

MAKES 4 TO 6 SERVINGS

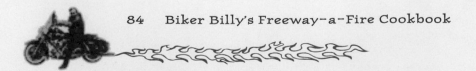

Righteous Rotelle

The shape of rotelle pasta makes it a perfect vehicle for carrying sauce. Just like a motorcycle is a perfect vehicle for carrying me. And the sauce is like me, too, after a long motorcycle ride: sun-dried, hot, and aromatic. The sun-dried tomatoes and chipotle peppers are a winning combination. Onion, garlic, and classic Italian seasonings (including a big dose of basil) are cooked in olive oil to create a sauce that is as potent as a race-prepped Ducati. Add a layer of mozzarella and Parmesan cheeses, just like racing leathers, and you're ready for the checkered flag. So rev up your culinary engines and race into the kitchen and ride with the Righteous Rotelle.

¼ cup extra-virgin olive oil

2 medium-size onions, minced

3 tablespoons chopped garlic

1 to 2 chipotle peppers packed in adobo sauce (to your taste), minced

¾ cup sun-dried tomatoes packed in oil, minced

1 teaspoon salt

½ teaspoon ground black pepper

1 teaspoon dried oregano

1 teaspoon dried parsley

⅓ cup dried basil

1½ cups water

1 pound rotelle pasta

3 cups shredded mozzarella cheese

¼ cup freshly grated Parmesan cheese

Heat the olive oil in a small sauté pan over high heat. Add the onions and cook until the onions begin to brown, 3 to 5 minutes. Reduce the heat to medium. Add the garlic and cook 1 to 2 minutes. Add the chipotle peppers and sun-dried tomatoes and cook until the onion is golden brown, 1 to 2 minutes. Add the salt, black pepper, oregano, parsley, basil, and water and bring to a boil. Reduce the heat to low. Cover and simmer until the sauce thickens, 10 to 15 minutes.

Preheat the oven to 350°F. Fill a large pot with water and bring to a boil over high heat. Cook the pasta according to package directions until it is

al dente. Drain and rinse with cold water to stop the cooking process and remove excess starch. Allow the pasta to drain thoroughly.

Put the pasta in a baking dish and cover with the sauce. Stir well to coat the pasta with sauce and cover with the mozzarella and Parmesan cheeses. Bake until the cheeses are melted and begin to brown, 20 to 25 minutes. Serve piping hot with garlic bread (page 200 or 201).

MAKES 4 TO 6 SERVINGS

Burning Bow Ties

I could have named this recipe Fiery Farfel. But, to misquote William Shakespeare, a pasta dish this fiery would be tasty by any name. The sun-dried tomatoes, baby carrots, and asparagus are both delicious and colorful. The sauce benefits from the dynamic duo of garlic and basil coupled with the earthy portobello mushroom and sun-dried tomatoes. And the Biker Billy jalapeño adds all the fire you could desire. The result is a vision of bow tie pasta perfectly dressed in formal wear—just like a biker in vintage black leather.

¾ cup sun-dried tomatoes, cut into ¼-inch-thick slices

¼ cup dried basil

3 tablespoons dried parsley

½ cup boiling water (see page 15)

⅓ cup extra-virgin olive oil

1 Biker Billy jalapeño pepper, stemmed and thinly sliced

1 cup baby carrots, quartered lengthwise

1 bunch asparagus (about 1 pound), trimmed of thick woody ends and cut into 1-inch pieces, tips reserved

6 scallions, trimmed

1 medium-size portobello mushroom cap, cut into ¼-inch-thick squares

½ cup chopped garlic (I use prechopped garlic from a jar)

2 teaspoons salt

1 teaspoon ground black pepper

1 pound bow tie pasta

¼ cup water

Combine the sun-dried tomatoes, basil, and parsley in a small bowl and cover with the boiling water. Allow to cool to room temperature.

Fill a large pot with water and bring to a boil over high heat.

continued

Heat the olive oil in a large sauté pan over medium heat. Add the jalapeño, carrots, and asparagus stems and stir well to coat with oil. Remove the dark green tops from the scallions and cut them into 1-inch-thick slices; set aside. Cut the white and light green sections into 1-inch pieces and add to the sauté pan. Stir well and cook until the vegetables begin to brown, 8 to 10 minutes. Add the rehydrated sun-dried tomatoes, basil, and parsley with their soaking water, reserved asparagus tips, mushroom, garlic, salt, and black pepper and stir well. Reduce the heat to medium and cook until the asparagus pieces are tender, 8 to 10 minutes.

While the vegetables cook, cook the pasta in the boiling water according to package directions until it is al dente. Rinse with hot water to remove excess starch. Allow the pasta to drain thoroughly.

Add the reserved dark green scallion pieces and ¼ cup water to the sauté pan and stir well. Simmer until the dark green scallion pieces begin to wilt, 2 minutes. Combine the pasta and vegetables in a large serving bowl, toss well, and serve immediately.

MAKES 4 TO 6 SERVINGS

Not Really Ravioli

Your dinner guests will not really believe you when you tell them these are your own homemade ravioli. They will be sure that you bought them at some fancy gourmet shop. But don't be disappointed. Tomorrow, while they conduct their futile search for that gourmet shop, you'll be able to enjoy more of these homemade Not Really Ravioli.

The warm reddish pasta wrapped around the satisfying blend of seasoned mozzarella cheese and minced broccoli makes these ravioli a really special treat. Serve them with your favorite sauce, or for a memorable appetizer, make smaller ones, then fry them in butter, and serve them with some Chipotle Pasta Sauce (page 78) for dipping.

For the filling:

2 cups shredded mozzarella cheese
2 cups broccoli florets, minced (see Note)
1 small onion, minced
1 poblano pepper, stemmed, seeded, and minced
2 tablespoons chopped garlic
½ cup packed fresh basil leaves, minced
¼ cup snipped fresh chives
¼ cup fresh oregano leaves, minced
¼ cup extra-virgin olive oil
1 teaspoon salt
1 teaspoon ground black pepper

For the dough:

2 chipotle peppers, stemmed
⅓ cup boiling water (see page 15)
1½ teaspoons salt
1 tablespoon paprika
3 large eggs
3 teaspoons extra-virgin olive oil

continued

2 cups all-purpose flour, plus extra for
    kneading and dusting
1 egg, beaten, optional (see Note)

To make the filling, combine the cheese, broccoli, onion, and poblano pepper in a large mixing bowl. Add the garlic, basil, chives, oregano, olive oil, salt, and black pepper. Mix until well blended. Cover and refrigerate for at least 1 hour, as the filling will be easier to handle when well chilled.

For the dough, place the chipotle peppers in a small bowl and cover with the boiling water. Allow to cool to room temperature.

If you are preparing the pasta by hand, puree the rehydrated peppers and the soaking water in a blender until no large pieces of chipotle remain, 1 minute. Add the salt, paprika, eggs, and olive oil and puree until smooth, 1 minute. Place the flour in a large bowl, and form a well in the center. Pour the pepper puree into the well. Cut the pepper puree into the flour using a dough cutter or two knives. When a dough has formed, remove it from the bowl and knead on a lightly floured surface for 2 or 3 minutes. The dough should not be sticky; if it is, work in a little extra flour as you knead it until it is smooth and dry to the touch. Place the dough in a covered bowl or a sealable plastic bag and let rest for 30 minutes.

If you are preparing the pasta using a food processor, puree the rehydrated peppers and the soaking water in the workbowl of the processor equipped with a chopping blade until no large pieces of chipotle remain, 1 minute. Add the salt, paprika, eggs, and olive oil and puree until smooth, 1 minute. Add the flour, ½ cup at a time, processing for about 1 minute after each addition. Continue to process until the dough forms a ball that revolves around the processor bowl (it may be necessary to stop processing periodically to scrape down the sides of the bowl). If the dough sticks to the processor bowl, add a little flour and process again. The dough should not be sticky and should freely separate from the food processor bowl and blade. Place the dough in a covered bowl or a sealable plastic bag and let rest for 30 minutes.

To assemble the ravioli, divide the dough into 4 pieces (when rolled, these should produce manageable-size sheets of dough). Using a floured rolling pin on a lightly floured surface, roll 1 piece of dough into a rectangle about ⅛ inch thick. Roll from the center toward the outside and turn the dough a quarter-turn between each rolling. Always make sure there is enough flour on the rolling pin and surface to prevent sticking.

Cut the rolled pasta into 2-inch squares (this measurement can be varied to produce larger or smaller ravioli). Place 1 spoonful of filling on the center of each pasta square (the size of the spoonful should be adjusted according to the size of the pasta square). There should be an even border

of pasta around the filling that is wide enough to allow you to easily seal the edges. Pick up one side of the pasta and fold it over the filling and pinch the edges closed (it is important that the filling is sealed inside the pasta). Place the assembled ravioli on a flour-dusted plate. They should not touch each other or they will stick together. Repeat with the remaining dough and filling until all the ravioli are assembled.

Fill a large pot with water and bring to a boil over high heat. Place the ravioli, a few at a time, into the pot of boiling water, while gently stirring with a wooden spoon. By adding the ravioli a few at a time, the water should remain at a rolling boil and the stirring should prevent them from sticking to the pot or to each other. Cooking time is determined by the thickness of the dough and your preference for a firm or soft pasta. The ravioli will cook quickly (2 to 4 minutes) and float to the top when done. The only way to know if they are done is to test one by eating it; start testing as soon as most of them are floating near the top. It is better to err on the side of firmness. Drain the ravioli thoroughly and serve immediately with your favorite sauce.

MAKES ABOUT 36 TWO-INCH RAVIOLI

NOTE: The florets from one average-size bunch of broccoli should produce 2 cups of minced broccoli. Use some of the tender upper stalk if the florets produce less than the desired 2 cups. Since the filling is only lightly cooked when the ravioli are boiled, avoid using the woody lower portion of the stalk, which would not cook properly. The easiest way to mince the broccoli is in a blender or a food processor equipped with a chopping blade.

NOTE: Sometimes the dough does not seal readily. This can happen for several reasons: (1) Too much flour was added in the final stage of kneading to remove stickiness. (2) Too much flour was used during rolling. (3) The dough is drying because the kitchen is hot and dry. But, regardless of the reason, when the dough will not seal, simply brush the border around the filling with beaten egg and pinch closed. After a short drying time, the ravioli should stay sealed while cooking.

Lucifer's Lasagna

Lasagna can be a meal unto itself. And this one surely is. The alternating layers of pasta, sautéed vegetables, and creamy ricotta cheese are complemented by the fiery sauce. There is just enough sauce to tie it all together without drowning it. The whole carefully constructed dish is smothered with a sinful layer of melted mozzarella cheese. Just like you would be proud of a high-performance bike you assembled from the ground up, you will be proud to serve this devilishly delicious dish. And if you think it tastes good when you first serve it, the leftovers will be so delectable they will virtually burn rubber out of the fridge.

There are three main steps in preparing this lasagna before baking: the sauce, the vegetables and the assembly. Although it seems like a lot of time and work is required, it is not as bad as it seems. The sauce can simmer while you cook the vegetables and cook the pasta. The assembly is fun and therefore seems fast to me. Since this dish is so good and easy, what are you waiting for—a poke with a pitchfork?

For the sauce:

1 large bunch broccoli

3 dried New Mexico peppers, stemmed, seeded, and torn into small pieces

1 cup boiling water (see page 15)

3 chipotle peppers packed in adobo sauce, minced

¼ cup extra-virgin olive oil

3 medium-size onions, coarsely chopped

1 cup sliced mushrooms

2 tablespoons chopped garlic

One 28-ounce can whole peeled tomatoes, coarsely chopped, with their juice

1 tablespoon dried parsley

1 teaspoon dried basil

1 teaspoon dried oregano

1 bay leaf

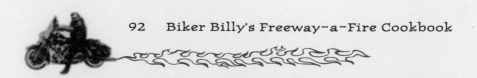

1 teaspoon salt

1 teaspoon ground black pepper

For the vegetables:

¼ cup extra-virgin olive oil

2 cups baby carrots, halved lengthwise

1 medium-size onion, thinly sliced

2 tablespoons chopped garlic

3 cups sliced mushrooms

2 medium-size zucchini, cut into ¼-inch-thick slices

1 red bell pepper, cored, seeded, and diced

1 yellow bell pepper, cored, seeded, and diced

For assembly:

1 pound lasagna noodles

2 cups ricotta cheese

1 pound mozzarella cheese, thinly sliced

To prepare the sauce, trim the broccoli, remove the florets, break them into bite-size pieces, and set aside (the florets are used with the vegetables). Thinly slice the stalk.

Place the New Mexico peppers in a small bowl and cover with the boiling water. Set aside and allow to cool to room temperature.

In a blender or a food processor equipped with a chopping blade, puree the chipotle and rehydrated New Mexico peppers with the soaking water until no large pieces of pepper remain, 1 minute.

In a large saucepot, heat the olive oil over high heat. Add the broccoli stalk and stir well to coat with oil. Cook for 3 minutes. Add the onions and mushrooms and stir well. Cook until the onions are transparent, 3 to 5 minutes. Add the garlic and cook until the garlic begins to brown, 1 to 2 minutes. Add the pureed peppers, tomatoes, parsley, basil, oregano, bay leaf, salt, and black pepper and bring to a boil. Reduce the heat to medium and simmer for 30 minutes, stirring often. Remove and discard the bay leaf. Keep the sauce warm over low heat while you prepare the vegetables.

To prepare the vegetables, in a large sauté pan, heat the olive oil over high heat. Place the carrots in the sauté pan and stir well to coat with oil. Cook for 2 to 3 minutes. Add the onion, garlic, and mushrooms and cook until the onions are tender, 3 to 5 minutes. Using a slotted spoon, transfer

the vegetables to a covered dish and set aside, trying to leave as much oil in the sauté pan as possible. Put the zucchini and bell peppers into the sauté pan and stir well to coat with oil. (You may add a small amount of extra oil, but go easy, since too much oil will make the finished lasagna greasy.) Cook for 3 minutes. Add the reserved broccoli florets and stir well. Cook until the broccoli florets darken, 3 to 5 minutes. Remove from the heat and return the mushroom mixture to the sauté pan, toss together, and allow to cool to room temperature. The vegetables should still be crisp and firm.

To assemble, fill a large pot with water and bring to a boil, over high heat. Cook the pasta according to package directions until it is al dente. Rinse with cold water to stop the cooking process and remove excess starch. Allow the pasta to drain thoroughly.

Preheat the oven to 350°F.

Cover the bottom of a large baking dish with some of the sauce. Arrange a single layer of pasta noodles on the sauce. Add a layer of vegetables and cover with pasta. Cover the pasta with sauce, add a layer of ricotta cheese; then cover the ricotta with another layer of pasta. Continue to alternate vegetable layers with sauce and ricotta cheese layers. Cover the final layer of pasta with sauce and then with the mozzarella cheese.

Bake until the mozzarella cheese is melted and begins to brown, 30 to 45 minutes. Allow to cool a few minutes before cutting. Lucifer's Lasagna is a killer served with garlic bread (page 200 or 201).

MAKES 12 TO 18 SERVINGS

Saddlebag Meals: Pies, Pockets, and Stuffed Pastries

I like the lean, mean look of custom bikes. The clean lines of the frame, fat rear tires, long front ends, and the motor capture, in sculpture, the power of motion. But when it comes to a bike for me to ride, it's got to have saddlebags. And even with amply sized saddlebags, I need a few little extra pockets to stuff goodies in. I even have a detachable tour-pak (trunk) for my Harley-Davidson Road King and an assortment of extra bags to strap on just in case I need extra capacity on a long trip. Sometimes I use that space to carry home groceries (even if I take a fifty-mile detour on the way to or from the store). I have even brought home pizza on the bike. Since I like to take long journeys on my bike, I have become somewhat of an expert on packing (more accurately called stuffing) the bike. And I have transformed those highway-hauling skills into culinary creations.

Since most of you are not crazy enough to try to carry home a pizza on your bike, I have two pizza recipes here for you. And if you wondered what a pizza looks like after I take it for that fifty-mile detour through twisty mountain roads, try the Unholy Stromboli recipe. Still looking for your slice of the pie? Try the Rude Rutabaga Pie or the Hot Chili Pie, and have an extra slice for me. If you're looking to pack a saddlebag lunch, I have four well-stuffed pocket and pastry recipes to fire up your travels. So, if you ascribe to the motto Ride to Eat and Eat to Ride, then run—don't walk—to the kitchen and start Cooking with Fire. Then pack up your saddlebags and satisfy your taste for adventure on the culinary highway.

Hot Chili Pie

If you like chili, burritos, and salsa, then this is the pie for you. The flavors are so robust that pot pies seem chicken by comparison. Quiche looks pale and wimpish in the presence of this dark, rich pie, which clearly stands head and shoulders above all the others. Hot Chili Pie will rule lunch, brighten brunch, master dinner, and make midnight snacks an explosive event.

The golden, flaky pie crust is the perfect complement to the fiery flavors of the filling. Smoky chipotle flavor boosted by Liquid Smoke combine with the Mexican herbs and spices to deliver a south-of-the-border blast. The ample measure of cheese richly rounds out the flavors. It is a good thing that this recipe makes two pies, since everyone will want a second slice.

¼ cup olive oil

2 medium-size onions, diced

2 chipotle peppers packed in adobo sauce, minced

2 tablespoons chopped garlic

2 tablespoons Liquid Smoke

½ teaspoon ground cumin

½ teaspoon ground coriander

1 tablespoon dried parsley

1 tablespoon dried cilantro

½ teaspoon salt

½ teaspoon ground black pepper

¼ cup water

One 16-ounce can red kidney beans, drained and rinsed

One 16-ounce can cannellini beans, drained and rinsed

One 28-ounce can whole peeled tomatoes, coarsely chopped, with their juice

1 package pie crust mix (for a double-crust 9-inch pie)

3 cups shredded mild cheddar cheese

Heat the olive oil in a large sauté pan over high heat. Add the onions and chipotle peppers and cook until the onions are golden brown, 6 to 8 minutes. Add the garlic and cook for 1 minute. Add the Liquid Smoke, cumin, coriander, parsley, cilantro, salt, black pepper, and water and stir well. Cook until the liquid is gone and the onions begin to fry again. Add the kidney and cannellini beans and stir well. Cook until the mixture begins to stick to the pan, 6 to 8 minutes. Add the tomatoes, stir well, and bring to a boil. Reduce the heat to medium. Simmer, stirring often, until the sauce thickens, about 30 minutes. Remove from the heat and allow to cool to room temperature (if the filling is hot, it will melt the pie crust during assembly). Add the cheese and stir until well blended.

Preheat the oven to 450°F.

Prepare the pie crust mix according to package directions for two 9-inch pie crusts. Place the crusts in two 9-inch pie pans and flute the edges by pinching the dough between your thumb and forefinger. Divide the filling mixture between the two pie crusts and cover equally with the cheese. Bake until the cheese is melted and the crust is golden brown, 15 to 20 minutes. Serve warm.

MAKES TWO 9-INCH PIES; 8 TO 12 SERVINGS

A Paterson motorcycle police officer with his new Harley-Davidson police bike, Paterson, New Jersey, circa 1972.

Rude Rutabaga Pie

Odds are that most of you have seen rutabagas, root vegetables that look like turnips grown near Three Mile Island. But I am sure few of you have ever cooked them. Well, this recipe will give you a chance to try out these atomic-size vegetables. Cooked rutabaga has a texture that is similar to that of potatoes, but with a flavor all its own.

1 large rutabaga, peeled and cut into ½-inch cubes
1 teaspoon salt
2 tablespoons butter
1 teaspoon crushed red pepper
½ teaspoon ground cumin
½ teaspoon ground black pepper
1 leek, washed well and thinly sliced
1 red bell pepper, cored, seeded, and cut into ½-inch squares
1 package pie crust mix (for a double-crust 9-inch pie)
2 cups shredded mild cheddar cheese

Put the rutabaga in a large pot and cover with water. Place over high heat and bring to a boil. Add ½ teaspoon of the salt and boil for 30 to 40 minutes until tender. Drain and set aside.

Melt the butter in a large sauté pan over medium heat. Add the crushed red pepper, cumin, black pepper, and remaining ½ teaspoon salt and cook for 1 minute. Add the leek and bell pepper and cook for 2 to 3 minutes. Add the rutabaga and cook until the rutabaga begins to brown, 3 to 5 minutes. Remove from the heat.

Preheat the oven to 350°F.

Prepare the pie crust mix according to package directions for two 9-inch pie crusts. Place the crusts in two 9-inch pie pans and flute the edges by pinching the crust between your thumb and forefinger. Divide the filling mixture between the two pie crusts and cover equally with the cheese. Bake until the cheese is melted and the crust is golden brown, 15 to 20 minutes. Serve warm.

MAKES TWO 9-INCH PIES; 8 TO 12 SERVINGS

That's a Pizza

It never fails—you spend all evening in the garage working on your bike while also building a healthy appetite and losing all track of time. Then you are overcome with a near-lethal case of pizza munchies, so you grab the phone and hit the auto-dialer button for your favorite pizza joint. *Ring ring ring ring ring*, a quick glance at your watch, *ring ring ring*, they closed two hours ago.*&%$#@! What are you going to do now? Well, just run into the kitchen and start making your own pizza. You can even customize it like you would your bike. And it may even be ready faster than some places will get around to delivering to your part of town. After you've had one bite, you'll exclaim Alright, That's a Pizza!

The sauce recipe makes enough for two average pies or one saucy pie. The dough recipe makes enough for one pie. For two pies, double the ingredient amounts and divide the dough in half before rolling it out. I usually make two pies, since everybody always wants just one more slice. Of course, you should add any or all of your favorite toppings.

1 cup warm water, 115° to 120°F (see Note)

1 packet active dry yeast

2 cups all-purpose flour, plus extra for kneading

1 ancho pepper, stemmed, seeded, and torn into small
   pieces

¼ cup boiling water (see page 15)

¼ cup extra-virgin olive oil, plus extra for coating

1 medium-size onion, diced

2 tablespoons chopped garlic

1 cup roasted red peppers, drained

½ cup sun-dried tomatoes packed in oil

1 teaspoon dried oregano

1 tablespoon dried parsley

½ teaspoon salt

½ teaspoon ground black pepper

2 tablespoons cool water

1 pound mozzarella cheese, shredded

continued

If you are preparing the pizza dough by hand, combine the warm water and yeast in a small mixing bowl. Using a wire whisk or fork, mix until the yeast is completely dissolved. Place the flour in a large bowl, forming a well in the center. Pour the yeast mixture into the well. Cut the liquid into the flour using a dough cutter or two knives. When a dough has formed, remove it from the bowl and knead on a lightly floured surface for 2 to 3 minutes. The dough should not be sticky; if it is, work in a little extra flour as you knead it until it is soft and dry to the touch.

If you are preparing the pizza dough using a food processor, combine the warm water and yeast in the workbowl of the processor equipped with a chopping blade, and process until the yeast is completely dissolved, 30 seconds. Add the flour, ½ cup at a time, processing for about 1 minute after each addition until the dough forms a ball that revolves around the processor bowl. It may be necessary to stop processing periodically to scrape down the sides of the bowl. If the dough sticks to the processor bowl, add a little flour and process again. The dough should not be sticky and should freely separate from the food processor bowl and blade. When a dough has formed, remove it from the food processor and knead on a floured surface for 2 to 3 minutes. The dough should not be sticky; if it is, work in a little extra flour as you knead it until it is soft and dry to the touch.

Using a bowl that is at least twice the size of the dough ball, coat the inside with olive oil. Put the dough in the bowl and roll around to coat with oil. Cover and let rise in a warm place for 15 to 20 minutes, or until it doubles in volume.

Remove the dough from the bowl, place on a lightly floured surface, and knead for 1 minute. Return to the bowl, cover, and let rise in a warm place until it doubles in volume again, another 15 to 20 minutes. Prepare the sauce while the dough rises.

Preheat the oven to 500°F.

To prepare the sauce, place the ancho pepper in a small bowl and cover with the boiling water. Allow to cool to room temperature.

Place the olive oil in a large sauté pan over medium heat. Add the ancho pepper and the soaking water, onion, garlic, roasted peppers, sun-dried tomatoes, oregano, parsley, salt, and black pepper. Cook until the onions begin to brown, 5 to 7 minutes. Remove from the heat and add 2 tablespoons cool water. Stir well and transfer to a blender or a food processor equipped with a chopping blade. Puree until the sauce has no large pieces, 1 minute. If you prefer a really chunky-style pizza, do not puree the mixture.

To assemble the pizza, lightly coat a 12-inch pizza pan with olive oil. Using a floured rolling pin on a lightly floured surface, roll the dough into a 12-inch-diameter circle. Roll from the center toward the outside and turn the dough a quarter-turn between each rolling. Always make sure there is

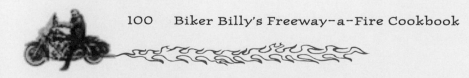

enough flour on the rolling pin and surface to prevent sticking, but be aware that too much flour can produce a dry, dusty crust. Transfer the dough to the oiled pizza pan. Press the dough into the pan, using your fingers to form a slight ridge around the edge to hold in the sauce.

Ladle your desired amount of sauce onto the dough and spread evenly. Cover with a layer of cheese and bake until the cheese is melted and the crust is golden brown, 15 minutes. Remove from the oven, slice, and serve piping hot.

MAKES ONE 12-INCH PIZZA; 4 SERVINGS

NOTE: Yeast is a live product, and successful results depend on using water that is at the correct temperature. In most cases, 115° to 120°F is correct, but always read the package instructions and use a good-quality food thermometer to check the water temperature.

Mexican Pizza

On a midnight munchy run south of the border, I met some culinary desperadoes. After an evening of trading highway cooking stories, I rode off into the sunrise with this tasty recipe. Okay, would you believe I banged my head on a kitchen cabinet door, and when I woke up, I had this idea? Well, believe what you like, but one slice of this pizza will make you believe in asking for seconds.

1 cup masa harina (see Note)
1 cup water
1 tablespoon dried cilantro
1 tablespoon dried parsley
1 ancho pepper, stemmed, seeded, and torn into small pieces
2 chipotle peppers, stemmed
1 pasilla pepper, stemmed, seeded, and torn into small pieces
1 cup boiling water (see page 15)
3 tablespoons olive oil
2 medium-size onions, thinly sliced
One 15-ounce can red kidney beans, drained and rinsed
2 tablespoons chopped garlic
¼ teaspoon ground coriander
½ teaspoon ground cumin
1½ teaspoons salt
½ teaspoon ground black pepper
1 cup tomato puree
2 to 3 cups shredded mild cheddar cheese
Olive oil or spray cooking oil for greasing

To prepare the dough, combine the masa harina and water in a medium-size mixing bowl and mix with a dough cutter or two knives until a dough forms. Knead in the bowl for 1 minute, cover, and set aside.

To prepare the sauce, place the cilantro, parsley, ancho, chipotle, and

pasilla peppers in a small bowl and cover with the boiling water. Allow to cool to room temperature.

In a blender or a food processor equipped with a chopping blade, puree the rehydrated herbs and peppers with the soaking water until no large pieces of pepper remain, 1 minute.

Heat 2 tablespoons of the olive oil in a large sauté pan over high heat. Add the onions and cook until golden brown, 5 to 7 minutes. Remove from the heat and, using a slotted spoon, transfer the onions to a small bowl and set aside, leaving as much oil as possible in the sauté pan. Return the sauté pan to medium heat and add the remaining 1 tablespoon olive oil, the beans, garlic, coriander, cumin, salt, and black pepper and cook for 5 minutes. Add the tomato puree and the pepper puree, stir well, and reduce the heat to low. Simmer until the sauce thickens, 10 minutes.

Preheat the oven to 350°F.

To assemble the pizza transfer the dough to a greased pizza pan and cover with a piece of wax paper the same size as the pan. Using a rolling pin over the wax paper, roll the dough into the pan. Roll from the center toward the outside and turn the pan a quarter-turn between each rolling. Carefully remove the wax paper and press the dough into the pan's edge, using your fingers to form a slight ridge to hold in the sauce.

Spread the bean mixture evenly over the dough. Add a layer of cheese and arrange the reserved onions on top. Bake until the cheese is melted and begins to brown 10 minutes.

Remove from the oven, slice, and serve piping hot, just like gringo pizza. Olé!

MAKES ONE 12-INCH PIZZA; 4 TO 6 SERVINGS

NOTE: Check the package directions for the ratio of masa harina to water and adjust if necessary.

Unholy Stromboli

This stuff is so evil and delicious that you'll think a motorcycle messenger straight from the burning bowels of hell delivered it. After a few bites you may start to hear the roar of straight pipes and feel your pulse pounding. Soon you'll have the overwhelming desire to eat this everyday. But don't panic, thinking you forgot the phone number of the pizza joint that delivered it, because you're the devilish chef who cooked it. Around this time you should dip your head into some ice water and cool off because the Unholy Stromboli has possessed you.

For the dough:

1 ancho pepper, stemmed, seeded, and torn
   into small pieces
½ cup boiling water (see page 15)
1 cup warm water, 115° to 120°F (see page 101)
1 packet active dry yeast
4 cups all-purpose flour, plus extra for kneading
1 teaspoon sugar
1 teaspoon salt
2 tablespoons extra-virgin olive oil

For the filling:

3 tablespoons extra-virgin olive oil
2 red cherry peppers, stemmed and minced
2 medium-size onions, diced
1 medium-size zucchini, halved lengthwise
   and cut into ½-inch-thick slices
1 cup sliced mushrooms
2 tablespoons chopped garlic
½ cup sun-dried tomatoes packed in oil, minced
1 red bell pepper, cored, seeded,
   and cut into ½-inch squares

1 yellow bell pepper, cored, seeded, and cut into
½-inch squares
1 teaspoon salt
1 teaspoon ground black pepper

For assembly:

2 cups shredded mozzarella cheese
1 cup packed fresh basil leaves, shredded ½ inch
thick
Olive oil for coating and brushing

To prepare the dough, place the ancho pepper in a small bowl and cover with the boiling water. Allow to cool to room temperature.

If you are preparing the dough by hand, in a blender puree the rehydrated peppers and the soaking water until no large pieces of ancho remain, 1 minute. Combine the warm water and yeast in a small mixing bowl. Using a wire whisk or fork, mix until the yeast is completely dissolved. Combine the flour, sugar, and salt in a large bowl and form a well in the center. Pour the yeast mixture and pepper puree into the well. Cut the liquid into the flour using a dough cutter or two knives. When a dough has formed, remove it from the bowl and knead on a lightly floured surface for 2 to 3 minutes. The dough should not be sticky; if it is, work in a little extra flour as you knead it until it is soft and dry to the touch.

If you are preparing the dough using a food processor, puree the rehydrated peppers and the soaking water in the workbowl of the processor equipped with a chopping blade, until no large pieces of ancho remain, 1 minute. Add the warm water and yeast and process for 30 seconds, or until the yeast is completely dissolved. Add the sugar, salt, and the flour, ½ cup at a time, processing for about 1 minute after each addition until the dough forms a ball that revolves around the processor bowl. It may be necessary to stop processing periodically to scrape down the sides of the bowl. If the dough sticks to the processor bowl, add a little flour and process again. The dough should not be sticky and should freely separate from the food processor bowl and blade. When a dough has formed, remove it from the food processor and knead on a lightly floured surface for 2 to 3 minutes. The dough should not be sticky; if it is, work in a little extra flour as you knead it until it is soft and dry to the touch.

Using a bowl that is at least twice the size of the dough ball, coat the inside with olive oil. Put the dough in the bowl and roll around to coat with oil. Cover and let rise in a warm place until it doubles in volume, 15 to 20 minutes. *continued*

Remove the dough from the bowl onto a lightly floured surface and knead for 1 minute. Return to the bowl, cover, and let rise in a warm place until it doubles in volume again, 15 to 20 minutes.

To prepare the filling, heat the olive oil in a large sauté pan over medium heat. Add the cherry peppers, onions, zucchini, and mushrooms. Cook until the onions are tender, 3 to 5 minutes. Add the garlic, sun-dried tomatoes, bell peppers, salt, and black pepper. Cook until the bell peppers are tender, 3 to 5 minutes. Remove from the heat and allow to cool (the filling must be cool before you attempt assembly or it will melt through the uncooked dough).

Preheat the oven to 400°F.

To assemble the stromboli, in a large bowl, combine the vegetable mixture, cheese, and basil and toss together until well mixed.

Divide the dough in half (when rolled and assembled, this will produce 2 stromboli of a manageable size). Lightly coat two large cookie sheets with olive oil. Using a floured rolling pin on a lightly floured surface, roll the dough, 1 piece at a time, into a rectangle about ¼ inch thick. Roll from the center toward the outside and turn the dough a quarter-turn between each rolling. Always make sure there is enough flour on the rolling pin and surface to prevent sticking, but be aware that too much flour can produce a dry, dusty stromboli. Transfer the dough to one of the oiled cookie sheets. Place half of the filling on the dough, leaving a 2-inch border on one of the long sides, and a 1-inch border on the other three sides. Starting from the long side with the 1-inch border, roll the stromboli toward the 2-inch border. The long seam should be on the bottom; close the ends by pressing them down and center the stromboli on the cookie sheet. Repeat for the other stromboli. Brush lightly with olive oil and bake until golden brown, 30 minutes. Serve piping hot with your favorite sauce on the side for dipping.

MAKES 2 STROMBOLI; 4 TO 6 SERVINGS

Camel Pockets

If camels had pockets, what would they carry? That's the opening line of a stupid joke, but this recipe is no joke. These tasty stuffed pastry pockets are crammed with Middle Eastern–style flavors. Their golden color and wonderful aromas will transform your dining room into an exotic desert oasis. The fire from the cayenne pepper will warm you like the rays of a brilliant Arabian sun. As the sweat rolls into your eyes, you may see riders raising a cloud of dust as they cross distant sand dunes. But it's all only a cayenne pepper–induced mirage. Start your own caravan to culinary adventure: cook up a batch of these pockets and watch your nomadic tribe gather in the oasis.

¼ cup extra-virgin olive oil
2 medium-size onions, diced
One 19-ounce can garbanzo beans, drained, liquid reserved
3 tablespoons chopped garlic
1½ teaspoons salt
1 teaspoon ground black pepper
1 teaspoon ground cayenne pepper
1 teaspoon ground cumin
½ teaspoon ground coriander
1 tablespoon dried parsley
1 tablespoon hot Hungarian paprika
½ cup water
8 ounces feta cheese, crumbled
1 package pie crust mix (for a double-crust 9-inch pie)
All-purpose flour for rolling

Heat the olive oil in a large sauté pan over high heat. Add the onions and garbanzo beans and stir well to coat with oil. Cook until the onions are golden brown, 4 to 6 minutes. Add the garlic, salt, black pepper, cayenne pepper, cumin, coriander, parsley, paprika, water, and the reserved liquid from the garbanzo beans. Stir well to dissolve the spices. Reduce the heat

to medium, stir well, and cook until the liquid has evaporated and the sauce has thickened, 4 to 6 minutes. Remove from the heat and allow to cool to room temperature. Add the feta cheese, mix well, transfer to a covered bowl, and refrigerate for 1 hour.

Prepare the pie crust mix according to package directions for two 9-inch pie crusts. Place the dough in a covered bowl and refrigerate for 30 minutes.

Preheat the oven to 425°F.

Divide the dough in half (when rolled, these should produce manageable-size sheets of dough). Using a floured rolling pin on a lightly floured surface, roll the dough, 1 piece at a time, into a rectangle about ⅛ inch thick. Roll from the center toward the outside, and turn the dough a quarter-turn between each rolling. Always make sure there is enough flour on the rolling pin and surface to prevent sticking, but be aware that too much flour can produce a dry, dusty pocket.

Using a biscuit cutter or the rim of a glass, cut the rolled dough into 3-inch circles (this measurement can be varied to produce larger or smaller camel pockets). You can knead the dough scraps together and reroll them. Place a spoonful of filling on the center of each dough circle (the size of a spoonful should be adjusted according to the size of the dough circle). There should be an even border of dough around the filling that is wide enough to allow you to easily seal the edges. Pick up one side of the dough and fold it over the filling and pinch the edges closed. It is important that the filling be sealed inside the dough. Place the assembled camel pockets on a floured plate; they should not touch each other or they may stick together. Repeat until all the camel pockets are assembled. Arrange the camel pockets in a single layer on a cookie sheet with a ½-inch space between them.

Bake until the crust is golden brown, 20 to 30 minutes. Serve piping hot.

MAKES 36 THREE-INCH POCKETS; 4 TO 6 SERVINGS

Hollering Chipotle Pockets

These crusty, cheesy, chipotle-powered pockets will have you hollering for seconds (or milk if you are a "tender tongue"). Oh, don't be afraid now, one chipotle pepper makes them nice and zesty, but it won't hurt you. However, if you want to holler FIRE, just add a few more chipotle peppers. The buttery pie crust–style dough makes these pockets a really rich treat. The recipe is designed to make small pockets, but you can make larger pockets if you desire.

For the filling:

3 tablespoons extra–virgin olive oil
1 chipotle pepper packed in adobo sauce, minced,
    plus 2 tablespoons adobo sauce, reserved
1 medium–size onion, diced
2 tablespoons chopped garlic
1 teaspoon dried cilantro
1 teaspoon dried parsley
1 teaspoon dried oregano
½ teaspoon dried thyme
½ teaspoon salt
1 teaspoon ground black pepper
One 16–ounce can dark red kidney beans, drained
    and rinsed
1 cup canned stewed tomatoes, coarsely chopped
1 cup water
1 cup shredded mild cheddar cheese

For the dough:

2 tablespoons water
2 cups all–purpose flour, plus extra for kneading
1 teaspoon salt
¾ cup (1½ sticks) butter, cut into 6 pieces

continued

To prepare the filling, in a large sauté pan, heat the olive oil over medium heat. Add the chipotle pepper and onion and cook until the onion is tender, 3 to 5 minutes. Add the garlic, cilantro, parsley, oregano, thyme, salt, and black pepper. Stir well and cook until the onions are golden brown, 3 to 5 minutes. Add the kidney beans, tomatoes, and water and bring to a boil. Reduce the heat to low and simmer until the sauce thickens, 7 to 10 minutes. Remove from the heat and allow to cool to room temperature (if the filling is hot it will melt the dough during assembly). Add the cheese and stir until well blended.

Put the reserved adobo sauce and 2 tablespoons water in a small bowl. Stir until well blended and set aside.

Preheat the oven to 350°F.

If you are preparing the dough by hand, in a medium-size mixing bowl, combine the flour and salt. Whisk together for 30 seconds to thoroughly mix the dry ingredients. Add the butter pieces and cut together with two knives or a dough cutter until the butter is completely cut into the flour and it has a granular texture. Form a well in the center of the flour and pour in the adobo mixture. Stir until a dough forms. Test the dough to see if it is ready to use by pinching a small amount with your fingers; if it holds together, it is ready to use. It may be necessary to add some additional water, 1 tablespoon at a time. Knead after each addition and then test again.

If you are preparing the dough using a food processor, combine the flour and salt in the workbowl of the processor equipped with a chopping blade. Pulse two or three times to mix completely. Add the butter, arranging the pieces evenly around the food processor bowl. Process until the butter is cut into the flour, creating a granular texture, 1 to 2 minutes. While the blades are spinning, pour in the adobo mixture and process until a dough forms and begins to move around the bowl as a clump, approximately 1 minute. Test the dough to see if it is ready to use by pinching a small amount with your fingers; if it holds together, it is ready to use. It may be necessary to add some additional water, 1 tablespoon at a time. Process after each addition, then test again.

Remove the dough from the bowl and knead on a lightly floured surface just long enough to form a ball (overkneading will ruin the texture of the crusts).

To assemble the pockets, divide the dough into 4 pieces (when rolled, these should produce manageable-size sheets of dough). Using a floured rolling pin on a lightly floured surface, roll the dough, 1 piece at a time, into a rectangle about ⅛ inch thick. Roll from the center toward the outside and turn the dough a quarter-turn between each rolling. Always make sure there is enough flour on the rolling pin and surface to prevent sticking, but be aware that too much flour can produce a dry, dusty pocket.

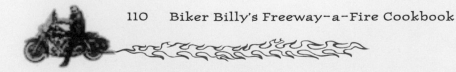

Cut the rolled dough into 2-inch circles using a biscuit cutter or the rim of a glass (this measurement can be varied to produce larger or smaller pockets). You can knead the dough scraps together and reroll them. Place a spoonful of filling on the center of each dough circle (the size of a spoonful should be adjusted according to the size of the dough circle). There should be an even border of dough around the filling that is wide enough to allow you to seal the edges easily. Pick up one side of the dough and fold it over the filling and pinch the edges closed. It is important that the filling be sealed inside the dough. Place the assembled pockets on a floured plate; they should not touch each other or they will stick together. Repeat until all the pockets are assembled. Transfer the pockets to a greased cookie sheet. Bake until golden brown, 20 to 25 minutes. Serve piping hot.

MAKES ABOUT 48 TWO-INCH POCKETS, 8 TO 12 SERVINGS

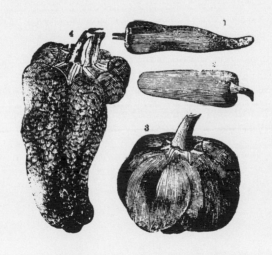

Sleazy Cheesy Pockets

These are nothing like those tame, neat stuffed pockets in the freezer section of the grocery store. What you have here is a cross between tortured tarts and potpie from hell. First, the innocent veggies are covered with a chile pepper gravy and two kinds of cheese. Then they are wrapped in a buttery pie crust dough and baked to fiery perfection. The baking aromas will invite you into the kitchen like the beat of music beckons you into a sleazy saloon. Go ahead, answer the call—I dare ya!

For the filling:

1 ancho pepper, stemmed, seeded, and torn into small pieces
1 pasilla pepper, stemmed, seeded, and torn into small pieces
1 dried New Mexico pepper, stemmed, seeded, and torn into small pieces
1 chipotle pepper, stemmed
1 cup boiling water (see page 15)
2 tablespoons butter
3 medium-size shallots, minced
2 tablespoons chopped garlic
2 tablespoons all-purpose flour
1 cup water
1 teaspoon dried chives
½ teaspoon dried basil
½ teaspoon dried thyme
½ teaspoon dried marjoram
1 teaspoon salt
1 teaspoon ground black pepper
2 cups sliced cremini (brown) mushrooms
6 scallions, trimmed and cut into 1-inch pieces
1 red bell pepper, cored, seeded, and cut into 1-inch squares

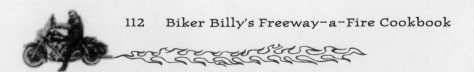

1 yellow bell pepper, cored, seeded, and cut into
   1-inch squares
1 large bunch broccoli, florets only, cut into bite-size
   pieces
1 cup shredded mild cheddar cheese
1 cup shredded mozzarella cheese

For the dough:

3 cups all-purpose flour, plus extra for kneading
2 teaspoons salt
1 cup (2 sticks) butter, cut into 16 pieces
⅓ cup water

To prepare the filling, place the ancho, pasilla, and New Mexico and chipotle peppers in a small bowl and cover with the boiling water. Allow to cool to room temperature.

In a blender or a food processor equipped with a chopping blade, puree the rehydrated peppers and the soaking water until no large pieces of chipotle remain, 1 minute.

In a large sauté pan, melt the butter over high heat. Add the shallots and garlic, and cook until the shallots begin to brown, 3 to 5 minutes. Reduce the heat to medium. Add the flour and stir well. Cook until the flour turns a light brown, about 2 minutes. Add the pureed peppers. Stir well to dissolve the flour.

Add the chives, basil, thyme, marjoram, salt, and black pepper and stir well. Add the mushrooms, scallions, bell peppers, and broccoli florets and stir well. Simmer until the broccoli begins to darken, 5 to 7 minutes. The broccoli florets should be tender but not soft. Remove from the heat and allow to cool. Add the cheddar and mozzarella cheeses and mix well.

Preheat the oven to 425°F.

If you are preparing the dough by hand, in a medium-size mixing bowl, combine the flour and salt. Whisk together for 30 seconds to thoroughly mix the dry ingredients. Add the pieces of butter and cut together with two knives or a dough cutter until the butter is completely cut into the flour and it has a granular texture. Form a well in the center of the flour and pour in the water. Stir until a dough forms.

If you are preparing the dough using a food processor, combine the flour and salt in the workbowl of the processor equipped with a chopping blade. Pulse two or three times to mix completely. Add the butter, arranging the pieces evenly around the food processor bowl. Process until the butter is cut into the flour, creating a granular texture, 1 to 2 minutes. While the blades are spinning, pour in the water and process until a dough forms and begins to move around the bowl as a ball, approximately 1 minute.

Remove the dough from the bowl and knead on a lightly floured surface just long enough to form a ball (overkneading will ruin the texture of the crusts).

To assemble the pockets, using a floured rolling pin on a lightly floured surface, roll the dough into a long cylinder and cut into 16 equal pieces. Flatten each piece into a pancake shape and then roll the dough into a rectangle ⅛ inch thick. Roll from the center toward the outside and turn the dough a quarter-turn between each rolling. Always make sure there is enough flour on the rolling pin and surface to prevent sticking, but be aware that too much flour will produce a dry, dusty pocket. Place a spoonful of filling on the center of each dough piece (the size of a spoonful should be adjusted according to the size of the dough piece). Fold the sides of the dough up onto the filling. Pinch the dough together where the edges meet, leaving a small opening in the center to allow steam to escape during baking. Transfer each pocket to a greased cookie sheet. Repeat until all the pockets are assembled. Bake until the tops begin to brown, 20 to 25 minutes. Serve piping hot.

MAKES 16 POCKETS; 4 TO 8 SERVINGS

Pita Pockets in Pain

No Pain, No Gain may be the motto of the exercise crowd, but for me the motto is Learn to Burn. And these tasty stuffed pita pockets have been working out really hard so they can give you just the right burn. They are packed to the point of bursting with delicious veggies and bean curd, and the chipotle-soy sauce makes them a powerful culinary bodybuilder. So exercise your appetite and learn to burn with these yummy stuffed pita pockets. If you feel any pain just loosen your belt; it works for me.

For the sauce:

3 chipotle peppers, stemmed
¼ cup boiling water (see page 15)
½ cup cool water
1 tablespoon cornstarch
1 teaspoon ground black pepper
½ teaspoon ground ginger
1 teaspoon chopped garlic
½ cup soy sauce

For the filling:

¼ cup peanut oil
1 pound extra-firm bean curd, drained
   and cut into ½-inch cubes
1 cup baby carrots, quartered
1 cup sliced mushrooms
One 15-ounce can baby corn, drained
1 red bell pepper, cored, seeded,
   and cut into ½-inch squares
6 scallions, trimmed and cut into ¼-inch-thick
   slices
1 bunch broccoli, florets only, cut into bite-size
   pieces

continued

For assembly:

6 pitas

To prepare the sauce, place the chipotle peppers in small bowl and cover with the boiling water. Allow to cool to room temperature.

In a blender or a food processor equipped with a chopping blade, puree the rehydrated peppers and the soaking water until no large pieces of chipotle remain, 1 minute.

Put ½ cup cool water in a small bowl and add the cornstarch, stirring until the cornstarch is completely dissolved. Set aside.

In a small saucepot, combine the pepper puree, black pepper, ginger, garlic, and soy sauce. Bring to a boil over high heat. Reduce the heat to low and simmer for 5 minutes, stirring often.

Stir the cornstarch and water mixture again and then slowly pour into the saucepot, stirring constantly until well blended. Raise the heat to medium and simmer, stirring constantly, until the sauce thickens, 1 to 2 minutes. Reduce the heat to very low and keep warm, stirring often.

To prepare the filling, heat the peanut oil in a large wok over high heat. Add the bean curd and toss well to coat with oil. Stir-fry until the bean curd is browned, 8 to 10 minutes. Add the carrots and stir-fry for 2 minutes. Add the mushrooms, corn, bell pepper, scallions, and broccoli and stir-fry until the broccoli begins to darken, 3 to 5 minutes. The vegetables should still be crisp and firm. Pour ½ cup of the chipotle-soy sauce over the vegetables and toss to coat.

To assemble the pockets, warm the pita bread in an oven or toaster. Cut each pita in half and carefully open it. Place ½ cup of the filling in each pita half. Serve with extra sauce on the side.

MAKES 6 SERVINGS

Zesty Eggplant Pastries

Wrapped in a golden, flaky crust, these pastries are treats both for the eye and the tummy. They look like innocent apple turnovers, but they are really zesty entrees filled with a wild biker-style concoction. Equally good at home for lunch or dinner, they are also perfect for packing in your saddlebags. Imagine stopping at a scenic overlook and enjoying these Zesty Eggplant Pastries while you drink in the beauty of nature. Just remember to pack something cool to drink. This recipe prepares meal-size pastries, but you could make them smaller and serve them as appetizers or snacks.

¼ cup extra-virgin olive oil

1 jalapeño pepper, stemmed and thinly sliced

2 medium-size onions, thinly sliced

3 tablespoons chopped garlic

1½ teapoons salt

½ teaspoon ground black pepper

1 tablespoon dried parsley

1 teaspoon dried oregano

1 teaspoon dried basil

1 tablespoon hot Hungarian paprika

One 6-ounce can tomato paste

2 cups boiling water

1 large eggplant, quartered and sliced

4 cups shredded mozzarella cheese

One 16-ounce package frozen phyllo,
   thawed (see page 25)

½ cup (1 stick) butter, melted

Heat the olive oil in a large sauté pan over high heat. Add the jalapeño and onions and cook until the onions are golden brown, 6 to 8 minutes. Add the garlic and cook for 1 minute. Add the salt, black pepper, parsley, oregano, basil, paprika, tomato paste, and water and stir well. Bring to a boil. Add the eggplant and reduce the heat to medium. Cover and simmer until the eggplant is tender and the sauce has thickened, stirring often, 12 to 15 minutes. Remove from the heat and allow to cool to room temperature. Add the cheese and toss well to combine.

continued

Preheat the oven to 350°F.

Grease a large baking sheet with some of the melted butter. Peel 2 or 3 sheets of phyllo together as one piece from the package and lay the sheets on a working surface, with the long direction going left to right. Cut in half across the width, creating 2 pieces, like the pages of an open book. Using a pastry brush, brush some melted butter on the phyllo. Place ½ cup of the eggplant and cheese mixture onto each piece of phyllo, centered right to left one-third of the way down the length of each piece. Fold both near corners of the phyllo over the filling, forming a triangle. Fold the filled triangle over onto the rest of the sheet of phyllo and fold the remaining corners onto the triangle. Brush with melted butter, transfer to a baking sheet with the buttered side down, and brush the top with more butter. Repeat until all the triangles are assembled.

Bake until golden brown, 10 to 15 minutes. Allow to cool 1 to 2 minutes before removing from the baking sheet. Serve warm.

MAKES 16 TRIANGLES

Bean Curd from Beyond

B ean curd seems like a strange food to some people. Then, bikers seem strange to some folks, too. But once you have a chance to meet a few bikers, talk for a while, and maybe even share some food with them, you will soon see that they are regular folks. Well, you can have the same experience with bean curd. If you have tried it before and didn't like it, chances are good that you had poorly seasoned (or unseasoned) soft bean curd. Bean curd has little flavor on its own, and what it does have is not something to write home about. The softer-textured varieties can have an unsatisfying, mushy feel in your mouth. So why eat bean curd? From a nutritional stand-point, bean curd is a low-fat, low-calorie, cholesterol-free food that is rich in high-quality protein and contains healthy quantities of calcium and other minerals. Even with food-value credentials like that, many people just can't get beyond bean curd's lack of taste and texture.

Let me tell you a biker secret about bean curd. Because it has so little fla-vor of its own, it can be transformed into many different-tasting dishes. You just have to season it well. The texture issue can be resolved by buying extra-firm bean curd. Be sure to check out the section on bean curd in The Biker's Pantry on page 19.

This chapter will give you a quick tour of some of the tasty adventures you can have by applying my fire to bean curd.

Hot Thai Fry

Come ride with me far away to the Pacific Rim, where exotic flavors abound. This delicious combination of crispy stir-fried vegetables and crunchy deep-fried bean curd is covered with a wild nutty sauce. Grab your food processor and rev up that shredding disk, because this recipe is sure to burn culinary rubber and wheelie you into gustatory paradise.

For the sauce:

1 ancho pepper, stemmed, seeded, and torn into small pieces
1 dried long, slim red cayenne pepper, stemmed and crushed
½ cup boiling water (see page 15)
1 tablespoon chopped garlic
1 tablespoon peeled and finely chopped fresh ginger
¼ cup peanut oil
1 teaspoon ground black pepper
½ cup chunky peanut butter
¼ cup light teriyaki sauce
½ cup warm water

For the vegetables:

Peanut oil for deep-frying
1 large broccoli stalk
2 tablespoons peanut oil
1 cup shredded carrots
1 small zucchini, shredded
1 small yellow squash, shredded
4 scallions, trimmed and cut into ¼-inch-thick slices
1 red bell pepper, cored, seeded, and julienned

For the bean curd:

1 yellow bell pepper, cored, seeded, and julienned
1 pound extra-firm bean curd, drained and cut into
½-inch-thick "French fries"

To prepare the sauce, place the ancho and cayenne peppers in a small bowl and cover with the boiling water. Allow to cool to room temperature.

In a blender or a food processor equipped with a chopping blade, puree the rehydrated peppers and their soaking water, garlic, and ginger. In a small pot, warm the peanut oil over medium heat. Carefully add the puree and black pepper. Fry (the oil may splatter) for about 3 minutes, stirring often. Add the peanut butter, stirring until well blended. Add the teriyaki sauce and warm water, continuing to stir. Reduce the heat to low, stirring often, while you prepare the vegetables.

In a deep pot or deep-fryer, preheat several inches of peanut oil to 365°F.

Remove the broccoli florets from the stalk. Break or cut the florets into bite-size pieces and set aside. Trim any leaves or hard, dry parts from the stalk. Use a food processor equipped with a shredding blade to shred the stalk, or shred by hand.

Heat the 2 tablespoons peanut oil in a large sauté pan over high heat. Add the shredded broccoli and carrots, stir well to coat with oil, and stir-fry for 2 to 3 minutes. Add the zucchini, yellow squash, scallions, broccoli florets, and bell pepper and stir-fry for 3 to 5 minutes.

While the vegetables are stir-frying, carefully place a few pieces of the bean curd "fries" into the deep-fryer at a time. Fry the bean curd until golden brown, 2 to 4 minutes, then drain on a paper towel.

On a large serving plate, form a bed with the vegetables. Arrange the fried bean curd on top and cover with the sauce. Toss to distribute the sauce and serve immediately.

MAKES 4 TO 6 SERVINGS

Ancho Lime Surprise

One of my good friends, and a valued member of my TV production crew, was informed by his doctor that he had diabetes. Fortunately, his condition was at a stage where he could control it with diet and exercise. However, this presented him with what looked like a life filled with dull food. I created this dish to demonstrate that he could still enjoy food, using the dinner guideline (3 ounces of meat, 2 cups of vegetables, 1 cup of grain, and 2 tablespoons of fat) that his doctor provided him as a starting point. I swapped bean curd for the meat and came up with this tasty dish. I have added no extra salt, as salt intake was also an issue for him.

I am not a doctor, and I don't even play one on TV, so if you are on a strict diet, check this out with your doctor first. This recipe should give you an example of what delicious foods can be enjoyed within a restricted diet. So Eat Hot and Well!

1 ancho pepper, stemmed, seeded, and torn into small pieces

½ cup boiling water (see page 15)

½ teaspoon ground black pepper

1 tablespoon chopped garlic

Juice of 1 lime

1 pound extra-firm bean curd, drained and cut into ½-inch-thick "French fries"

1 large broccoli stalk

1 small zucchini

¼ cup extra-virgin olive oil

½ cup baby carrots, halved lengthwise

1 red onion, diced

1 ripe plum tomato, peeled (see page 18)

1 yellow bell pepper, cored, seeded, cut into ½-inch squares

2 cups cooked rice

Place the ancho pepper in a small bowl and cover with the boiling water. Allow to cool to room temperature.

In a blender or a food processor equipped with a chopping blade, puree the rehydrated ancho pepper and the soaking water, black pepper, garlic, and lime juice.

Place the bean curd in a bowl and cover with the puree. Toss gently to coat all the bean curd pieces completely. Allow to marinate for at least 30 minutes, tossing occasionally to ensure that all the pieces remain coated with the puree.

Trim the broccoli, removing the florets and breaking them into bite-size pieces. Set aside. Cut the stalk into irregular chunks (rotating the stalk between cuts and changing the angle of the cut). Trim the zucchini and cut into irregular chunks (rotating between cuts and changing the angle of the cut).

In a large sauté pan, heat the olive oil over high heat. Place the carrots in the sauté pan, stir well to coat with oil, and cook for 1 to 2 minutes. Add the broccoli stalk and cook for 1 to 2 minutes. Add the zucchini and onion and cook for 1 to 2 minutes.

Reserving the marinade, transfer the bean curd to the sauté pan, a few pieces at a time, stirring to coat with oil. Cook for 3 to 5 minutes.

Meanwhile, in a blender or a food processor equipped with a chopping blade, combine the reserved marinade and the tomato and puree until smooth, about 1 minute.

Add the broccoli florets, bell pepper, and puree to the sauté pan. Simmer until the broccoli florets begin to turn dark green, 2 to 3 minutes. On a large serving platter, make a bed with the rice and top with the vegetables and bean curd. Serve immediately.

MAKES 4 SERVINGS

Bombay Bean Curd

This colorful dish is a collision of two cultures, a sort of culinary traffic accident. From the Eastern tradition, the spinach sauce bring you the flavors of India. Farther east, the bean curd is an Asian favorite with an Indian-style impact. Boom! The meeting of the two will explode across your palate and you'll swear you hear distant sirens. Don't wait for an emergency team to arrive, be a Good Samaritan and help yourself to a second serving.

For the sauce:

2 tablespoons extra-virgin olive oil

1 medium-size onion, minced

2 tablespoons chopped garlic

2 poblano peppers, stemmed, seeded, and minced

1 teaspoon ground cumin

1 teaspoon ground coriander

1 teaspoon salt

1 teaspoon ground black pepper

One 10-ounce package frozen chopped spinach,
   thawed and drained

½ cup water

½ cup half-and-half

¼ cup unsweetened shredded coconut

For the bean curd:

1 cup whole wheat flour

1 tablespoon sweet paprika

1 teaspoon ground cumin

1 teaspoon ground turmeric

1 teaspoon salt

1 teaspoon ground black pepper

¼ cup extra-virgin olive oil

1 small onion, minced

1 fresh red cayenne pepper, stemmed and thinly
   sliced

1 pound *extra-firm bean curd, drained and*
   cut into ½-inch cubes
3 *cups cooked white Texmati rice*

To prepare the spinach sauce, heat the olive oil in a large sauté pan over medium heat. Add the onion, garlic, and poblano peppers and cook until the onion is tender, 3 to 5 minutes. Add the cumin, coriander, salt, black pepper, spinach, and water. Simmer until the liquid is almost gone, 8 to 10 minutes. Remove from the heat. Add the half-and-half and coconut while stirring. Transfer to a blender or a food processor equipped with a chopping blade and puree until smooth, about 2 minutes. Transfer to a small covered pot over low heat and keep warm, stirring often.

To prepare the bean curd, in a large mixing bowl, combine the flour, paprika, cumin, turmeric, salt, and black pepper, blend thoroughly with a wire whisk, and set aside. Place several pieces of the bean curd into the flour mixture and toss until well coated. Transfer to a plate that has been dusted with the flour mixture. Repeat until all of the bean curd has been floured.

Heat the olive oil in a large sauté pan over high heat. Add the onion and cayenne pepper and cook until golden brown, 3 to 5 minutes. Remove from the heat and use a slotted spoon to transfer the onion and cayenne to a small bowl. Allow as much oil as possible to remain in the pan.

Return the sauté pan to a high heat. Add the floured bean curd and fry until browned on all sides, 5 to 7 minutes. Handle the bean curd gently to avoid damaging the delicate crust.

Form a bed with the rice in a shallow serving dish, arrange the bean curd in a single layer, and cover with the spinach sauce. Sprinkle with the reserved onion and cayenne pepper and serve immediately.

MAKES 4 SERVINGS

Hong Kong Bean Curd

Just as the mighty city of Hong Kong rises out of the South China Sea, so do the flavors of this dish rise above the bed of brown rice. The light peppery taste of the watercress blends with the hot red pepper to make you feel like you are riding through a hot Southeast Asian night. And cooking this dish is a lot easier than navigating a bike through downtown Hong Kong. So take your taste buds on an Asian tour de force by whipping up some Hong Kong Bean Curd—and don't spare the hot pepper.

> 1 pound extra-firm bean curd, drained
> 2 cups water
> 2 tablespoons cornstarch
> 4 tablespoons (½ stick) butter
> 1 teaspoon crushed red pepper, or more to taste
> 1 teaspoon ground ginger
> 1 teaspoon salt
> ½ teaspoon ground white pepper
> 6 scallions
> 2 tablespoons chopped garlic
> 2 cups packed watercress, trimmed of thick stems
> 1 red bell pepper, cored, seeded, and julienned
> 3 cups cooked brown rice

Place the bean curd on a cutting board with the large side up. Cut on the diagonal into 4 triangles, then place each triangular piece on its longest side and cut in half from the tip toward the longest side. Slice each triangular chunk into 4 slices, giving you a total of 32 triangles.

Put 1 cup of the water in a small bowl and add the cornstarch. Stir until the cornstarch is completely dissolved and set aside.

In a large sauté pan, melt the butter over high heat. Add the red pepper, ginger, salt, and white pepper and stir well. Carefully place the bean curd in a single layer in the hot butter. Fry until the bean curd begins to brown, 3 to 5 minutes. Turn the bean curd pieces over and fry another 3 to 5 minutes.

While the bean curd is frying, trim the scallions. Remove the dark green tops, cut into ¼-inch-thick slices, and set aside. Cut the white and light

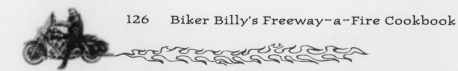

green sections into ½-inch pieces and add to the sauté pan. Add the garlic and stir well. Cook until the scallions begin to brown, 3 to 5 minutes.

Add the watercress, bell pepper, and remaining 1 cup water and stir well. Bring to a boil. Reduce the heat to medium, cover, and simmer until the watercress is tender, 5 to 7 minutes.

Stir the cornstarch and water mixture and then slowly pour it into the sauté pan while stirring. Stir until well blended. Reduce the heat to low. Add the reserved dark green scallion slices and simmer, stirring often, until the sauce thickens. Serve on a bed of the brown rice.

MAKES 4 TO 6 SERVINGS

Tramontin Harley-Davidson in Clifton, New Jersey, circa 1924. Pictured from left to right is the first generation of the Tramontin family Harley dealers: Ernest "Red" Tramontin; his wife, Pierina; Jimmy, the dog; their son, Bub; Peppi Tramontin; and Ida Tramontin.

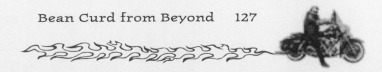

The Bean Curd from Beyond

I call this The Bean Curd from Beyond because dried bean curd is as alien to most people as little green men are. You may not believe in UFOs now, but this recipe will make you a believer—in Unidentified Frying Objects, that is. Give this recipe a try—you may experience a close encounter of the bean curd kind.

For the sauce:

1 pasilla pepper, stemmed, seeded, and torn into small pieces
1 ancho pepper, stemmed, seeded, and torn into small pieces
1 dried, de árbol pepper, stemmed and crushed
½ cup boiling water (see page 15)
½ cup cool water
1 tablespoon cornstarch
2 tablespoons sesame oil
1 medium-size onion, minced
2 tablespoons chopped garlic
1 teaspoon ground ginger
½ teaspoon ground black pepper
2 tablespoons light teriyaki sauce
¼ cup honey

For the bean curd:

8 to 10 ounces dried bean curd (see page 20)
2 tablespoons peanut oil
1 cup baby carrots, halved lengthwise
One 8-ounce can sliced water chestnuts, drained
2 cups sliced mushrooms
One 15-ounce can baby corn, drained
1 red bell pepper, cored, seeded, and diced

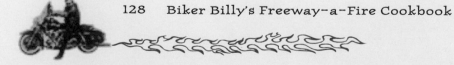

1 yellow bell pepper, cored, seeded, and diced
6 scallions, trimmed and cut into ¼-inch-thick
slices
4 cups cooked rice

To prepare the sauce, place the pasilla, ancho, and de árbol peppers in a small bowl and cover with the boiling water. Allow to cool to room temperature.

Put the cool water in another small bowl and add the cornstarch. Stir until the cornstarch is completely dissolved and set aside.

Heat the sesame oil in a small sauté pan over medium heat. Add the onion and garlic and cook until the onion is tender, 3 to 5 minutes. Add the rehydrated peppers with the soaking water, ginger, black pepper, teriyaki sauce, and honey and simmer for 2 minutes.

Transfer to a blender or a food processor equipped with a chopping blade and puree until smooth, 2 minutes. Return to the sauté pan over low heat. Stir the cornstarch and water mixture and then slowly pour it into the sauté pan, stirring, until well blended. Keep warm over a very low heat, stirring often.

To prepare the bean curd, place the bean curd on a cutting board with the large side up. Cut on the diagonal into 4 triangles, then place each triangular piece on its longest side and cut in half from the tip toward the longest side. Slice each triangular piece into 4 slices, so you have a total of 32 triangles.

Heat the peanut oil in a large wok over high heat. Add the bean curd and toss well to coat with oil. Stir-fry until the bean curd begins to brown, 2 to 3 minutes. Add the carrots and water chestnuts and stir-fry for 2 minutes. Add the mushrooms, corn, bell peppers, and scallions and stir-fry until the mushrooms darken, 3 to 5 minutes. The vegetables should still be crisp and firm.

Pour the sauce over the vegetables and toss to coat. Serve immediately on a bed of the rice.

MAKES 4 SERVINGS

Scrambled Beyond Belief

If you love scrambled eggs, but aren't supposed to eat them, this recipe will lift your heavy heart. A pound of bean curd equals more than 6 jumbo eggs in weight, but has a fraction of the fat and no cholesterol. If you use a nonstick pan, you can reduce the amount of margarine for an even lower-fat dish. The color and texture are so close to those of scrambled eggs it is beyond belief, and the taste makes eggs look like chicken. Best of all, the fire from the chipotles is a great morning wake-up call. Serve this in place of eggs at breakfast, or stuff it into a pita for a great hot sandwich anytime.

> 2 chipotle peppers, stemmed
> ¼ cup boiling water (see page 15)
> 6 scallions
> 3 tablespoons margarine or butter
> 1 pound extra-firm bean curd, drained and crumbled
> 1 teaspoon ground turmeric
> 1 teaspoon ground cumin
> 1 teaspoon ground ginger
> 1 teaspoon dried chervil
> 1 teaspoon salt
> 1 teaspoon ground black pepper

Place the chipotle peppers in a small bowl and cover with the boiling water. Allow to cool to room temperature.

In a blender or a food processor equipped with a chopping blade, puree the rehydrated peppers and the soaking water until no large pieces of chipotle remain, 1 minute.

Remove the dark green tops from the scallions, cut into ¼-inch-thick slices, and set aside. Mince the white and light green sections.

Melt the margarine in a large sauté pan over medium heat. Add the minced scallions and bean curd and stir well to coat with margarine. Cook until the scallions begin to brown, 5 to 7 minutes. Add the pepper puree, turmeric, cumin, ginger, chervil, salt, and black pepper and stir well to blend in the spices. Reduce the heat to low and simmer until the liquid is gone, 3 to 5 minutes. Sprinkle with the dark green scallion tops and serve piping hot.

MAKES 4 TO 6 SERVINGS

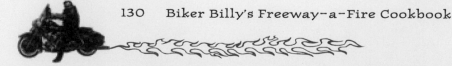

Surprise Sauce

This sauce looks, at first glance, like a fattening cream sauce, but the surprise is that it is made with bean curd. Ladle it over some veggies and you will have a high-protein, high-fiber, and low-fat meal. In spite of all that healthy stuff, it is really tasty, with a warm glow from the cayenne pepper. The Flamethrower Veggies (page 133) go well with the sauce, or use your imagination and try the sauce over other dishes. Just remember that if your crew yells "Yuck!" at the mention of bean curd, you can surprise them with this sauce.

> 2 tablespoons margarine or butter
> 1 tablespoon dried minced chives
> 1 teaspoon ground savory
> 1 teaspoon ground sage
> 1 teaspoon dried marjoram
> ½ teaspoon dried thyme
> 1 tablespoon dried parsley
> 1 teaspoon dried basil
> ½ teaspoon salt
> ½ teaspoon ground cayenne pepper
> ½ teaspoon ground white pepper
> 2 tablespoons hot water
> 1 pound soft bean curd, rinsed, drained,
>   and cut into 1-inch cubes
> ¼ to ½ cup water

Fill the bottom half of a double boiler (not quite halfway) with boiling water and place over medium heat (you don't want the top part of the double boiler to be in direct contact with the water). Every so often, check the water level to ensure that the pot does not boil dry. Keep another pot of water boiling on the stove so you can add water if necessary. Melt the margarine in the top of the double boiler. Add the chives, savory, sage, marjoram, thyme, parsley, basil, salt, cayenne, and white pepper and stir well. Add the hot water and stir well. Allow the herbs and spices to cook until they are completely rehydrated, 2 to 3 minutes.

continued

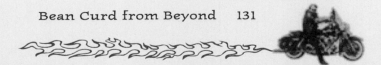

In a blender or a food processor equipped with a chopping blade, combine the bean curd and ¼ cup of the water and puree until smooth and creamy, about 1 minute. Add more water (up to ½ cup total) only if necessary to produce a smooth, creamy puree.

Slowly add the pureed bean curd to the rehydrated herbs and spices while stirring with a wire whisk. Simmer, stirring often, until the sauce is thoroughly warm, 5 to 7 minutes.

MAKES ABOUT 2 CUPS

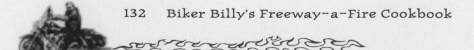

Flamethrower Veggies

I call these simple sautéed vegetables Flamethrower Veggies due to the blast of heat the Biker Billy jalapeño pepper gives them. You could core the Biker Billy pepper to reduce the heat or just use a wimpy, ordinary jalapeño. Although the veggies were intended to go with the Surprise Sauce (page 131), they can stand on their own as a fiery side dish.

> 1 large broccoli stalk
> 6 scallions
> 2 tablespoons canola oil
> 1 cup baby carrots, halved lengthwise
> 1 Biker Billy jalapeño pepper, stemmed and thinly
>   sliced
> 1 red bell pepper, cored, seeded, and julienned
> 1 yellow bell pepper, cored, seeded, and julienned
> Salt and ground black pepper to taste

Trim the broccoli, removing the florets and breaking them into bite-size pieces. Set aside. Cut the stalk into ¼-inch-thick slices.

Remove the dark green tops from the scallions and cut into ¼-inch-thick slices and set aside. Cut the white and light green sections into ½-inch pieces.

Heat the oil in a large sauté pan over medium heat. Add the carrots, Biker Billy jalapeño pepper, broccoli stalk, and scallions and cook until the scallions begin to brown, 5 to 7 minutes.

Add the broccoli florets, dark green scallion slices, and bell peppers and cook until the broccoli florets darken, 5 to 7 minutes. The broccoli florets should be tender, but not soft. Add salt and black pepper and serve immediately.

MAKES 4 TO 6 SERVINGS

The Passaic Valley Motorcycle Club Auxiliary, circa mid-1950s. Several of the ladies pictured here rode their own bikes and were members of the famous Motor Maids Motorcycle Club. Founded in 1940, Motor Maids Inc. is an international riding organization for women motorcyclists.

Rice Burners

From the name of this chapter, I bet you think I am going to say something derogatory about Japanese bikes and the people who ride them. Well, surprise surprise: just because I love my Harley and my friends at Harley-Davidson, it doesn't mean that I have ill will toward riders of other brands. In fact, I consider all motorcycle riders to be my friends, and I believe we all need to stand together and protect our rights. With the air clear, now let's get going and burn some rice.

This chapter is filled with fiery rice treats for you, from blazing side dishes to one-dish meals. You'll want to answer the call when my Stuffed Hell's Bells toll. The Rocket Risotto will launch you into orbit. My Rowdy Red Rice will give you a new perspective on rice and beans. Hopefully Dirty Biker Rice will help some folks clean up their attitudes toward bikers, while Blasted Rice will show you how one of my readers likes to blow away the mealtime blues.

Rocket Risotto

Here's a rice dish tasty enough to send you up into orbit. Climb aboard the Rocket Risotto and boost your taste buds with some high G-force flavors. A true risotto requires imported Italian Arborio rice to achieve the rich, creamy texture. Making this dish with any other type of rice would be like repairing a Ducati with Buick parts. Yuck! The broth adds high-test fuel to this recipe, and can also be used whenever you need a killer broth or stock. Start the countdown to an Italian-style biker feast and blast off with Rocket Risotto. While you're up there, grab a bird's-eye view of all the good motorcycle roads you haven't ridden yet.

For the broth:

8 cups water
3 dried New Mexico peppers, stemmed
3 chipotle peppers, stemmed
1 leek, trimmed, washed well, and thinly sliced (see page 23)
2 carrots, cut into ½-inch-thick slices
2 celery stalks with leaves, trimmed and cut into ½-inch-thick slices
1 tablespoon black peppercorns
2 tablespoons dried parsley
1 tablespoon dried chives
1 teaspoon dried basil
1 teaspoon dried oregano
1 bay leaf
1 tablespoon chopped garlic
½ teaspoon salt

For assembly:

1 chipotle pepper, stemmed
¼ cup boiling water (see page 15)
5 tablespoons butter

1 carrot, thinly sliced

1 medium-size onion, minced

2 tablespoons chopped garlic

1 celery stalk, trimmed and cut into ½-inch-thick slices

2 cups sliced cremini (brown) mushrooms

1 red bell pepper, cored, seeded, and diced

2 cups Arborio rice

½ cup freshly grated Parmesan cheese

Salt and ground black pepper to taste

To prepare the broth, place the 8 cups of water in a large soup pot over high heat. Add the New Mexico and chipotle peppers and bring to a simmer. Reduce the heat to low and add the leek, carrots, celery, peppercorns, parsley, chives, basil, oregano, bay leaf, garlic, and salt. Simmer, covered, for 1 to 2 hours, stirring often (the longer you simmer the broth, the richer it will be). Strain the broth and discard the solids (this should yield 6 cups of broth; if it does not, add enough water to increase the volume to 6 cups). Keep warm over very low heat.

To assemble the risotto, place the chipotle pepper in a small bowl and cover with the boiling water. Allow to cool to room temperature.

In a blender or a food processor equipped with a chopping blade, puree the rehydrated pepper and the soaking water until no large pieces of chipotle remain, 1 minute.

Melt the butter in a large sauté pan over medium heat. Add the carrot and cook for 2 minutes. Add the onion and cook until just tender, 2 to 3 minutes. Add the chipotle puree, garlic, celery, and mushrooms, and cook until the mushrooms are tender, 3 to 4 minutes. Add the bell pepper and rice, stir well, and cook for 2 minutes. Add 2 cups of the broth, raise the heat to high, and bring to a boil. Reduce the heat to low. Simmer, uncovered, stirring often, adding 2 more cups of broth as needed (see Note), until the rice is firm and the sauce is thick and creamy, 20 to 25 minutes. Just before serving, sprinkle on the Parmesan cheese, season with salt and pepper, and stir well. Serve steaming hot.

MAKES 4 TO 6 SERVINGS

NOTE: Four cups of broth will not always be enough to cook 2 cups of rice, so you may need to add more broth. In order to achieve rice that is firm and not mushy, add enough extra liquid to create a creamy consistency. The Arborio rice has a naturally high starch content, and stirring releases the starches that combine with the broth to form a thick, creamy texture.

Rowdy Red Rice

This is a strange take on the concept of rice and beans. The rice has the warm, gentle fire of ancho and pasilla peppers, which also impart an earthy flavor. The peas are enveloped in a creamy herb sauce that calms the Rowdy Red Rice. The deep red color of the rice highlighted by the red bell pepper makes a nice visual contrast to the green of the peas and sauce.

Prepare the peas while the rice is simmering so that they will arrive at the table at their peak of texture and flavor. The fire level of this dish is mellow to start, and the cream sauce will mellow it even more—that makes it a good introduction to the pleasures of fire. Much like a gentle ride around the block can introduce someone to the joys of motorcycling. Share the joy!

For the rice:

3 tablespoons butter

1 medium-size onion, minced

2 tablespoons chopped garlic

1 cup white Texmati rice

1 teaspoon salt

½ teaspoon ground black pepper

1 ancho pepper, stemmed, seeded, and crushed

1 pasilla pepper, stemmed, seeded, and crushed

2½ cups water

1 red bell pepper, cored, seeded, and diced

For the peas:

2 tablespoons butter

1 teaspoon dried tarragon

½ teaspoon ground savory

½ teaspoon ground sage

½ teaspoon salt

¼ teaspoon ground white pepper

1 cup half-and-half

2 cups frozen peas, thawed

To prepare the rice, melt the butter in a large sauté pan over high heat. Add the onion and sauté until it is tender, 2 to 3 minutes. Add the garlic and rice and stir well to coat with butter. Cook until the rice begins to brown, 2 to 3 minutes. Add the salt, black pepper, ancho and pasilla peppers and stir well. Add the 2½ cups water and the bell pepper. Stir well and bring to a boil. Reduce the heat to low. Cover and simmer until all the liquid has been absorbed, 15 to 20 minutes.

To prepare the peas, melt the butter in a small saucepot over medium heat. Add the tarragon, savory, sage, salt, and white pepper and cook for 1 to 2 minutes, using care not to brown the herbs. Add the half-and-half and stir until well blended. Add the peas and stir well. Reduce the heat to low and simmer until the half-and-half has reduced and thickened, 10 to 15 minutes.

In a large serving dish, create a bed with the rice. Spoon the peas and cream sauce on top and serve immediately.

MAKES 4 TO 6 SERVINGS

Dirty Biker Rice

It's sad to say, but some people view motorcycle riders as "dirty bikers." And
having typecast us as bad guys, they go ahead and treat us as second-class
citizens. Imagine being denied access to parks, restaurants, hotels, health
insurance, and even parking in front of your own home because you drive a
Ford or Chevy. Well, it happens to people simply because they ride motorcycles. One would hope that discrimination was largely a thing of the past in
America. However, when it comes to bikers, it still plagues us. So, if you ever
hear someone spouting antibiker rhetoric, just cook them this recipe. Then,
after they have eaten their words (so to speak), politely ask them to recon-
sider their prejudices regarding bikers.

2 chipotle peppers, stemmed
¼ cup boiling water (see page 15)
1 large bunch broccoli
4 tablespoons (½ stick) butter
4 to 6 scallions, trimmed and cut into ½-inch-thick
   slices
1 cup (about 4 ounces) minced shiitake mushroom
   caps
2 tablespoons chopped garlic
1 cup Texmati rice
1½ teaspoons salt
1 teaspoon ground black pepper
½ teaspoon ground cumin
¼ teaspoon ground coriander
1 tablespoon dried parsley
1 tablespoon dried cilantro
1 teaspoon dried basil
1 cup water
1 tablespoon Liquid Smoke
1 tablespoon blackstrap molasses
One 12-ounce bottle beer
1 red bell pepper, cored, seeded, and diced
½ cup boiling water

Place the chipotle peppers in a small bowl and cover with the boiling water. Allow to cool to room temperature.

In a blender or a food processor equipped with a chopping blade, puree the rehydrated peppers and the soaking water until no large pieces of chipotle remain, 1 minute.

Remove the broccoli florets from the stalk. Break or cut the florets into bite-size pieces and set aside. Trim any leaves or hard dry parts from the broccoli stalk. Using a food processor equipped with a chopping blade, or mincing by hand, finely chop the stalks.

Heat the butter in a large sauté pan over medium heat. Add the scallions and cook until the scallions are tender, 3 to 4 minutes. Add the mushrooms and minced broccoli stalks and stir well to coat with butter. Cook until the scallions are golden brown, 3 to 5 minutes. Add the chipotle puree, garlic, and rice and stir well to coat with butter. Cook until the rice is lightly browned, 5 to 8 minutes.

Add the salt, black pepper, cumin, coriander, parsley, cilantro, basil, 1 cup water, Liquid Smoke, molasses, and beer and stir well. Raise the heat to high and bring to a boil. Stir well, reduce the heat to medium, and simmer, covered, for 10 minutes.

Add the bell pepper, broccoli florets, and ½ cup boiling water and stir well. Reduce the heat to low and cook, covered, for 5 minutes, stirring occasionally. Remove from heat and let rest, covered, for 5 to 10 minutes. Serve immediately.

MAKES 4 TO 6 SERVINGS

Blasted Rice

This Viewer Recipe Contest Winner came from a woman who couldn't get my show on her cable system. After seeing me on *The Tonight Show* with Jay Leno, she bought my first book and sent in this recipe. Well, as you can expect, I changed her recipe a bit while I cooked it on my show. I hope Kelly from Homewood, Illinois, likes my adaptation. The crew sure did, since this blasted off their plates like a Titan missile. Alright!

    4 tablespoons (½ stick) butter
    1 small onion, minced
    1 chipotle pepper packed in adobo sauce, minced
    2 tablespoons chopped garlic
    ⅓ cup orzo pasta
    1 cup Texmati rice
    2 tablespoons light soy sauce
    1 teaspoon Liquid Smoke
    ½ teaspoon dried basil
    ½ teaspoon dried oregano
    1 tablespoon dried parsley
    ½ teaspoon dried thyme
    1 teaspoon salt
    1 teaspoon ground black pepper
    2¾ cups water
    1 red bell pepper, cored, seeded, and diced
    1 ripe medium-size tomato, pureed
    2 scallions, trimmed and cut into ¼-inch-thick slices

Melt the butter in a large sauté pan over high heat. Add the onion and chipotle pepper and cook until the onion begins to brown, 3 to 5 minutes. Reduce the heat to medium and add the garlic, orzo, and rice and stir well to coat with butter. Cook until the rice is lightly browned, 3 to 5 minutes.

Add the soy sauce, Liquid Smoke, basil, oregano, parsley, thyme, salt, black pepper, and water. Raise the heat to high and bring to a boil. Add the

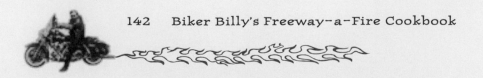

bell pepper and pureed tomato, stir well, and reduce the heat to low. Cover and simmer until all the liquid has been absorbed, 10 to 15 minutes. Transfer to a large serving dish, sprinkle with the scallions, and serve immediately.

MAKES 4 TO 6 SERVINGS

New Jersey, circa 1939. Bub Tramontin helps a crashed rider pick up his bike during a dirt-track race, while the officer is looking to wave off oncoming racers.

Stuffed Hell's Bells

Ask not for whom the stuffed bells toll, for they toll for you. And believe me, when these bells from hell toll, you will want to answer the call. If you like basil you will go nuts when you cook these succulent beauties; just wait until you taste them. The cayenne peppers give the stuffing a nice kick that works well with the flavorful Texmati rice. Along with the mellow warmth of the ancho-spiked sauce, this comfort food would warm the cockles of even the Devil's heart.

For the stuffing:

2 tablespoons extra-virgin olive oil
2 fresh long, slim red cayenne peppers,
    stemmed, seeded, and thinly sliced
2 medium-size onions, minced
2 tablespoons chopped garlic
1 teaspoon salt
1 teaspoon ground black pepper
1 cup white Texmati rice
2 cups water
1 cup packed fresh basil leaves, coarsely chopped

For the sauce:

2 ancho peppers, stemmed, seeded, and torn into
    pieces
¼ cup boiling water (see page 15)
One 28-ounce can whole peeled tomatoes, drained,
    juice reserved, and coarsely chopped
2 tablespoons extra-virgin olive oil
2 medium-size onions, diced
2 tablespoons chopped garlic
½ teaspoon salt
½ teaspoon ground black pepper

For assembly:

    4 large yellow bell peppers, cored and seeded,
      ½ inch removed from the tops
    ¼ cup freshly grated Parmesan cheese (optional)

To prepare the stuffing, heat the olive oil in a large saucepan over medium heat. Add the cayenne peppers, onions, and garlic and cook until the onions are tender, 3 to 5 minutes. Add the salt, black pepper, and rice and cook until the onions begin to brown, 2 to 3 minutes. Add the 2 cups water, raise the heat to high, and bring to a boil. Add the basil, stir well, cover tightly, and reduce the heat to low. Simmer, covered, until all of the water has been absorbed, 15 to 20 minutes (do not stir the rice when you check if the water has been fully absorbed, since stirring releases the starch and will make the rice sticky).

To prepare the sauce, place the ancho peppers in a small bowl and cover with the boiling water. Allow to cool to room temperature.

In a blender or a food processor equipped with a chopping blade, puree the rehydrated ancho peppers, the soaking water, and the reserved juice from the tomatoes until no large pieces of ancho remain, 1 minute.

Heat the olive oil in a large sauté pan over high heat. Add the onions and stir well to coat with oil. Cook until the onions are golden brown, 3 to 5 minutes. Add the ancho puree, garlic, salt, black pepper, and chopped tomatoes to the sauté pan. Bring to a boil, reduce the heat to low, and simmer until the sauce just thickens, 8 to 10 minutes.

Preheat the oven to 350°F.

To assemble the peppers, stuff each bell pepper with the rice mixture (the filling should form a small dome on top). Cover the bottom of a 9-inch square baking dish with half of the sauce (if you have extra rice filling after stuffing the peppers, spread it over the sauce). Place the stuffed bell peppers in the baking dish and ladle the remaining sauce around the peppers. Bake until the bell peppers are tender, 20 to 30 minutes. Five minutes before you remove the peppers from the oven, sprinkle Parmesan cheese, if you desire, on top of the peppers. Serve piping hot.

MAKES 4 SERVINGS

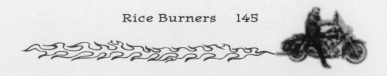

Bobby Tramontin wins another race aboard Mellow Yellow, during unauthorized drag races at Pocono Raceway, Pocono, Pennsylvania, circa early 1970s.

Amber Waves of Grain

Riding across this great country on my Harley, I have been almost overwhelmed by the miles and miles of farmland covered with amber waves of grain. It is easy to see why America is the breadbasket to the world. Beyond using them to make bread, grains can also produce wonderful dishes with a surprising variety of flavors. The first grain that comes to mind is wheat, and there are several dishes here based on wheat. Bulgur wheat is a personal favorite, and it is the star of three recipes: Stuffed Cabbage à la Biker, Hot Nutty Bulgur, and Bourbon Bulgur. For more information about this protein-rich, high-fiber grain, check out The Biker's Pantry on page 19. There is another form of wheat that is often mistaken for pasta—couscous. This is probably one of the easier grains to cook. After trying my Kooky Couscous recipe, you will also be crazy for couscous. And what collection of biker grain recipes would be complete without barley? Most barley consumed today arrives at the table with a head on it. Yes, it's beer. The three barley recipes here will give you a different type of buzz, the fiery kind. (And if you enjoy barley in the form of beer or distilled spirits, please leave your motor vehicles safely parked, thanks!) I've also included Kasha, a.k.a. buckwheat, an Eastern European staple that has a wonderful unique flavor and aroma. Try my Killer Kasha for a fiery new take on an Old World classic. The recipes in this chapter should give you a sampling of some of the feasts that can be created with grains. After dinner, consider planning a motorcycle tour across America and see those amber waves of grain firsthand.

Kooky Couscous

The image of Lawrence of Arabia astride a beautiful Brough Superior motorcycle conjures up dreams of desert days and wild Arabian nights. Imagine spending your day riding across exotic North Africa on a motorcycle safari. As the sun sets, you return to an oasis camp, your senses burning with excitement, your body parched and possessed by a powerful appetite. A warm desert breeze gently blows through camp, rustling the palm trees and carrying an aroma of Arabian delights. After a deep drink from the well, you settle by the campfire and are handed a steaming plate of food. That first delicious mouthful bursts across your palate with flavors that bring back all the excitement of the day's ride. Soon the fiery food illuminates you from within, like the campfire ignites the desert night. Wanna feel the desert wind on your face? Try this crazy couscous dish and you'll swear you hear the wind in the palms.

For the sauce:

2 chipotle peppers, stemmed
¼ cup boiling water (see page 15)
4 tablespoons (½ stick) butter
½ cup sun-dried tomatoes
1 tablespoon chopped garlic
1 tablespoon sweet paprika
½ teaspoon salt
½ teaspoon ground white pepper
1 cup light cream

For the couscous:

2¼ cups water
2 tablespoons butter
2 tablespoons dried parsley
1 tablespoon onion flakes
½ teaspoon salt
½ teaspoon ground white pepper
One 10-ounce box couscous

For the vegetables:

    2 tablespoons light olive oil
    2 carrots, julienned
    1 cup sliced mushrooms
    2 scallions, trimmed and cut into ½-inch thick slices
    1 yellow bell pepper, cored, seeded, and julienned
    1 red bell pepper, cored, seeded, and julienned
    1 large broccoli stalk

To prepare the sauce, place the chipotle peppers in a small bowl and cover with the boiling water. Allow to cool to room temperature.

Melt the butter in a small sauté pan over low heat. Add the sun-dried tomatoes and garlic and stir well to coat with butter. Cook for 5 minutes, stirring often. Add the rehydrated chipotle peppers and the soaking water. Increase the heat to high and bring almost to a boil. Reduce the heat to medium and simmer for 2 minutes. Transfer to a blender or a food processor equipped with a chopping blade and puree until no large pieces of chipotle remain, 1 minute. Return the puree to the sauté pan over low heat. Add the paprika, salt, and white pepper and stir well. Slowly add the cream while stirring. Keep warm over a very low heat while you sauté the vegetables.

To prepare the couscous; place the 2¼ cups water in a medium-size pot over high heat and bring to a boil. Add the butter, parsley, onion flakes, salt, white pepper, and couscous. Stir well, cover, and remove from the heat. Allow to sit for 5 minutes. Use a fork to fluff up the couscous and set aside.

To prepare the vegetables, heat the olive oil in a large sauté pan over high heat. Add the carrots and stir well to coat with oil. Cook for 2 minutes. Add the mushrooms and scallions; cook for 1 minute. Add the bell peppers and broccoli, and cook until the broccoli begins to darken and the vegetables are tender, 2 to 3 minutes.

On a large serving dish, form a bed with the couscous. Arrange the vegetables on top of the couscous, leaving a 1-inch border of couscous uncovered. Ladle the sauce over top and serve immediately.

MAKES 4 TO 6 SERVINGS

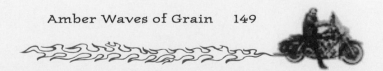

Biker Barley

Barley is a wonderful grain that many of us encounter only in soups, as in mushroom barley soup. In keeping with those traditional flavors, this recipe uses mushrooms, leek, and onion to give it that rich, earthy flavor so the barley will feel right at home. Adding the combination of ancho and chipotle peppers works in unison with the gentle herbs to create a biker-style taste sensation. You can serve this as a main dish or as a hearty side dish.

1 ancho pepper, stemmed, seeded, and torn into
    small pieces
1 chipotle pepper, stemmed
½ cup boiling water (see page 15)
4 tablespoons (½ stick) margarine
1 medium-size onion, diced
1 leek, trimmed, washed well, and cut into
    ¼-inch-thick slices (see page 23)
4 cups sliced mushrooms (about 10 ounces)
2 tablespoons chopped garlic
1 teaspoon salt
1 teaspoon ground black pepper
1 tablespoon dried parsley
1 tablespoon Liquid Smoke
1 teaspoon ground sage
1 cup pearl barley
2½ cups hot water

Place the ancho and chipotle peppers in a small bowl and cover with the boiling water. Allow to cool to room temperature.

In a blender or a food processor equipped with a chopping blade, puree the rehydrated peppers and the soaking water until no large pieces of pepper remain, 1 minute.

In a large sauté pan, melt the margarine over high heat. Add the onion and leek and cook until the onion begins to brown, 3 to 5 minutes. Reduce the heat to medium. Add the pureed peppers, mushrooms, and chopped garlic and cook until the mushrooms darken and are tender, 3 to 5 minutes.

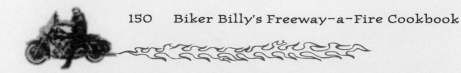

Add the salt, black pepper, parsley, Liquid Smoke, sage, barley, and 2½ cups hot water and stir well. Raise the heat to high and bring to a boil. Reduce the heat to low, cover, and simmer until the barley is tender, 45 to 50 minutes. Serve immediately.

MAKES 4 TO 6 SERVINGS

Ballistic Barley Pilaf

The Biker Billy jalapeño pepper makes this pilaf truly ballistic. If you leave
the jalapeño seeds and core in the recipe, it would be an ICBM (Intensely
Caliente Biker Meal). This one-dish meal (or explosive side dish) combines
a blend of fresh-tasting herbs with savory sautéed onion, shallot, garlic, and
portobello mushroom. The texture of the barley is perfect for a pilaf and the
colors of the vegetables add eye appeal. So fire your missiles and blast din-
nertime boredom away with Ballistic Barley Pilaf.

> 2 tablespoons extra-virgin olive oil
> 1 medium-size onion, diced
> 1 shallot, minced
> 1 Biker Billy jalapeño pepper, stemmed, seeded, and
>   minced
> 4 garlic cloves, minced
> 1 red bell pepper, cored, seeded, and diced
> 1 portobello mushroom, diced
> 1 teaspoon dried basil
> 1 teaspoon dried chervil
> ½ teaspoon dried marjoram
> 1 teaspoon salt
> 1 teaspoon ground black pepper
> 2 cups cooked pearl barley
> 1 cup frozen peas and carrots, thawed

Heat the olive oil in a large sauté pan over medium heat. Add the onion,
shallot, and Biker Billy jalapeño pepper and stir well to coat with oil. Sauté
until the onions begin to brown, 5 to 7 minutes. Add the garlic, bell pepper,
portobello mushroom, basil, chervil, marjoram, salt, and black pepper and
stir well to coat with oil. Cook until the mushroom begins to darken, 3 to 5
minutes. Add the cooked barley and peas and carrots, and stir well. Reduce
the heat to low and cook until the vegetables are just tender, 3 to 5 minutes.
Serve piping hot.

MAKES 4 TO 6 SERVINGS

Barley Bites

I originally conceived of this recipe as an appetizer. But one time I poured too much batter into the frying pan and created a great side dish, too. You could make these really bite-size for an appetizer serving or potato pancake–size like I did. Try these in place of hash browns with your preride breakfast and add some zoom to your morning. In fact, they are at home anytime you would serve potatoes or rice.

> 1 jumbo egg
> 1 chipotle pepper packed in adobo sauce, minced
> 2 sun–dried tomatoes packed in oil, minced
> ½ cup water
> ¼ teaspoon ground cumin
> ¼ teaspoon ground coriander
> ½ teaspoon dried cilantro
> ½ teaspoon salt
> ½ teaspoon ground black pepper
> ½ teaspoon baking powder
> ½ cup all–purpose flour
> 2 scallions, trimmed and cut into
>   ¼–inch–thick slices
> 1 tablespoon chopped garlic
> 1 cup cooked pearl barley
> Olive oil for frying

In a medium-size mixing bowl, combine the egg, chipotle pepper, sun-dried tomatoes, and water. Beat with a fork until well blended. Add the cumin, coriander, cilantro, salt, black pepper, baking powder, and flour. Beat with a fork until a smooth batter forms. Add the scallions, garlic, and pearl barley and stir until well combined.

In a medium-size frying pan, heat ¼ inch of olive oil over medium heat. Place a tablespoon of the barley mixture into the oil and flatten gently with the back of a spoon. Repeat until the pan is full. Fry until the edges start to brown, 2 to 3 minutes. Turn and fry the other side for another 2 to 3 minutes. Drain on a paper towel and serve piping hot.

MAKES 4 SERVINGS

Killer Kasha

Kasha, also known as buckwheat, is a hearty grain with a unique, almost nutty flavor. Judging by how many supermarkets I had to visit to find kasha, it seems like few people cook this wholesome grain nowadays. That is a shame, since it has a lot of flavor to offer. If you follow current nutritional guidelines, grains should comprise the largest portion of your daily food intake. Since grains can seem like a sea of sometimes all-too-similar amber waves, the uniqueness of kasha can be a refreshing change. This dish is a classic Eastern European dish that I have customized with biker-style fire and spice. I hope you enjoy it and that it expands your culinary field of grains.

> 3 tablespoons butter
> 1 to 2 chipotle peppers packed in adobo sauce
>   (to your taste), minced
> 2 large onions, diced
> 10 garlic cloves, minced
> 1 large portobello mushroom, diced
> 2 shallots, minced
> 1 red bell pepper, cored, seeded, and diced
> ¼ cup snipped fresh chives
> 2 teaspoons salt
> 1½ teaspoons ground black pepper
> 1 cup whole grain kasha
> 2 cups water
> 1 pound bow tie pasta

Bring a large pot of water to a boil over high heat.

In a large sauté pan, melt the butter over medium heat. Add the chipotle peppers and cook for 2 minutes. Add the onions and cook until the onions are tender, 3 to 5 minutes. Add the garlic, portobello mushroom, shallots, bell pepper, chives, salt, black pepper, and kasha and stir well to coat with butter. Cook until the kasha is lightly toasted, 3 to 5 minutes. Add the 2 cups water, raise the heat to high, and bring to a boil. Reduce the heat to low and simmer until all the liquid has been absorbed, 10 to 12 minutes.

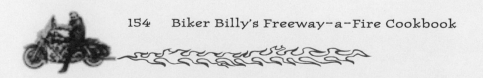

While the kasha simmers, cook the pasta in the pot of boiling water according to package direction until it is al dente. Drain and rinse with hot water to remove excess starch. Allow the pasta to drain thoroughly.

In a large serving bowl combine the pasta and kasha, toss well, and serve immediately.

MAKES 4 TO 6 SERVINGS

Hot Nutty Bulgur

Move over rice, this is the side dish of the future. Bulgur wheat itself has a nice nutty flavor and a satisfying texture. The almonds and raisins add an Indian influence, while the mint gives a hint of the Middle East. Toss in the American kick of the ancho and chipotle peppers and you have an international motorcycle rally of flavors. Take your tongue on a biker-style world tour and serve up this flavorful dish.

    1 ancho pepper, stemmed, seeded,
        and torn into small pieces
    1 chipotle pepper, stemmed
    ¼ cup boiling water (see page 15)
    4 tablespoons (½ stick) margarine or butter
    1 cup bulgur wheat
    ½ cup slivered almonds
    1¼ cups water
    1 tablespoon honey
    2 teaspoons dried mint
    ½ cup golden raisins
    ½ teaspoon salt
    ¼ teaspoon ground black pepper

Place the ancho and chipotle peppers in a small bowl and cover with the boiling water. Allow to cool to room temperature.

In a blender or a food processor equipped with a chopping blade, puree the rehydrated peppers and the soaking water until no large pieces of pepper remain, 1 minute.

In a large sauté pan, melt the margarine over medium heat. Add the bulgur wheat and almonds and stir thoroughly to coat with margarine. Toast the bulgur wheat, stirring frequently, until lightly browned, 2 to 3 minutes. Add the pepper puree, water, honey, mint, raisins, salt, and black pepper. Stir well, raise heat to high, and bring to a boil. Reduce the heat to low and simmer, covered, until all the liquid is absorbed, 15 to 20 minutes. Serve piping hot.

MAKES 4 TO 6 SERVINGS

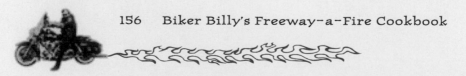

Bourbon Bulgur

This deep, dark bulgur wheat dish has an intoxicating flavor. Like a fine bourbon, it should be savored slowly. The orange bell pepper adds a colorful sparkle, while the chipotle sparks up the fire. Ask for seconds before you finish the first serving, or you may miss last call with this dish.

The alcohol evaporates while this dish cooks, but the flavor of the bourbon remains. And remember, if you enjoy alcohol as a beverage, let time cook it out of your system before you drive or ride. Eat Hot and Ride Sober!

1 ancho pepper, stemmed, seeded, and torn into small pieces

2 chipotle peppers, stemmed

½ cup boiling water (see page 15)

3 tablespoons butter

1 medium-size onion, minced

3 cups minced mushrooms (about 10 ounces)

2 tablespoons chopped garlic

1½ cups bulgur wheat

2 cups water

1 teaspoon dried chives

1 tablespoon dried parsley

1½ teaspoons salt

1 teaspoon ground black pepper

1 teaspoon Liquid Smoke

1 tablespoon blackstrap molasses

2 tablespoons bourbon

1 orange bell pepper, cored, seeded, and diced

Place the ancho and chipotle peppers in a small bowl and cover with the boiling water. Allow to cool to room temperature.

In a blender or a food processor equipped with a chopping blade, puree the rehydrated peppers with the soaking water until no large pieces of pepper remain, 1 minute.

In a large sauté pan, melt the butter over high heat. Add the onion and cook until the onion begins to brown, 3 to 5 minutes. Reduce the heat to medium. Add the pureed peppers, mushrooms, and garlic. Cook until the mushrooms darken and are tender, 3 to 5 minutes. Add the bulgur wheat and stir well to coat with butter. Cook until the bulgur wheat begins to brown, 3 to 5 minutes. Add the water, chives, parsley, salt, black pepper, Liquid Smoke, molasses, bourbon, and orange bell pepper. Stir well, raise the heat to high, and bring to a boil. Reduce the heat to very low, cover, and simmer until all the liquid has been absorbed, 10 to 15 minutes. Serve piping hot.

MAKES 4 TO 6 SERVINGS

R. Lee Wimmer in his navy uniform aboard his 1929 Harley-Davidson JD model, circa early 1940s. Lee likes to make pancakes before Saturday morning rides.

Stuffed Cabbage à la Biker

When you were a child, the sight of stuffed cabbage on the dinner table was right up there with broccoli as a mealtime turnoff. But one bite of these hot babies will make you roar up to the table and say, "Stuff me with cabbage!" So tie on your black leather bib and get ready for a stick-to-your-ribs, biker-style staple. Just don't offer them to the kids if you plan on having seconds.

1 head cabbage
6 tablespoons (¾ stick) margarine or butter
1 teaspoon cumin seeds
1 teaspoon black peppercorns
2 cardamom pods, crushed
2 dried long, slim red cayenne peppers,
   stemmed and crushed
1 cup bulgur wheat
2 cups water
½ teaspoon salt
2 medium-size onions, chopped
2 tablespoons chopped garlic
½ cup pitted black olives
Firecracker Salsa (page 232)
1 cup shredded mild cheddar cheese

To prepare the cabbage leaves, wash the cabbage thoroughly. Remove the outermost layer of leaves, cut out the core of the cabbage, and discard them all. Place the head of cabbage in a large pot and add enough cold water to cover the cabbage. Remove the cabbage, turn the heat to high, and bring the water to a boil. Return the head of cabbage to the boiling water, core side down (if necessary, use a wooden spoon to submerge the cabbage). Boil for about 5 minutes, and, using two large slotted spoons, carefully remove the cabbage from the water and drain. When the cabbage is cool enough to handle, carefully peel off one leaf at a time (the outer leaves should be tender enough to peel off without tearing). When you reach the first leaf that won't come off without tearing, return the cabbage to the pot and boil for a few more minutes. Repeat until 12 to 18 of the leaves have been removed. Quarter and coarse chop the remaining cabbage and set aside.

continued

To prepare filling, in a large sauté pan, melt 2 tablespoons of the margarine over medium heat. Add the cumin, peppercorns, cardamom, and cayenne peppers and cook until the peppercorns start to pop and the spices are fragrant, 3 to 5 minutes. Using a slotted spoon, remove the spices and set aside. Melt 2 more tablespoons margarine in the pan. Add the bulgur wheat and stir thoroughly to coat with margarine. Toast the bulgur wheat, stirring frequently, until it is lightly browned, 2 to 3 minutes. While the bulgur wheat is toasting, grind the reserved spices, using a coffee grinder or a mortar and pestle.

In a medium pot bring water to a boil. Add the ground spices, bulgur wheat, and salt; reduce the heat to low and stir well. Cover and cook until all the water has been absorbed, 15 minutes.

Melt the remaining 2 tablespoons margarine in the sauté pan over medium heat. Add the onions and cook until the onions are tender, 2 to 3 minutes. Add the garlic, olives, and reserved chopped cabbage and cook until the cabbage is tender, 5 to 7 minutes. Remove from the heat and combine with the bulgur wheat.

To assemble the stuffed cabbage, preheat the oven to 350°F. Take a cabbage leaf and place a large spoonful of the filling in the center of the leaf. Fold the bottom corners over the filling and roll up the leaf. Repeat until you have used up all of the stuffing and leaves.

Cover the bottom of a 9 by 13 by 2-inch baking pan with a thin layer of salsa. Arrange the stuffed cabbage in a single layer, then cover with more salsa, and then the cheese. Bake until the cheese begins to brown, about 10 minutes.

MAKES 12 TO 18 STUFFED CABBAGE LEAVES

Handlebar Grub:
Burgers, Balls, and Loaves

Riding my motorcycle helps me get a grip on life. No matter how complex or confounding things get in today's hyperactive world, I know that my bike will help me get through it all. Even when the driveway in front of my garage is full of snow and ice, I can still go into the garage and sit on the bike and get a handle on things. In other words, the bike is a comfort to my soul. After the bike, my next big comfort tool is food. Take one look at me and you can tell I know how comforting food can be. Hey, would you really trust a skinny cook?

The recipes in this chapter are "get a grip"–type foods—hence, Handlebar Grub. They are also comforting enough to help you come to grips with life, or at least your appetite. The Banshee Bean Curd Burgers and Bulgur Biker Burgers require a two-fisted grip. The Mean Bean Meatballs and Bombay Balls are further apart in culinary style than grips on the colossal Harley Softtail on the front of the Las Vegas Harley Café. And if you want comfort food to help you get a grip, try the Red Hot Red Bean Loaf or the Vulgar Bean Curd Loaf. Remember when life becomes too much to handle, going for a ride will blow away your troubles and my fiery food will blow away your hunger.

Banshee Bean Curd Burgers

You'll howl like a banshee when you eat these burgers. As a safety precaution, before cooking them, lock all doors and windows and post sentries. The aroma of these burgers frying has been known to cause the neighbors to come screaming over like banshees. Of course, you could just make extra and invite the whole neighborhood for dinner; it's a lot easier than trying to control a riot.

You can pump up the volume on the banshee wail by adding more chipotle peppers to the recipe or by pouring some Smoky Chipotle Sauce (page 231) on the burgers.

> 1 chipotle pepper, stemmed
> ¼ cup boiling water (see page 15)
> 2 extra-large eggs
> ½ teaspoon ground savory
> ½ teaspoon dried thyme
> ½ teaspoon salt
> ½ teaspoon ground black pepper
> 1 cup shredded carrots
> 3 cups shredded dried bean curd (see page 20)
> ¼ cup whole wheat flour, plus extra for dusting
> Canola or peanut oil for frying
> Hamburger buns (optional)

Place the chipotle pepper in a small bowl and cover with the boiling water. Allow to cool to room temperature.

In a blender or a food processor equipped with a chopping blade, puree the rehydrated pepper and the soaking water until no large pieces of chipotle remain, 1 minute. Add the eggs, savory, thyme, salt, and black pepper, and process until well blended, about 1 minute.

In a large mixing bowl, combine the carrots and bean curd and toss together well. Add the pepper puree and toss together well. Add the flour and mix until the flour is fully incorporated. Cover and refrigerate for 30 minutes.

Place some flour in a shallow bowl. Take a handful (between ½ and ⅔ cup) of the mixture and form it into a burger. Dip the burger in the flour and

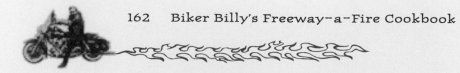

turn once or twice until the burger is well covered. Place the burger on a plate that is lightly dusted with flour. Repeat until 6 to 8 burgers are formed.

Heat enough oil to generously coat the bottom of a large frying pan over high heat. Place a few of the burgers in the hot oil at a time (do not crowd them in the pan). Fry on each side until they are golden brown, using care when you turn them to avoid breakage, 2 to 3 minutes. Drain on a paper towel. Serve piping hot on buns, if you desire.

MAKES 6 TO 8 BURGERS

Bulgur Biker Burgers

Veggie burgers are all the rage now. Many restaurants serve them and there are at least a dozen varieties in the supermarket. This burger recipe combines a nice texture with good protein and fiber in a relatively low-fat package. But don't mistake these for some kind of tasteless health food, no sir! The earthy flavors of the mushrooms and chipotle pepper are highlighted by the Indian tones of the curry powder. If you're looking for a burger with a handlebarful of flavor, whip up a batch of these babies.

    1 cup bulgur wheat
    1 cup boiling water (see page 15)
    1 tablespoon Liquid Smoke
    1 chipotle pepper packed in adobo sauce, minced
    1 small onion, minced
    2 tablespoons chopped garlic
    ½ cup coarsely chopped mushrooms
    1 teaspoon ground turmeric
    ½ teaspoon ground sage
    1 teaspoon curry powder
    ¼ teaspoon dried oregano
    1½ teaspoons salt
    1½ teaspoons ground black pepper
    2 large eggs
    8 ounces extra-firm bean curd, crumbled
    1 cup minced mushrooms
    2 tablespoons whole wheat flour
    Canola or peanut oil for frying
    Hamburger buns (optional)

In a small mixing bowl, combine the bulgur wheat, water, and Liquid Smoke and stir well. Cover and allow the bulgur wheat to absorb all the liquid, about 30 minutes.

In a blender or a food processor equipped with a chopping blade, combine the chipotle pepper, onion, garlic, chopped mushrooms, turmeric, sage, curry powder, oregano, salt, and black pepper and puree for 1 minute. Add the eggs and puree until smooth, about 1 minute.

In a large mixing bowl, combine the pepper puree, bulgur wheat, bean curd, minced mushrooms, and flour and mix well. Cover and refrigerate for 1 hour to allow the burger mix to firm up. Form into 6 to 8 burgers. In a large frying pan, heat ¼ inch of canola or peanut oil over high heat. Fry the burgers 2 to 3 minutes on each side, or until browned. Serve on buns, if desired.

MAKES 6 TO 8 BURGERS

Mean Bean Meatballs

Pop some of these little devils on top of your favorite pasta dish and they'll look so mean they'll scare the sauce right off the spaghetti. But don't be afraid of them because they are every bit as tasty as they are mean-looking. About the only person they'll scare is the butcher, since there is no meat in them. These are higher in fiber and lower in fat than those made of meat. The bean and bulgur wheat combination is also a good source of protein, making these a great choice for fueling up a hungry biker.

The mix needs to be well chilled to form solid meatballs. Breading them before frying helps hold them together and forms a crispy seal to keep the oil from saturating them. Keeping the oil hot and not crowding them also prevents them from being oily. I have given you two choices for breading: I like the crunchier texture of the cornmeal, but flour works great, too. Using egg whites only to hold the breading on will reduce cholesterol. If you want to make them with meat, simply replace the 1 cup bulgur wheat and 1 cup boiling water with 2 cups lean ground meat (making sure to increase the frying time to ensure thorough cooking).

1 cup bulgur wheat
1 cup boiling water (see page 15)
1 ancho pepper, stemmed, seeded, and torn into
   small pieces
1 pasilla pepper, stemmed, seeded, and torn into
   small pieces
1 dried New Mexico pepper, stemmed, seeded, and
   torn into small pieces
½ cup boiling water
2 tablespoons extra-virgin olive oil
2 small onions, coarsely chopped
2 tablespoons chopped garlic
½ teaspoon salt
½ teaspoon ground black pepper
½ teaspoon ground cumin
1 tablespoon dried parsley
1 teaspoon dried cilantro

One 16-ounce can black beans, drained, liquid
   reserved
Peanut or canola oil for frying (see page 21)
2 large eggs, beaten
Cornmeal or all-purpose flour for breading

In a medium-size bowl, combine the bulgur wheat with the 1 cup boiling water, stir well, and cover tightly. Set aside until the water has been fully absorbed, about 20 to 30 minutes (see Note). Place the ancho, pasilla, and New Mexico pepper in a small bowl and cover with the ½ cup boiling water. Allow to cool to room temperature.

Put the olive oil in a small sauté pan over medium heat. Add the rehydrated peppers, soaking liquid, onions, and garlic, and cook for 2 to 3 minutes. Add the salt, black pepper, cumin, parsley, cilantro, and the reserved bean liquid. Simmer until the liquid is reduced to a very thick consistency, 3 to 5 minutes. Remove from the heat and allow to cool.

Transfer the mixture to a food processor equipped with a cutting blade and puree for 1 minute. Add the beans and pulse 6 times (this will combine the ingredients into a thick paste but leave the beans somewhat intact). Add the bean mixture to the bulgur wheat, mix well, and refrigerate for at least 1 hour.

In a deep pot or a deep-fryer, heat several inches of oil to 365°F. Take a spoonful of the mixture and form into a 2-inch ball. Dip the ball in the beaten eggs and roll in the cornmeal or flour. Place the ball on a plate that is lightly dusted with cornmeal or flour. Repeat until all of the mixture is used. Place a few of the balls in the hot oil at a time, using care not to crowd them. Fry until they are golden brown, 2 to 3 minutes. Drain on a paper towel and serve piping hot.

MAKES ABOUT 36 MEATBALLS

NOTE: When using bulgur wheat, check the package directions regarding the ratio of water to uncooked wheat. I have noticed some variance among brands. This is due to the fact that bulgur wheat is cracked whole grain wheat that is precooked. The amount of precooking may vary among manufacturers. Most packages have two preparation techniques, one for "hot cereal" and another for "side dish." For this recipe, I am preparing it according to the side-dish method.

Bombay Balls

This exotic dish may share the form of meatballs and spaghetti, but it is as different as a Harley is from a Volkswagen. The golden-brown chickpea balls, resting on a bed of rice and covered with a creamy white sauce speckled with poppy seeds, are visually pleasing. That is only the beginning. The battered balls are bursting with Indian flavors and a nice blast of fire. The rich sauce is mild, but tangy, with a coconut flair. You may have to ride only a few blocks to find the ingredients, but the taste will make you feel like you're on an adventure in an exotic far-off land.

For the balls:

1 small onion, minced
One 19-ounce can chickpeas, drained and rinsed
½ teaspoon ground cumin
¼ teaspoon ground ginger
1 teaspoon crushed red pepper
½ teaspoon salt
½ teaspoon ground black pepper
¼ cup plain dried bread crumbs
1 large egg, beaten

For the batter:

1 cup complete pancake mix
1 teaspoon ground cumin
1 teaspoon ground turmeric
½ teaspoon ground coriander
1 teaspoon ground cayenne pepper
1 teaspoon sweet paprika
1 teaspoon salt
1 teaspoon ground black pepper
1 cup water

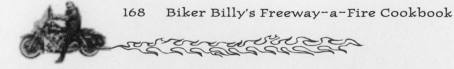

For the sauce:

1 tablespoon unsalted butter

1 medium-size onion, minced

1 teaspoon ground cumin

½ teaspoon ground coriander

½ cup half-and-half

1 cup plain yogurt

½ cup unsweetened shredded coconut

1 tablespoon poppy seeds

For assembly:

Canola oil for frying

3 cups cooked rice

To prepare the balls, in a large mixing bowl, combine the onion, chickpeas, cumin, ginger, crushed red pepper, salt, black pepper, and bread crumbs. Mash together with a potato masher or a fork until it forms a coarse mixture (use care not to overmash it). Add the egg and mix until well blended. Cover and refrigerate for 1 hour.

To prepare the batter, in a medium-size mixing bowl, combine the pancake mix, cumin, turmeric, coriander, cayenne, paprika, salt, and black pepper. Mix together with a wire whisk. Add the water and blend with the wire whisk until a smooth batter forms. Cover and let rest while you prepare the sauce.

To prepare the sauce, in a small saucepot, melt the butter over low heat. Add the onion, cumin, and coriander and cook until the onions are transparent, 10 to 15 minutes. Transfer the onion mixture to a blender, add the half-and-half, and puree until smooth. Return to the saucepot and reduce the heat to very low. Add the yogurt, coconut, and poppy seeds and stir until well blended. Cook, stirring often, while you prepare and fry the balls.

To assemble, heat several inches of oil in a deep pot or deep-fryer to 365°F. Take a spoonful of the chickpea mixture and form a 1-inch ball using your hands. Repeat until all the mixture is used. Dip a few of the balls in the batter. Using a fork, remove the balls from the batter, then transfer each battered ball onto an oiled spoon and lower it into the hot oil. Place a few of the battered balls in the hot oil at a time, using care not to crowd them. Fry until golden brown, 2 to 3 minutes. Drain on a paper towel and repeat until all the balls are fried. Arrange the balls on a bed of the rice and cover with the sauce. Serve piping hot.

MAKES 4 TO 6 SERVINGS

Red Hot Red Bean Loaf

If Little Red Riding Hood had had this loaf in her saddlebags when she rode to Grandma's house, she would have turned the big bad wolf into a lapdog. And you can easily tame the growling appetites of your wolf pack with it, too. The flavors and texture of this loaf are satisfying enough to make it a favorite at your house, like it is at mine.

This loaf is a solid source of protein. Rice and beans by themselves are a good complement of proteins, and with the addition of eggs and cheese in this recipe, you know it is really high-performance food. Not only is the nutrition high-performance, but the flavor is, too. Serve this dish just as you would meatloaf or use it to make killer sandwiches.

    4 tablespoons (½ stick) butter
    1 medium-size onion, diced
    1 yellow bell pepper, cored, seeded, and diced
    1 cup diced mushrooms
    2 chipotle peppers packed in adobo sauce, minced
    4 sun-dried tomatoes packed in oil, minced
    2 tablespoons chopped garlic
    1 teaspoon salt
    ½ teaspoon ground black pepper
    1 tablespoon all-purpose flour
    1 cup water
    One 16-ounce can small red beans, drained and
        rinsed
    2 extra-large eggs
    1 tablespoon dried parley
    1 tablespoon dried chives
    ½ teaspoon ground sage
    3 cups cooked rice
    2 cups shredded mild cheddar cheese

In a large sauté pan, melt the butter over high heat. Add the onion and cook until the onion begins to brown, 3 to 5 minutes. Add the bell pepper and mushrooms and cook until the mushrooms begin to darken, 3 to 5

minutes. Add the chipotle peppers, sun-dried tomatoes, garlic, salt, and black pepper and stir well. Cook until the garlic begins to brown, 2 to 3 minutes.

Add the flour and stir well. Continue to stir until the flour is lightly browned, about 2 minutes. Add the water and stir until the flour is dissolved. Reduce the heat to low. Add the beans, stir well, and simmer until the sauce has thickened, 5 to 7 minutes. Remove from the heat and allow to cool to room temperature.

In a medium mixing bowl, combine the eggs, parsley, chives, and sage. Beat together well and set aside.

Preheat the oven to 350°F. Grease two 1-quart loaf pans.

In a large mixing bowl, combine the bean mixture with the rice and cheese. Toss together until well mixed. Add the egg mixture and stir until well blended.

Divide the loaf mixture evenly between the two loaf pans and press lightly to form solid loaves. Bake until the tops are lightly browned, 45 to 60 minutes.

MAKES 2 LOAVES

Vulgar Bean Curd Loaf

A meatloaf made without meat? I can just hear some cattle rancher screaming, "Oprah!" all over again. Well, the only thing that is vulgar about this recipe is the language that rude rancher is using. The flavors and textures of this bean curd loaf create stick-to-your-ribs satisfaction. The bean curd and bulgur wheat are a high-protein and high-fiber combination that is lower in fat and cholesterol than ground meat. And the chipotle pepper combines with the herbs and spices to produce a zesty flavor, with the almonds highlighting the nutty bulgur wheat. Serve this just like you would traditional meatloaf, or use it to make hearty lunch sandwiches.

For the loaf:

2 tablespoons olive oil
1 chipotle pepper packed in adobo sauce, minced
1 medium-size onion, minced
2 tablespoons chopped garlic
½ cup slivered almonds
1 cup bulgur wheat
2 cups water
1 tablespoon dried parsley
1 teaspoon dried chives
1 teaspoon ground ginger
1 teaspoon dried basil
1 teaspoon dried thyme
1½ teaspoons salt
1 teaspoon ground black pepper
3 carrots, shredded
1 pound extra-firm bean curd, drained and shredded

For the sauce:

2 tablespoons olive oil
2 tablespoons whole wheat flour

1 teaspoon ground turmeric

1 teaspoon ground sage

1 teaspoon ground savory

1 teaspoon hot Hungarian paprika

½ cup water

Olive oil or spray cooking oil for greasing

To prepare the loaf, heat the olive oil in a large sauté pan over medium heat. Add the chipotle pepper, onion, and garlic and cook until the onion is tender, 3 to 5 minutes. Add the almonds and cook for 1 to 2 minutes. Add the bulgur wheat and cook until the bulgur begins to brown, 2 to 3 minutes. Add the 2 cups water, raise the heat to high, and bring to a boil. Reduce the heat to low, add the parsley, chives, ginger, basil, thyme, salt, and black pepper and stir well to distribute the spices. Cover and simmer until all the liquids have been absorbed, 10 to 15 minutes. Remove from the heat and allow to cool to room temperature.

In a large mixing bowl, combine the carrots, bean curd, and the bulgur wheat mixture and toss together well.

Preheat the oven to 375°F. Grease two 1-quart loaf pans.

To prepare the sauce, heat the olive oil in a small sauté pan over low heat. Add the flour and stir well with a wire whisk. Add the turmeric, sage, savory, and paprika and cook, while whisking, until lightly browned, about 2 minutes. Add the ½ cup water and stir well to form a thick sauce. Pour the sauce over the bulgur mixture and stir well to thoroughly distribute the sauce.

Divide the loaf mixture evenly between the two loaf pans and press lightly to form solid loaves. Bake until the tops are lightly browned, 45 minutes.

MAKES 2 LOAVES

Atomic Eggplant Submarine

Just like a 1950s B-movie monster, this creation from the secret biker laboratory will wreak havoc, at least with your appetite. The almost glow-in-the-dark, atomic-powered breading is what brings the eggplant to life. The submarine sauce is poised for a nuclear first strike. And the cheese is past the brink of meltdown. So don your radiation suit, call up the National Guard, sound the air-raid sirens, and turn your kitchen into a mad scientist's laboratory. Whip up an Atomic Eggplant Submarine and torpedo your taste buds with these open-faced hoagies from hell.

This is perfect handlebar grub to prepare for an after-ride gathering. Just cook the eggplant and sauce the day before, refrigerate separately, and assemble while your riding buddies start bench racing.

For the eggplant:

1 cup whole wheat flour
½ cup Italian-style dried bread crumbs
1½ teaspoons dried oregano
1½ teaspoons onion powder
1½ teaspoons garlic powder
1½ teaspoons dried parsley
1½ teaspoons salt
1 tablespoon hot Hungarian paprika
1½ teaspoons ground cayenne pepper
1½ teaspoons ground black pepper
2 extra-large eggs, beaten
1 medium-size eggplant, cut into ¼-inch-thick
   slices
Olive oil for frying

For the sauce:

2 tablespoons extra-virgin olive oil
1 medium-size onion, minced
⅓ cup sun-dried tomatoes packed in oil, minced

2 chipotle peppers packed in adobo sauce, minced
1 tablespoon chopped garlic
1 teaspoon dried parsley
1 teaspoon dried oregano
½ teaspoon salt
½ teaspoon ground black pepper
1½ cups canned crushed tomatoes

For assembly:

1 large loaf Italian bread, cut in half lengthwise
2 cups shredded mozzarella cheese

To prepare the eggplant, in a large mixing bowl, combine the whole wheat flour, bread crumbs, oregano, onion powder, garlic powder, parsley, salt, paprika, cayenne pepper, and black pepper. Stir together with a wire whisk until completely blended. Transfer half of the breading mixture to a wide, shallow bowl that is larger than the biggest slice of eggplant. Set aside the rest of the breading.

Coat each eggplant slice with the beaten eggs, place it in the bowl of breading mixture, and cover with some of the reserved breading mixture. Pat gently to adhere the breading and transfer to another plate. Repeat until all the eggplant is breaded.

Heat ½ inch of oil in a large frying pan over medium heat. Put the breaded eggplant pieces into the frying pan and fry until the edges begin to turn golden brown, 3 to 5 minutes. Carefully turn the breaded eggplant over and fry the other side until golden brown. (It may be necessary to add more oil as you work.) Drain well on paper towels.

To prepare the sauce, heat the olive oil in a small sauté pan over medium heat. Add the onion and cook until it is tender, 3 to 5 minutes. Add the sun-dried tomatoes, chipotle peppers, and garlic and stir well to coat with oil. Cook for 5 minutes, stirring often. Add the parsley, oregano, salt, black pepper, and crushed tomatoes and stir well. Cover and simmer until the sauce thickens, stirring often, 10 to 15 minutes.

Preheat the oven to 400°F.

Place the Italian bread halves on a baking sheet. Spread a layer of sauce on each piece of bread and top with a layer of fried eggplant. Cover the eggplant with more sauce and smother with the cheese. Bake until the cheese is melted, 10 to 15 minutes. Serve piping hot.

MAKES 4 TO 6 SERVINGS

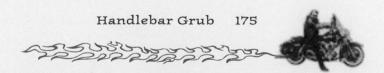

Bobby Tramontin at age 4½ outside the Tramontin Harley-Davidson Dealership in Clifton, New Jersey, circa late 1940s. The bike is an English paratroopers bike that was cut down to fit Bobby; the tank is made from a 1937 Pontiac headlight. As Bub tells it, Bobby was riding a three-wheeler in front of the store when a customer said, "You should have a motor on that kid." Bobby told his dad and Bub built this bike for him.

V-Twin Vegetables

No other motorcycle engine design evokes as many emotions, images, or opinions as the V-twin. It is my favorite choice of engine and the heartbeat of my beloved Harley Police bike. Although Harley produced single-cylinder engines long ago, and may again someday, it is the Harley V-twin that forms the core of this American icon. The sound of these motors rumbling across the landscape is instantly recognizable. That sound simultaneously stirs feelings of home and wanderlust in my soul. It is the only sound that gets me going more than the sound of onions sizzling in a cast-iron frying pan. This chapter is dedicated to that V-twin, and it is full of high-powered dishes. So while you're out on your next ride, stop by a farm stand and buy some fresh vegetables. Or better yet, grow them in your own V-twin garden and surprise your riding buddies with these fiery dishes.

Tormented Eggplant

Your riding buddies will be quite surprised by these barbecued devils. Sitting on the grill, they look like whole, plain eggplant, no thrill there. But when you remove them from the grill and slice 'em open, oh boy, it's party time! The sharp tang of the jalapeños blends wonderfully with the earthy tones of the sun-dried tomatoes. The process of slowly roasting on the grill allows the eggplant to become infused with all those great flavors.

Sliced crosswise, ½ to 1 inch thick, these Tormented Eggplants make the perfect centerpiece for a plate of grilled vegetables, or a welcome side dish with any pasta or Italian-style main course. I also enjoy making sandwiches with them. However, when you serve them, the only torment will be deciding who gets the last serving.

You can prepare them the day before you grill them.

> 2 medium-size eggplants
> ¼ cup extra-virgin olive oil
> 2 jalapeño peppers, stemmed and thinly sliced
> 1 medium-size onion, diced
> ⅓ cup sun-dried tomatoes packed in oil, minced
> 2 tablespoons chopped garlic
> ½ teaspoon salt
> ½ teaspoon ground black pepper
> 1 tablespoon dried oregano
> ½ cup packed fresh basil leaves, coarsely chopped
> 5 to 6 ounces mozzarella cheese, cut into ¼-inch cubes
> Toothpicks for securing

Cut the blossom end (opposite to the stem end) off each eggplant. (It is best to cut inwards at an angle, so that the end, when it is removed, resembles a cone. This will help the open end to seal better after the eggplant is stuffed.) Using a long, thin sharp knife, carve out most of the flesh from inside each eggplant. Be careful to leave the skins intact (and unpunctured), with a ½-inch-thick layer of flesh still attached. These hollowed egg-

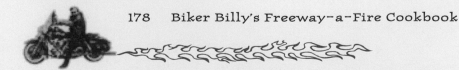

plants form "shells" that will be stuffed later. Set the shells aside and coarsely chop the scooped-out flesh.

Heat the olive oil in a large sauté pan over high heat. Add the jalapeño peppers, onion, and sun-dried tomatoes and cook until the onion begins to brown, 3 to 5 minutes. Add the garlic, salt, black pepper, oregano, and the chopped eggplant and cook until the eggplant is tender, 3 to 5 minutes. Remove from the heat and allow to cool. Add the basil and mozzarella cheese and toss together.

Stuff each eggplant shell with the filling. Close the eggplants by replacing the ends, using the toothpicks to hold them in place. Place on a hot grill and adjust the distance from the fire to ensure slow roasting. Grill (turning often to expose all sides to the flame) until the eggplant is tender on all sides, 30 minutes.

Cut the roasted eggplant crosswise into thick slices and serve them immediately—remembering to remove the toothpicks.

MAKES 2 STUFFED EGGPLANTS; ABOUT 6 TO 8 SERVINGS

Dorothy Tramontin, Bub's wife and Bobby's mom, on her bike in Seaside Heights, New Jersey, circa 1939.

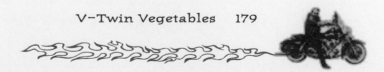

Tortured Tomatoes

If your motorcycle adventures take you to a far-off land where the natives test their manhood by walking on hot coals, then offer them this recipe. It is much less painful to grill these tomatoes than it is to grill your toes.

These are a great addition to any barbecue. The flavors will give you that summertime feel, even if you cook them on an indoor grill in December. So save your toes and torture the tomatoes.

1 pasilla pepper, stemmed, seeded,
    and torn into small pieces
1 teaspoon chopped garlic
¼ teaspoon dried oregano
½ teaspoon salt
½ teaspoon ground black pepper
1 teaspoon crushed red pepper
¼ cup boiling water (see page 15)
2 tablespoons extra-virgin olive oil
1 small onion, thinly sliced
2 large ripe tomatoes, cut in half (see Note)

Place the pasilla pepper, garlic, oregano, salt, black pepper, and crushed red pepper in a small bowl and cover with the boiling water. Allow to cool to room temperature.

Heat the olive oil in a small sauté pan over medium heat. Add the onion and cook until it is tender, 2 to 3 minutes. Add the rehydrated pepper mixture and soaking liquid and simmer for 2 minutes. Remove from the heat and transfer to a blender or a food processor equipped with a chopping blade. Puree until smooth, 60 to 90 seconds.

Place the tomato halves, cut side up, on a hot grill and spoon the puree on top. Grill, without turning, until the tomatoes are tender, 20 to 30 minutes. Serve piping hot.

MAKES 4 SERVINGS

NOTE: You may have to trim the tomato halves so that the cut surfaces will be level when placed on the grill. If they do not sit level on the grill, the sauce will run off and the flavor will be lost.

Hank and Lavonda's
Hot Tomato Stuff

Our good friends Hank and Lavonda always have this tasty treat on hand when Rachelle and I visit them. It is as sinfully easy to make as it is tasty. And we always look forward to it when we ride over to their house. After you try it, you will enjoy it, too.

     1 large ripe tomato, diced
     1 garlic clove, diced
     6 fresh basil leaves, minced
     2 tablespoons extra-virgin olive oil
     ¼ teaspoon ground cayenne pepper
     Salt and ground black pepper to taste
     1 medium-size loaf Italian bread, sliced ½ to ¾ inch
        thick and toasted

In a small bowl, combine the tomato, garlic, basil, olive oil, and cayenne pepper and mix well. Cover and refrigerate for at least 1 hour. Add salt and black pepper and serve on the toasted Italian bread.

MAKES 4 SERVINGS

Barbecued Zucchini Boats

On warm summer evenings, I love to cruise around on my Harley. There is something special about the air on a summer night that feels good rushing across my face. The gentle rumble of the motor is so relaxing. The fragrances of growing things mixed with the aromas of backyard barbecues make the air taste like candy. All these combine to give me a feeling of great satisfaction when my ride is done. The only problem is that they also make me hungry. Now that I have shared that with you, let me share these satisfying goodies with you. They'll fire up anything you serve with them and will leave you ready to ride.

1 ancho pepper, stemmed, seeded, and torn into small pieces
1 teaspoon dried cilantro
¼ cup boiling water (see page 15)
3 medium-size zucchini
2 tablespoons extra-virgin olive oil
1 to 2 fresh jalapeño peppers (to your taste), stemmed and minced
1 medium-size onion, minced
1 tablespoon chopped garlic
Salt and ground black pepper to taste
¾ cup shredded mild cheddar cheese

Place the ancho pepper and cilantro in a small bowl and cover with the boiling water. Allow to cool to room temperature.

In a blender or a food processor equipped with a chopping blade, puree the rehydrated pepper and the soaking water until no large pieces of ancho remain, 1 minute.

Cut each zucchini in half lengthwise. With a spoon, carve out most of the flesh from inside each zucchini half, using care to leave the skins intact with about a ⅜- to ½-inch-thick layer of flesh still attached. These hollowed zucchini halves form "shells" that will be stuffed later. Set the shells aside and coarsely chop the rest of the flesh.

Heat the olive oil in a small sauté pan over high heat. Add the ancho

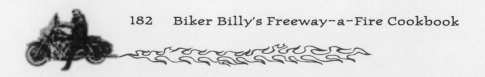

puree, chopped zucchini, jalapeños, onion, and garlic and cook until the onion begins to brown, 3 to 5 minutes. Add salt and black pepper. Remove from the heat and allow to cool.

Stuff each zucchini shell evenly with the filling. Cover with the cheese. Place on a hot barbecue grill and adjust the distance from the fire to ensure slow roasting. Grill until the zucchini shells are tender and the cheese is melted, 30 minutes.

MAKES 4 SERVINGS

Nuked Cukes

These stuffed devils make a wonderful side-dish surprise. Who expects baked stuffed cucumbers? The sweet garden flavor of the cucumbers, which makes them a frequent salad staple, combines beautifully with the fresh basil. Baking infuses them with the earthy tastes of the three peppers, and sun-dried tomatoes and mozzarella cheese tie it all together. They make a welcome companion to any biker-style pasta dish. Or you can slice them and serve them on some crusty Italian bread for a light, but satisfying, lunchtime sandwich.

1 ancho pepper, stemmed, seeded, and torn into small pieces

1 pasilla pepper, stemmed, seeded, and torn into small pieces

1 dried long, slim red cayenne pepper, stemmed and crushed

¼ cup boiling water (see page 15)

2 tablespoons extra-virgin olive oil

2 medium-size onions, diced

2 tablespoons chopped garlic

¼ cup sun-dried tomatoes, minced

1 teaspoon salt, plus more to taste

1 teaspoon ground black pepper

4 large cucumbers, peeled

1 cup packed fresh basil leaves, coarsely chopped

1 cup shredded mozzarella cheese

Place the ancho, pasilla, and cayenne peppers in small bowl and cover with the boiling water. Allow to cool to room temperature.

In a blender or a food processor equipped with a chopping blade, puree the rehydrated peppers and the soaking water until no large pieces of pepper remain, 1 minute.

Heat the olive oil in a large saucepan over medium heat. Add the onions and cook until they are tender, 3 to 5 minutes. Add the garlic and sun-dried tomatoes and cook until the onions begin to brown, 2 to 3 minutes. Add the pepper puree, salt, and black pepper and simmer until all the liquid has evaporated, 2 to 3 minutes. Remove from the heat and allow to cool.

Cut the cucumbers in half. Using a dull knife or a teaspoon, remove the seeds from the center of each cucumber half, using care not to tear or puncture the cucumber flesh. This will form hollow "shells."

Preheat the oven to 375°F.

Add the basil and mozzarella cheese to the sauté pan and toss to mix well. Stuff each cucumber half evenly with the filling. Place 2 stuffed cucumber halves on a sheet of aluminum foil, sprinkle lightly with salt, put the halves together, and wrap up tightly in the foil. Repeat with the remaining cucumbers. Place on a cookie sheet and bake for 1 hour. Serve piping hot.

MAKES 4 TO 8 SERVINGS

Devilish Pumpkin Fries

Besides making jack-o'-lanterns, most people think pie is the beginning and end of what you can do with pumpkins. This recipe should change a few minds and empty a few farm stands of their post–Halloween pumpkin glut. Since pumpkins store well, you can keep enjoying these devilish fries long after the hobgoblins are gone. So scare up some of your friends and carve 'em up. After just one bite, your grin will be so big that you'll scare all the jack-o'-lanterns in the neighborhood.

For the pumpkin:

2 tablespoons butter
1 teaspoon ground ginger
1 teaspoon ground cumin
1 teaspoon ground nutmeg
1 teaspoon ground allspice
1 teaspoon ground cayenne pepper
1 tablespoon sugar
2 teaspoons salt
1 teaspoon ground black pepper
4 cups water
4 cups fresh pumpkin, cut into 2 by ½-inch "French fries"

For the coating:

½ cup all-purpose flour
½ cup whole wheat flour
½ cup plain dried bread crumbs
2 teaspoons salt
2 teaspoons ground black pepper
½ teaspoon ground nutmeg
½ teaspoon ground cayenne pepper
1 teaspoon ground cumin
½ teaspoon ground cloves
Canola or peanut oil for frying

To prepare the pumpkin, melt the butter in a large pot over medium heat. Add the ginger, cumin, nutmeg, allspice, cayenne pepper, sugar, salt, and black pepper and stir to dissolve. Cook the spices, stirring often, using care not to burn them, 1 to 2 minutes. Add the water, raise the heat to high, and bring to a boil. Add the pumpkin, reduce the heat to low, and simmer until the pumpkin is tender, about 30 minutes. The pumpkin should be soft, but still hold its shape. (The goal is to cook it long and slow to infuse it with the flavors of the spices). Drain the pumpkin and rinse with cool water.

To prepare the coating, in a large mixing bowl, combine the flours and bread crumbs. Add the salt, black pepper, nutmeg, cayenne pepper, cumin and cloves and, using a wire whisk, stir the ingredients until well blended.

Place several pieces of pumpkin into the flour mixture and toss until well coated. Transfer to a plate that has been dusted with the flour mixture. Repeat until all of the pumpkin has been coated.

Heat the oil in a large sauté pan over high heat. Add the pumpkin and fry until browned on all sides, 5 to 7 minutes, using care to handle the pumpkin gently to avoid damaging the delicate crust. Drain on paper towels and serve immediately.

MAKES 4 SERVINGS

Lisa's Incredible Cauliflower

This is a recipe from a very dear friend of my wife Rachelle's and mine—Lisa Martinelli. One time when we were visiting Lisa and her husband, Steve, I noticed that their young children, Steven and Kristen, were happily eating cauliflower. Even baby Elizabeth was reaching for it. When I was a kid, you couldn't get me to eat cauliflower even at gunpoint. I shared my childhood aversion to this vegetable with Lisa, and she promised to make me a batch of her cauliflower. A few days later, Lisa appeared at our door with some of these incredible fried cauliflower florets. Well, Rachelle and I loved them and I asked for the recipe. Of course, I customized it by boosting the garlic and adding black pepper and cayenne pepper; I can never leave any recipe alone. I hope you enjoy these as much as I do. Just back down on the cayenne if you are making them for the little guys.

1 cup plain dried bread crumbs
2 tablespoons garlic powder
1 tablespoon onion powder
1 tablespoon dried parsley
1 tablespoon dried basil
1 teaspoon dried oregano
1 teaspoon salt
1 teaspoon ground cayenne pepper, or more to taste
1 teaspoon ground black pepper
1 medium-size head cauliflower, florets only,
   cut into bite-size pieces (see Note)
2 jumbo eggs, beaten
Canola oil for frying

In a large mixing bowl, combine the bread crumbs, garlic powder, onion powder, parsley, basil, oregano, salt, cayenne, and black pepper. Stir together with a wire whisk until completely blended. Transfer the breading mixture to a wide, shallow bowl.

Dip the cauliflower florets in the beaten eggs and roll in the breading mixture. Place the breaded cauliflower on a plate that is lightly dusted with the breading mixture. Repeat until all of the cauliflower is breaded.

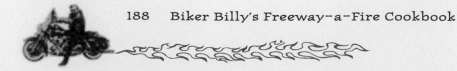

Heat ½ inch of oil in a large frying pan over medium heat. Put the breaded cauliflower into the frying pan and fry until the edges begin to turn golden brown, 3 to 5 minutes. Carefully turn the breaded cauliflower over and fry on the other side until golden brown. (It may be necessary to add more oil as you work.) Drain well on paper towels.

MAKES 4 TO 6 SERVINGS

NOTE: The measurements in this recipe produce enough breading to prepare a medium-size head of cauliflower with minimal waste. If you purchase a large cauliflower, you may need to use an additional egg.

Asparagus à la Dante

At that wonderful time of year when asparagus is in season and almost affordable, I become practically obsessed with cooking up this wonderful vegetable. Sometimes I dream of having asparagus crowns in my garden so I can always have some fresh at a good price. Well, you may have to pay a Devil's ransom for asparagus, but this recipe will taste so good that even the Devil would sell his soul for a second helping. So sharpen your pitchfork, and prepare to defend this dish from the evil minions who want to scarf it all down.

For the asparagus:

1 bunch asparagus (about 1 pound)

For the breading:

1 cup plain dried bread crumbs
1 teaspoon dried thyme
1 tablespoon dried parsley
1 teaspoon ground savory
1 teaspoon ground sage
1 tablespoon firmly packed light brown sugar
1 teaspoon salt
½ teaspoon ground cayenne pepper
1 teaspoon ground black pepper
2 extra-large eggs, beaten

For the sauce:

2 tablespoons butter
1 medium-size onion, diced
2 chipotle peppers packed in adobo sauce, minced
2 tablespoons chopped garlic
1 tablespoon all-purpose flour
3 tablespoons water

1 cup sour cream
½ teaspoon salt
Canola or peanut oil for frying

To prepare the asparagus, trim off and discard (see Note) the tough bottoms of the asparagus, usually about 1 inch off the end. In a large pot of boiling water, cook the asparagus 5 to 10 minutes (the thicker the asparagus, the longer the cooking time), or until just tender. Rinse with cold water to stop the cooking and drain.

To prepare the breading, in a large mixing bowl, combine the bread crumbs, thyme, parsley, savory, sage, brown sugar, salt, cayenne pepper, and black pepper. Stir together with a wire whisk until completely blended. Transfer the breading mixture to a wide, shallow bowl that is larger than the longest asparagus stalk.

Dip the asparagus in the beaten eggs and roll in the breading mixture. Place the breaded asparagus on a plate that is lightly dusted with the breading mixture. Repeat until all of the asparagus is breaded.

To prepare the sauce, in a small saucepot, melt the butter over medium heat. Add the onion and cook until golden brown, 5 to 7 minutes. Add the chipotle pepper and garlic and cook until the garlic begins to brown, 2 to 3 minutes. Add the flour and stir well. Continue to stir until the flour is lightly browned, about 2 minutes. Remove from the heat and stir in the water. Allow to cool for about 3 minutes. Transfer to a blender or a food processor equipped with a cutting blade. Pulse a few times to reduce the size of the onion pieces. Add the sour cream and salt and pulse until just blended. Return to the saucepot and warm gently over a very low heat, stirring often, while you fry the asparagus. (If you overheat the sour cream, you will "break the fat" and ruin the sauce, so slow heat is worth the wait.)

Heat ½ inch of oil in a large frying pan over medium heat. Put the breaded asparagus into the frying pan and fry until the edges begin to turn golden brown, 3 to 5 minutes. Carefully turn the breaded asparagus over and fry the other side until golden brown. (It may be necessary to add more oil as you work.) Drain well on paper towels.

Arrange the asparagus on a serving dish and cover with the sauce. Serve immediately.

MAKES 4 SERVINGS

NOTE: The tough bottom ends are not tender enough to eat, but they can be frozen for later use in making vegetable stock.

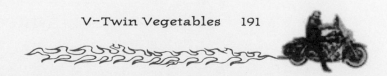

Hot Leeky Cabbage

Cabbage and leeks combine to create a powerful aroma when cooking. It will surely make any country boy hungry. The creamy leek sauce is pure paradise with a chipotle punch. Start cooking this savory cabbage dish and invite your riding buddies over. If they can't remember the way, tell them to follow their noses.

For the cabbage:

1 head savoy cabbage
1 medium-size onion, quartered and sliced
8 to 12 cups water
1 teaspoon caraway seeds
1 teaspoon celery seeds

For the sauce:

2 chipotle peppers, stemmed
¼ cup boiling water (see page 15)
1 cup half-and-half
1 teaspoon salt
½ teaspoon ground black pepper
6 tablespoons butter (¾ stick) butter
4 medium-size leeks, trimmed, washed well, and cut
    into ¼-inch-thick slices (see page 23)
2 tablespoons chopped garlic
2 tablespoons all-purpose flour

To prepare the cabbage, remove the outer 2 or 3 leaves from the head of cabbage. Quarter the cabbage, remove the core, and cut into ½-inch-thick slices. Place the cabbage and onion in a large pot and cover with water. Place the caraway and celery seeds in a tea infuser and put the infuser into the pot (this allows the caraway seeds to impart their flavor and then be easily discarded later). Place the pot over high heat and bring to a boil. Reduce the heat to medium, cover, and simmer, stirring occasionally, until

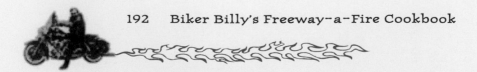

the cabbage is tender, 20 minutes. Remove the tea infuser and drain the cabbage, reserving 1 cup of the cabbage broth. Set aside.

To prepare the sauce, place the chipotle peppers in a small bowl and cover with the boiling water. Allow to cool to room temperature.

In a blender or a food processor equipped with a chopping blade, puree the rehydrated pepper and the soaking water until no large pieces of chipotle remains, 1 minute. Add the half-and-half, salt, and black pepper and process until well blended, about 1 minute. Set aside.

Melt 4 tablespoons of the butter in a large sauté pan over medium heat. Add the leeks and cook until the leeks begin to brown, 8 to 10 minutes. Add the garlic and cook until the leeks are golden brown, 2 to 3 minutes. Transfer to a heatproof bowl and set aside.

Melt the remaining 2 tablespoons butter in the sauté pan over medium heat. Add the flour and stir well. Continue to stir until the flour is a light brown, 2 to 3 minutes. Add the chipotle puree and stir well. Add 1 cup of the reserved cabbage broth and stir well. Return the leeks to the pan and stir well. Simmer, stirring often, until the sauce thickens, about 5 minutes. Add the cabbage to the sauté pan. Stir well to coat with the sauce and serve.

MAKES 4 TO 6 SERVINGS

Potato Tornado

These fiery spuds will blow away mere baked potatoes. The collision of habanero fire and the savory flavors of the sautéed onions and garlic creates a whirlwind of culinary delight. At first bite, you will feel the wind in your hair as you're carried away in the funnel cloud of the Potato Tornado.

> 4 tablespoons (½ stick) butter, plus extra for
>   greasing
> 1 dried habanero pepper, stemmed, seeded, and
>   crushed
> 1 small onion, minced
> 1 tablespoon chopped garlic
> ½ teaspoon salt
> ½ teaspoon ground black pepper
> 8 small red potatoes, very thinly sliced

Preheat the oven to 400°F. Grease a 9-inch pie pan with butter.

Melt the butter in a small sauté pan over medium heat. Add the habanero pepper, onion, garlic, salt, and black pepper. Cook until the onion is tender; 3 to 5 minutes.

Arrange the potato slices in an overlapping spiral pattern in the pie pan. Cover the potatoes evenly with the onion mixture. Bake until the potatoes are browned and tender, 40 to 45 minutes.

MAKES 4 TO 6 SERVINGS

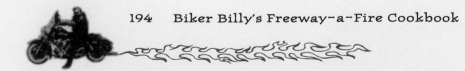

Snappy Stir-Fried Vegetables

These stir-fry vegetables are a colorful, light, fresh side dish all by themselves. If you add the Creamy Herb Fire Sauce (page 235), they become a fancy accompaniment to any main dish.

> 2 tablespoons extra-virgin olive oil
> 1 Biker Billy jalapeño pepper, stemmed, seeded, and minced
> 1 leek, trimmed, washed well, and cut into ¼-inch-thick slices (see page 23)
> 1 medium-size onion, quartered and thinly sliced
> 1 red bell pepper, cored, seeded, and julienned
> 1 yellow bell pepper, cored, seeded, and julienned
> 1 large bunch broccoli, florets only, cut into bite-size pieces
> Salt and ground black pepper to taste

In a large wok or frying pan, heat the olive oil over high heat. Add the Biker Billy jalapeño pepper, leek, onion, bell peppers, and broccoli florets.

Stir-fry until the vegetables are tender but still crispy, 5 to 7 minutes. Season with salt and pepper. Serve immediately.

MAKES 4 SERVINGS

Eggplant à la Diablo

To create a perfect Eggplant à la Diablo, you must start with eggplant wrapped in a golden-brown breading that is seasoned and fired-up to perfection. Then create a cheese filling that the Devil himself would ransom his soul for. Now spread a layer of that tormented cheese between two pieces of fiery eggplant. Voilà! You have assembled a dish that is so sinfully delicious it needs no sauce. Of course, you could serve it with sauce; just make sure the sauce is flavorful enough to withstand the Eggplant à la Diablo.

For the cheese filling:

2 pickled jalapeño peppers, stemmed and drained
½ teaspoon ground white pepper
½ teaspoon salt
2 tablespoons extra-virgin olive oil
½ cup packed fresh basil leaves, coarsely chopped
1 tablespoon chopped garlic
1 cup ricotta cheese
½ cup plain dried bread crumbs
1 cup shredded mozzarella

For the breading:

1 cup plain dried bread crumbs
1 teaspoon ground sweet paprika
1 teaspoon dried oregano
1 tablespoon dried parsley
½ teaspoon salt
½ teaspoon ground cayenne pepper
½ teaspoon ground black pepper
2 large eggs
2 tablespoons half-and-half
1 medium-size eggplant, cut into ¼-inch-thick slices
Olive oil for frying

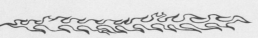

To prepare the filling, in a blender or a food processor equipped with a cutting blade, combine the jalapeño peppers, white pepper, salt, and olive oil. Pulse until the jalapeños are finely chopped. Add the basil, garlic, and ricotta cheese and pulse until well blended and creamy, 2 to 3 minutes. You may have to scrape down the sides of the bowl once or twice to completely blend the mixture. Transfer to a medium-size mixing bowl. Add the bread crumbs and mozzarella cheese and mix well. Cover and refrigerate for at least 30 minutes.

To prepare the breading, in a large mixing bowl, combine the bread crumbs, paprika, oregano, parsley, salt, cayenne pepper, and black pepper. Stir together with a wire whisk until completely blended. Transfer half of the breading mixture to a wide, shallow bowl that is larger than the biggest slice of eggplant. Set aside.

Combine the eggs and half-and-half in a small mixing bowl and beat with a wire whisk until completely blended. Transfer the egg mixture to another wide, shallow bowl.

Coat each eggplant slice with the egg mixture and place it in the bowl of breading mixture, and cover with some of the reserved breading mixture. Pat gently to adhere the breading and transfer to another plate. Repeat until all the eggplant is breaded.

Heat ½ inch of oil in a large frying pan over medium heat. Put the breaded eggplant pieces into the frying pan and fry a few slices at a time, until the edges begin to turn golden brown, 3 to 5 minutes. Carefully turn the breaded eggplant over and fry on the other side until golden brown. (It may be necessary to add more oil as you work.) Drain well on paper towels.

Preheat the oven to 350°F.

Arrange half of the fried eggplant pieces in a single layer on a baking dish (see Note). Cover each piece with a layer of cheese filling. Place the remaining pieces of eggplant on top of the cheese. Bake for 20 minutes. Serve piping hot.

MAKES 4 TO 6 SERVINGS

NOTE: I try to match the eggplant slices so the top and bottom pieces are the same size.

An unidentified motorcycle dealership, circa the 1920s, from the
Dugan family album.

Biker Breads

One of my weaknesses in life is bread. I love it so much that I could eat bread all day. The aromas of baking bread are hypnotizing to me; one whiff and the image of a steaming hot, freshly baked loaf with a mound of melting butter on top just pops into my head. I could be riding down the road and if the faint smell of baking bread reaches me, I will start looking for a restaurant. I'm a bread-aholic.

The only thing better than fresh-baked bread is garlic bread. Oh boy, do I love garlic bread. I could write a whole book on it, but for now I have included two recipes for your enjoyment; both have a nice measure of fire. Try them and you'll see why I think garlic bread turns any meal into a feast.

When my rides take me south, I am always on the lookout for good biscuits. It must be from childhood memories of Southern road trips. Hot biscuits make any meal special. In keeping with my love for garlic bread, both of the biscuit recipes have garlic in them. One has earthy tones of chipotle and the other has the nuclear blast of habanero—watch out, these are bad-ass biscuits. Another blast from my childhood food memories is Corn Doggies, shapely corn muffins with a hot attitude.

Speaking of muffins, I have included two tasty sweet muffins that will scare you right out of the kitchen: the Halloween treat Jack-O-Muffins, and Fire Broom Muffins. Enjoy them if you dare!

Wicked Garlic Bread

Italian food is naked without garlic bread. This biker-style, high-performance garlic bread is the perfect riding wear for any Italian food you serve. One bite and you will be addicted.

> 4 tablespoons (½ stick) butter
>
> 2 tablespoons minced garlic
>
> 2 sun-dried tomatoes packed in oil, minced
>
> 1 tablespoon dried parsley
>
> ¼ teaspoon dried basil
>
> ½ teaspoon crushed red pepper
>
> ¼ teaspoon ground black pepper
>
> 1 loaf crusty Italian bread, cut in half lengthwise (see Note)
>
> Freshly grated Parmesan cheese to taste

Preheat the oven to 375°F.

Melt the butter in a small sauté pan over very low heat. Add the garlic, sun-dried tomatoes, parsley, basil, and red and black peppers. Cook for 2 to 3 minutes, to infuse the butter with the seasonings without browning it. Pour the butter mixture over the bread halves and evenly distribute the solids. Sprinkle lightly with the grated Parmesan cheese and bake until the tops of the bread halves begin to brown, 3 to 5 minutes. Serve warm.

MAKES ABOUT 4 SERVINGS

NOTE: I have not specified the size of bread to use simply because you have to decide how heavily buttered you want your garlic bread. The smaller the loaf, the richer the flavor.

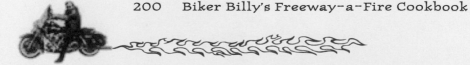

Lazarus's Garlic Bread

Okay, I confess, I love garlic bread! I can't eat Italian food without it and it seems like I can't make it the same way twice. This chunky garlic bread will revive your taste buds. The onion adds a nice balance to the slices of fresh garlic, and the sun-dried tomatoes make it even richer. Since there is no cheese in this recipe, the hot pepper's kick will be more pronounced.

> ½ cup (1 stick) butter
> ¼ cup minced onion
> ¼ cup garlic cloves, thinly sliced
> 1 tablespoon sun-dried tomatoes packed
>   in oil, minced
> 2 teaspoons crushed red pepper
> ½ teaspoon ground black pepper
> 1 loaf crusty Italian bread, cut in half lengthwise (see
>   Note)

Preheat the oven to 375°F.

Melt the butter in a small sauté pan over very low heat. Add the onion, garlic, sun-dried tomatoes, and red and black peppers. Cook for 2 to 3 minutes, to infuse the butter with the seasonings without browning it. Pour the butter mixture over the bread and evenly distribute the solids. Bake until the tops of the bread halves begin to brown, 3 to 5 minutes. Serve warm.

MAKES ABOUT 4 SERVINGS

NOTE: I have not specified the size of bread to use simply because you have to decide how heavily buttered you like your garlic bread. The smaller the loaf, the richer the flavor.

Burning Garlic Biscuits

These tasty devils perfectly combine the down-home flavor and comfort of scratch biscuits with the richness of garlic bread. I have prepared them with a habanero pepper, but you could easily substitute a jalapeño to reduce the firepower. They taste delicious and add a warm country-style feel to any meal. Best of all, they are simple to make.

For the filling:

4 tablespoons (½ stick) butter
¼ cup chopped garlic
1 fresh habanero pepper, stemmed, seeded,
    and finely minced

For the dough:

1¾ cups all-purpose flour, plus extra for kneading
½ teaspoon salt
1 tablespoon baking powder
1 tablespoon butter, cut into 4 pieces
¾ cup buttermilk

To prepare the filling, melt the butter in a small sauté pan over low heat. Add the chopped garlic and habanero pepper and cook until the garlic just begins to brown, 3 to 5 minutes. Remove from the heat and allow to cool to room temperature.

Preheat the oven to 450°F.

If you are preparing the dough by hand, in a medium-size mixing bowl, combine the flour, salt, and baking powder. Whisk together for 30 seconds to thoroughly mix the dry ingredients. Add the butter pieces and cut together with two knives or a dough cutter until the butter is completely cut into the flour and it has a granular texture. Form a well in the center of the flour and butter mixture and pour in the buttermilk. Stir until a dough forms, using two knives or a fork.

If you are preparing the dough using a food processor, in the workbowl

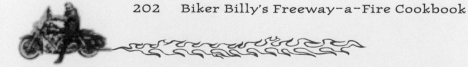

of the processor equipped with a chopping blade, combine the flour, salt, and baking powder. Pulse 2 or 3 times until completely mixed. Add the butter pieces, arranging them evenly around the food processor bowl. Process until the butter is cut into the flour, creating a granular texture, 1 to 2 minutes. While the blades are spinning, pour in the buttermilk and process until a dough forms and begins to move around the bowl as a ball, approximately 1 minute.

Remove the dough from the food processor or bowl and knead on a lightly floured surface just long enough to form a smooth ball (overkneading will ruin the texture of the biscuits). Divide the dough in half. With a floured rolling pin, roll out 1 piece of dough into a circle about ¼ inch thick. Transfer to a cookie sheet lined with baking parchment. Using a slotted spoon, cover the dough with the sautéed garlic and habanero mixture, reserving about 1 teaspoon of the mixture and the butter in the sauté pan. Roll the remaining piece of dough into a circle the same diameter as the first. Place the second piece of dough on top of the first, brush with the reserved butter, and top with the remaining 1 teaspoon garlic and habanero in mixture.

Bake until the top begins to brown, 10 to 12 minutes. Cut into 12 pieces and serve piping hot.

MAKES ABOUT 12 TWO-INCH BISCUITS; 4 SERVINGS

Twisted Biscuits

Oh, mamma! I love biscuits and I can eat them with every meal. When I want to add a down-home feel to a meal, I am often drawn to this most simple of breads. And as this recipe shows, biscuits are not only easy to make but you can also have some twisted fun with them. And these puppies *are* twisted. If you let your family know how easy they are to make, they will be twisting your arm to bake them all the time. So let the flour fly and twist up some biscuits.

For the filling:

2 tablespoons butter
1 medium-size onion, minced
1 chipotle pepper packed in adobo sauce, minced
2 tablespoons chopped garlic
½ teaspoon salt
½ teaspoon ground black pepper

For the dough:

2 cups all-purpose flour, plus extra for kneading
½ teaspoon salt
2 tablespoons baking soda
5 tablespoons butter, cut into 5 pieces
1 cup whole milk
1 tablespoon butter, melted

To prepare the filling, melt the butter in a small sauté pan over medium heat. Add the onion, chipotle pepper, garlic, salt, and pepper and cook until the onion is golden brown, 5 to 7 minutes. Remove from the heat and allow to cool.

Preheat the oven to 450°F.

If you are preparing the dough by hand, in a medium-size mixing bowl, combine the flour, salt, and baking soda. Whisk together for 30 seconds to thoroughly mix the dry ingredients. Add the butter pieces and cut together with two knives or a dough cutter until the butter is completely cut into the flour and it has a granular texture. Form a well in the center of the flour and pour in the milk. Stir until a dough forms, using two knives or a fork.

If you are preparing the dough using a food processor, combine the flour, salt, and baking soda in the workbowl of the processor equipped with a chopping blade. Pulse 2 or 3 times until completely mixed. Add the butter pieces, arranging them evenly around the food processor bowl. Process until the butter is cut into the flour, creating a granular texture, 1 to 2 minutes. While the blades are spinning, pour in the milk and process until a dough forms and begins to move around the bowl as one ball, approximately 1 minute.

Remove the dough from the food processor bowl and knead on a lightly floured surface just long enough to form a smooth ball (overkneading will ruin the texture of the biscuits).

Using a floured rolling pin on a lightly floured surface, roll the dough into a 12 by 18-inch rectangle. Cover the dough with the onion and chipotle mixture. Along the long side of the dough, fold one third of the dough over on top of the onion-chipotle mixture. Fold the other long side on top of the first one, much like folding a letter. Gently pat the dough together. Cut the dough across its length into 12 pieces. Transfer each piece of dough to a cookie sheet, giving each piece a quarter-turn. Brush them with the melted butter and bake until the tops begin to brown, 10 to 12 minutes. Serve piping hot.

MAKES 12 TWISTED BISCUITS

Jack-O-Muffins

A haunted muffin is the perfect treat for a midnight snack on Halloween or anytime. These pumpkin muffins will scare away the munchies while feeding your sweet tooth. Packed with pecans, almonds, and raisins, they are a chunky delight. The spices and cayenne pepper give them an aroma, taste, and kick that will both trick and treat your senses.

> 1¾ cups all-purpose flour
> ¾ cup firmly packed light brown sugar
> 1 teaspoon ground cayenne pepper
> 1 teaspoon ground cinnamon
> ½ teaspoon ground nutmeg
> ½ teaspoon ground cloves
> ½ teaspoon ground allspice
> ¾ teaspoon salt
> 2 tablespoons baking powder
> ¾ cup buttermilk
> 2 jumbo eggs
> ¼ cup golden molasses
> ¼ cup honey
> 1½ cups cooked pumpkin, canned or fresh
> 4 tablespoons (½ stick) butter, melted
> ½ cup pecans, coarsely chopped
> ½ cup sliced almonds
> ½ cup golden raisins

Preheat the oven to 350°F. Grease a 12-muffin tin.

If you are preparing the muffins by hand, in a large mixing bowl, combine the flour, brown sugar, cayenne pepper, cinnamon, nutmeg, cloves, allspice, salt, and baking powder. Whisk together for 30 seconds to thoroughly mix the dry ingredients. Form a well in the center of the flour mixture and pour in the buttermilk, eggs, molasses, honey, pumpkin, and melted butter; stir until a smooth batter forms. Add the pecans, almonds, and raisins and stir until they are evenly distributed throughout the batter.

If you are preparing the muffins using a food processor, combine the

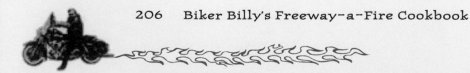

flour, brown sugar, cayenne pepper, cinnamon, nutmeg, cloves, allspice, salt, and baking powder in the workbowl of the processor equipped with a chopping blade. Pulse 2 or 3 times until completely mixed. While the blades are spinning, pour in the buttermilk, eggs, molasses, honey, pumpkin, and melted butter and process until a smooth batter forms, approximately 1 minute. Add the pecans, almonds, and raisins and pulse a few times until they are evenly distributed throughout the batter.

Divide the batter evenly into the 12-muffin tin. Bake until a toothpick inserted into a muffin comes out clean, 30 to 35 minutes. Allow to cool in the tin for 5 minutes before removing.

MAKES 12 MUFFINS

Fire Broom Muffins

Bran muffins with cayenne pepper in them? Doesn't that sound painful? Well, I guess if you ride a rigid-framed chopper and won't share your muffins, maybe. But these babies will not sweep through you like a burning broom. They have a nice warming glow to help fire up your mornings, as well as a little fiber for good health. Bake up a batch and watch them sweep away breakfast boredom.

1 cup whole wheat flour
¾ cup wheat bran
2 tablespoons firmly packed light brown sugar
1 teaspoon ground cayenne pepper
¼ teaspoon salt
1 teaspoon baking soda
1 cup buttermilk
1 jumbo egg
¼ cup dark molasses
4 tablespoons (½ stick) butter, melted,
   plus extra for greasing
½ cup pecans, coarsely chopped
⅓ cup golden raisins

Preheat the oven to 350°F. Grease a 12-muffin tin.

If you are preparing the muffins by hand, in a large mixing bowl, combine the flour, wheat bran, brown sugar, cayenne pepper, salt, and baking soda. Whisk together for 30 seconds to thoroughly mix the dry ingredients. In a small bowl, combine the buttermilk, egg, molasses, and melted butter and stir until well blended. Form a well in the center of the flour mixture and pour in the liquid mixture. Stir until a smooth batter forms. Add the pecans and raisins and stir until they are evenly distributed throughout the batter.

If you are preparing the muffins using a food processor, combine the flour, wheat bran, brown sugar, cayenne pepper, salt, and baking soda in the workbowl of the processor equipped with a chopping blade. Pulse 2 or 3 times to completely mix. While the blades are spinning, pour in the buttermilk, egg, molasses, and melted butter and process until a batter forms,

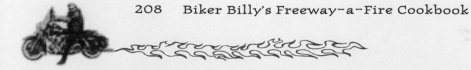

approximately 1 minute. Add the pecans and raisins and pulse a few times until they are evenly distributed throughout the batter.

Evenly divide the batter into the 12-muffin tin. Bake until a toothpick inserted into a muffin comes out clean, about 25 minutes. Allow to cool in the tin for 5 minutes before removing.

MAKES 12 MUFFINS

Four lady riders from the Tramontin family photo album, circa the 1950s.

Corn Doggies

No, these aren't those weird corn bread–battered, deep-fried hot dogs on a stick. They are heartwarming, delicious corn muffins that just make me corn doggedly happy when I bake them. Why? Because they remind me of wonderful childhood road trips down south to visit Grandma.

To make these doggies, it is best to use a special cast-iron baking pan that is shaped like little ears of corn. The one I have makes 7 corn ear–shaped biscuits. The big trick is to oil the pan and heat it in the oven before you pour the batter in. This produces a nice, crisp golden-brown crust. If you don't have a special corn-ear baking pan, the next best thing is a cast-iron frying pan.

Corn oil for greasing
½ cup all–purpose flour
¾ cup stone–ground cornmeal
2 tablespoons firmly packed light brown sugar
1 teaspoon ground cayenne pepper
½ teaspoon salt
2 tablespoons baking powder
⅔ cup buttermilk
2 jumbo eggs
¼ cup golden molasses
2 tablespoons butter, melted

Preheat the oven to 425°F. Grease a cast-iron corn-ear pan or frying pan with corn oil and heat in the oven.

If you are preparing the doggies by hand, in a large mixing bowl, combine the flour, cornmeal, brown sugar, cayenne pepper, salt, and baking powder. Whisk together for 30 seconds to thoroughly mix the dry ingredients. In a small bowl, combine the buttermilk, egg, molasses, and melted butter and stir until well blended. Form a well in the center of the flour mixture and pour in the liquid mixture. Stir until a smooth batter forms.

If you are preparing the doggies using a food processor, combine the flour, cornmeal, brown sugar, cayenne pepper, salt, and baking powder in the workbowl of the processor equipped with a chopping blade. Pulse 2 or 3 times to mix completely. While the blades are spinning, pour in the

buttermilk, eggs, molasses, and melted butter and process until a smooth batter forms, approximately 1 minute.

Carefully remove the cast-iron pan from the oven and pour off the excess oil. Pour the batter into the cast-iron pan. Bake until a toothpick inserted into a doggie comes out clean, about 15 minutes. Allow to cool in the pan for 5 minutes before removing.

MAKES ABOUT 7 CORN DOGGIES

Henrietta Weber on a 1932 Harley–Davidson VL model New Jersey
state police bike at the Walnut Grove restaurant on Route 46 in
Great Meadows, New Jersey, circa the 1930s.

Desserts to Die For

Jay Leno once kidded me on *The Tonight Show* about my obvious round size, asking, "How could a vegetarian be so, well, fat?" Well, part of the answer lies in the following recipes. I love desserts. All my teeth are of the sweet-tooth variety, and I am also a certified chocolate addict. When it comes to desserts, my eyes are always bigger than my stomach, but my stomach always rises (should I say spreads) to the occasion. Truly, if there is a type of food that will be my undoing (at least of my belt), it will be dessert. Does this sound familiar to you? Did you turn to this chapter first? If you answered YES to either of those questions, then welcome to the club, you're in good company.

Many of the recipes in this chapter use lots-o-butter. If you are a vegan or just watching your cholesterol, you can substitute margarine. However, butter will give the best taste and texture. Did I mention I love butter?

If you are wondering whether these recipes are hot, the answer is YES, every last one of them. Most of them use ground cayenne, a few use habanero, and one uses both. They are all enjoyable without the fire, but if you don't try them with it, you will be missing something special. The fire adds a rush to desserts. It's like a twisty road; it may be fun in a car, more interesting in a sports car, but on a bike, it really comes alive with excitement. But like riding, you should start out slow and learn your personal limits before you hop aboard a high-performance bike and run with the fast riders. Always ride your own ride and enjoy cooking with fire at your own level.

If you are unsure about fiery desserts, start with the cookie recipes. The cayenne pepper in these adds a warm afterglow that I find is a real treat. Don't worry, they are not too hot. And since cookies go so well with milk, you won't be far from relief if the cayenne gets you. When you begin to accept the concept of fiery desserts, try the Apricot Fire Tarts—the fruity flavor of the habanero pepper works so well with the apricots. Exploring the fiery roller-coaster of hot and sweet is like taking your taste buds for a ride, and it is one they will always remember and want to take again.

Umm Aaahs

I didn't have a name for this sweet dessert before I went into the garage to cook it on the show. But before we started taping, everyone in the audience who tried it spontaneously made a sound of delight that loosely translates to "Umm Aaah." So I named them Umm Aaahs. Silly, but true.

 ½ cup pine nuts
 1 cup honey
 ½ cup apple juice
 1 tablespoon butter, melted, plus extra for greasing
 1 teaspoon ground cayenne pepper
 1 teaspoon ground cinnamon
 2 tablespoons cornstarch
 4 large shredded wheat biscuits

Preheat the oven to 350°F. Grease a 9 by 7-inch baking dish.

In a blender or a food processor equipped with a chopping blade, combine ¼ cup of the pine nuts, honey, apple juice, butter, cayenne pepper, cinnamon, and cornstarch and puree for 1 minute. Place the biscuits in the baking dish. Pour the puree over the biscuits and cover with the remaining ¼ cup pine nuts. Brush with melted butter. Bake until golden brown and bubbling, 25 minutes. Allow to cool before serving.

MAKES 4 SERVINGS

Chocolate Killer Cookies

These are called killer cookies because they are so tasty that you could eat them until you pop; hence, murder by chocolate. But you won't die, because the fire from the cayenne pepper will restart your heart. So fire up the oven and bake these cookies. They would make the Grim Reaper envious.

> 2 ounces unsweetened chocolate
> ½ cup butter (1 stick), softened
> 1 cup sugar
> 1 teaspoon pure vanilla extract
> ½ teaspoon ground cayenne pepper
> ½ teaspoon salt
> ½ teaspoon baking powder
> 1 extra-large egg, beaten
> 1¼ cups all-purpose flour
> 1 cup white chocolate chips
> 1 cup chopped nuts (optional)
> Canola oil or butter-flavored cooking spray

Fill the bottom half of a double boiler (not quite halfway) with boiling water and place over medium heat (you don't want the top part of the double boiler to be in direct contact with the water). Every so often, check the water level to ensure that the pot does not boil dry. Keep another pot of water boiling on the stove so you can add water if necessary. Heat the unsweetened chocolate in the top of the double boiler. When the chocolate has melted, remove the pot from the heat (the chocolate will stay melted over the hot water until needed).

If you are preparing the cookies by hands, in a large bowl, mix the butter and sugar together with a wooden spoon until creamy. Add the vanilla, cayenne pepper, salt, and baking powder and mix together well. Add the melted chocolate and stir together until well blended. Add the egg and blend until smooth. Add the flour, ¼ cup at a time, mixing well with each addition, until a dough has formed. Add the white chocolate chips and the nuts, if using, and mix until they are evenly distributed throughout the dough.

If you are preparing the cookies using a food processor, place the butter

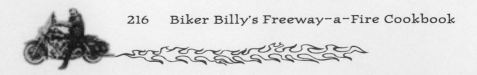

in the workbowl of the processor equipped with a chopping blade, and pulse several times. While the blades are running, slowly pour in the sugar and process until creamy. It may be necessary to scrape down the sides of the bowl a few times. Add the vanilla, cayenne pepper, salt, baking powder, and egg and process until well blended, 1 minute. Add the melted chocolate and process until well blended, 1 minute. Add the flour, ¼ cup at a time, processing for about 1 minute with each addition, until it is thoroughly blended. Continue to process until the dough forms a ball that revolves around the workbowl. It may be necessary to stop processing periodically to scrape down the sides of the bowl. Add the white chocolate chips and the nuts, if using, and pulse until they are evenly distributed throughout the dough (I have found that the chopping blades will cut the chips up if you pulse them too much). If the chips don't integrate into the dough with a few pulses, remove the dough from the food processor and finish by hand in a mixing bowl.

Preheat the oven to 375°F. Grease 2 cookie sheets.

Form a piece of dough into a 1-inch ball, flatten it between your palms, and place it on the cookie sheet. Continue with the remaining dough and arrange the cookies on the cookie sheets, with a ½-inch space between them. Bake 8 to 10 minutes for chewy cookies, and 10 to 12 minutes for crispier cookies. Transfer the cookies to a plate and allow to cool.

MAKES ABOUT 24 TWO-INCH COOKIES

Double Devil Chocolate Cookies

If you survived the Chocolate Killer Cookies (page 216) and are looking for a bigger chocolate fix, here it is. Double the chocolate and double the fire equals double the devilish delight. Maybe you should make a double batch because these cookies will disappear doubly fast. They are the cookie equivalent of a double-engine Harley drag bike.

> 4 ounces unsweetened chocolate
> ½ cup butter (1 stick), softened
> ½ cup sugar
> ½ cup firmly packed light brown sugar
> 1½ teaspoons pure vanilla extract
> 1 teaspoon ground cayenne pepper, plus more to
>   taste
> ½ teaspoon salt
> 1½ teaspoons baking powder
> 1 jumbo egg, beaten
> 1½ cups all-purpose flour
> 1 cup semisweet chocolate chips or chunks (if
>   available)
> Canola oil or butter-flavored cooking spray

Fill the bottom half of a double boiler (not quite halfway) with boiling water and place over medium heat (you don't want the top part of the double boiler to be in direct contact with the water). Every so often, check the water level to ensure that the pot does not boil dry. Keep another pot of water boiling on the stove so you can add water if necessary. Heat the chocolate in the top of the double boiler. When the chocolate has melted, remove the pot from the heat.

If you are preparing the cookies by hand, combine the butter and both sugars in a large bowl and mix together with a wooden spoon until creamy. Add the vanilla, cayenne pepper, salt, and baking powder and mix together well. Add the melted chocolate and stir until well blended. Add the egg and blend until smooth. Add the flour, ¼ cup at a time, mixing well with each addition, until a dough has formed. Add the chocolate chips and mix until the chips are evenly distributed throughout the dough.

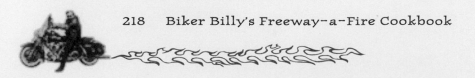

If you are preparing the cookies using a food processor equipped with a chopping blade, place the butter in the workbowl of the processor and pulse several times. While the blades are running, slowly pour in both sugars and process until creamy. It may be necessary to scrape down the sides of the bowl a few times. Add the vanilla, cayenne pepper, salt, baking powder, and egg and process until well blended, 1 minute. Add the melted chocolate and process until well blended, 1 minute. Add the flour, ¼ cup at a time, processing for about 1 minute with each addition, until thoroughly blended. Continue to process until the dough forms a ball that revolves around the workbowl. It may be necessary to stop processing periodically to scrape down the sides of the bowl. Add the chocolate chips and pulse until the chips are evenly distributed throughout the dough (the chopping blades will cut the chips up if you pulse them too much). If the chips don't integrate into the dough with a few pulses, remove the dough from the food processor and finish by hand in a mixing bowl.

Preheat the oven to 400°F. Grease 2 cookie sheets.

Form a piece of dough into a 1-inch ball, flatten it between your palms, and place it on the cookie sheet. Continue with the remaining dough and arrange the cookies in a single layer on the cookie sheets, with a ½-inch space between them. Bake for 8 to 10 minutes for chewy cookies, and 10 to 12 minutes for crispier cookies. Transfer the cookies to a plate and allow to cool.

MAKES ABOUT 24 TWO-INCH COOKIES

Peanut Purgatory Pie

This pie is somewhere between heaven and hell. It's so heavenly rich: The filling is gloriously creamy and both the crust and topping are sweet and buttery. It also packs a blast of pure hellfire in the double whammy of cayenne and habanero pepper. So if sin is on your dessert agenda, wander no further than this damned delicious dessert. Everybody pays for their sins, but if you want some salvation from this fiery plate (pun intended), serve Peanut Purgatory Pie with extra-tall glasses of ice-cold milk.

For the crust:

8 ounces graham crackers, crumbled
½ cup firmly packed light brown sugar
½ cup (1 stick) butter, melted
Butter for greasing

For the topping:

2 ounces bittersweet chocolate
4 tablespoons (½ stick) butter, softened
½ cup firmly packed light brown sugar
½ teaspoon ground cayenne pepper
½ cup all-purpose flour

For the filling:

1 dried habanero pepper, stemmed, seeded, and
  crushed
2 tablespoons boiling water (see page 15)
2 tablespoons light cream
One 8-ounce package cream cheese, cut into 8 pieces
1 cup smooth peanut butter
½ cup confectioners' sugar

To prepare the crust, combine the graham cracker crumbs and brown sugar in a blender or a food processor equipped with a chopping blade. Pulse several times until the crumbs are reduced to a coarse grain. Add the melted butter a little at a time, pulsing after each addition. (It may be necessary to scrape down the sides of the blender or processor workbowl between additions of butter.) After all the butter has been added, pulse several times to combine. To test the mixture to see if it is fully combined, pinch a small amount with your fingers; if it holds together, it is ready to use. Spread the crust mixture evenly on the bottom and sides of a 9-inch pie pan well greased with butter. Using your fingers or a spoon, pack the crumbs firmly to form a solid crust. A second pie pan can be used as a press to pack the crust more solidly. Chill the crust in the refrigerator for 15 to 30 minutes.

Preheat the oven to 350°F. Grease a cookie sheet.

To prepare the topping, fill the bottom half of a double boiler (not quite halfway) with boiling water and place over medium heat (you don't want the top part of the double boiler to be in direct contact with the water). Every so often, check the water level to ensure that the pot does not boil dry. Keep another pot of water boiling on the stove so you can add water if necessary. Heat the chocolate in the top of the double boiler. When the chocolate has melted, remove the pot from the heat.

If you are preparing the topping by hand, combine the butter, brown sugar, and cayenne pepper in a large bowl and mix together with a wooden spoon until creamy. Add the melted chocolate and stir until well blended. Add the flour and blend thoroughly until a dry, crumbly dough has formed.

If you are preparing the topping using a food processor, place the butter in the workbowl of the processor equipped with a chopping blade, and pulse several times. While the blades are running, slowly add the brown sugar, cayenne pepper, and melted chocolate and process until creamy, 1 minute. It may be necessary to scrape down the sides of the bowl a few times. Add the flour and process until a dry, crumbly dough forms, about 1 minute.

Sprinkle the dough crumbs onto the cookie sheet. Bake until crunchy, 15 minutes.

To prepare the filling, place the habanero pepper in a small bowl and cover with the boiling water. Allow to cool to room temperature.

In a blender or a food processor equipped with a chopping blade, puree the rehydrated habanero and the soaking water until no large pieces of habanero remain, 1 minute. Add the cream and cream cheese and pulse several times to combine. Add the peanut butter and pulse until combined. While the blades are spinning, slowly add the confectioners' sugar and process until smooth.

To assemble the pie, spread the filling into the refrigerated crust. Sprinkle the chocolate crumbs on top. Chill the pie in the refrigerator for 30 to 60 minutes.

MAKES ONE 9-INCH PIE; 6 SERVINGS

Desserts to Die For   221

Satan's Scones

The Devil made me do it, I swear. If you don't believe that the Devil himself is behind these sinfully rich scones, I can prove it. Here's the test: Bake up a batch. Gather a group of your friends and serve each of them a scone. Wait until they have had about two bites apiece and try to take back the scones. Now watch all hell break loose. Your formerly kind and gentle friends will become gourmet hellcats. Now, to save your butt, give them all a second helping of scones and a big glass of milk to cool them off.

If you have little kids in the house, spare them the sight of all this mayhem by distracting them with some of these scones made without the Satanic Glaze, since that is where all hellfire is. At least they'll still love you.

For the scones:

2 cups all-purpose flour
2 tablespoons baking powder
½ teaspoon salt
1 tablespoon sugar
6 tablespoons (¾ stick) butter
2 extra-large eggs
½ cup light cream
1 cup semisweet chocolate chips or chunks (if available)

For the glaze:

1 tablespoon light cream
½ teaspoon pure vanilla extract
¼ teaspoon ground cayenne pepper
1 teaspoon ground cinnamon
¾ cup confectioners' sugar

Tall glasses of milk (optional)

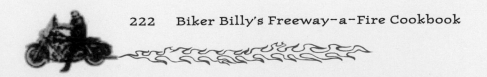

If you are preparing the scones by hand, in a large mixing bowl, combine the flour, baking powder, salt, and sugar and mix thoroughly with a wire whisk. Add the butter and cut in with a dough cutter or two knives until it reaches an even, granular texture. In a small mixing bowl, whisk together the eggs and cream. Reserve ¼ cup of the egg mixture and add the remainder to the flour mixture. Cut in until a crumbly dough forms. Add the chocolate chips and knead them into the dough with your hands until evenly distributed.

If you are preparing the scones using a food processor, combine the flour, baking powder, salt, and sugar in the workbowl of the processor equipped with a chopping blade, and pulse several times to mix thoroughly. Cut the butter into 4 pieces and place evenly around the inside of the workbowl and pulse until it reaches an even, granular texture. In a small mixing bowl, whisk together the eggs and cream. Reserve ¼ cup of the egg mixture and add the remainder to the flour mixture. Process until a crumbly dough forms. It may be necessary to stop processing periodically to scrape down the sides of the bowl. Add the chocolate chips and pulse until the chips are evenly distributed throughout the dough (I have found that the chopping blades will cut the chips up if you pulse them too much). If the chips don't integrate into the dough with a few pulses, remove the dough from the food processor and finish by hand in a mixing bowl.

Preheat the oven to 450°F.

Transfer the dough to a cookie sheet covered with baking parchment. Using your hands, press the dough into a 1-inch-thick rectangle. Use care to keep the edges from being too thin, as they will dry out during baking. Cut the rectangle diagonally from corner to corner through the center in an **X** pattern, forming 4 triangular pieces. Then cut from side to side, through the center, forming 8 triangular pieces. Use a spatula to separate the cut scones, creating a ¼-inch gap between them (the scones may crumble a little when you slide them apart; just repair the damage by gently pressing them back together). Brush the ¼ cup reserved egg mixture onto the scones. Bake until they begin to brown at the edges, 15 minutes. Remove from the oven and allow to cool. Meanwhile, prepare the glaze.

To prepare the glaze, heat the cream and vanilla in a small saucepot over low heat. Add the cayenne pepper and cinnamon and mix thoroughly with a wire whisk. Add the sugar and whisk together until a smooth glaze forms.

To assemble, arrange the scones on a serving plate with a 1-inch space between them. Drizzle the glaze over the scones and refrigerate until the glaze hardens, 5 to 10 minutes. Serve with tall glasses of milk.

MAKES 8 SCONES

Apricot Fire Tarts

I love to eat apricots fresh in season, but for most of the year, dried apricots have to do. These Apricot Fire Tarts are extra-sweet thanks to the honey and apple juice. The two habanero peppers create a prodigious level of fire, so if you're not a true fire-eating biker, start with just one pepper.

Butter for greasing
2 fresh habanero peppers, stemmed
¾ cup honey
¾ cup apple juice
2 tablespoons cornstarch
1 cup golden raisins
2 cups dried apricots (about 1 pound), minced
1 package pie crust mix (for a double-crust
   9-inch pie)
All-purpose flour for dusting
Vanilla ice cream (optional)

Preheat the oven to 350°F. Grease a 12-muffin tin with butter.

In a blender or a food processor equipped with a chopping blade, combine the peppers, honey, juice, and cornstarch and puree until no large pieces of pepper remain, 1 minute. Combine the fruit in a medium-size mixing bowl. Pour the puree over the fruit and stir well. Set aside.

Prepare the pie crust mix according to package directions for two 9-inch pie crusts. Divide the dough into 12 equal pieces. Using a floured rolling pin on a lightly floured surface, roll the dough, 1 piece at a time, into a circle about ⅛ inch thick. (When rolled these should produce circles of dough big enough to line a single muffin cup.) Roll from the center toward the outside and turn the dough a quarter-turn between each rolling. Always make sure that there is enough flour on the rolling pin and surface to prevent sticking. Place a dough circle in each muffin cup and flute the edges by pinching the dough between your thumb and forefinger. Divide the filling mixture among the 12 tart crusts. Bake until the crust is golden brown, 25 to 30 minutes. Allow to cool for 5 to 10 minutes, topping each tart with a scoop of ice cream, before serving.

MAKES 12 TARTS

Peaches in Paradise

This is a real down-home Southern treat that always reminds me of heading to Daytona Beach, Florida, for Bike Week. As winter grips the frozen North, I dream of warm Southern beaches and beautiful peaches. Yes, it is surely a biker's paradise to feel the warm sunshine on your face as you ride along the ocean in March and gaze upon the unbridled beauty of nature.

Well, this sweet dessert will give you a taste of Southern biker paradise, and the habanero pepper will warm you up like the Florida sunshine. The combination of biscuit and crumb toppings gives this bike-style dessert a V-twin rumble. Enjoy the Peaches in Paradise; they are wonderful served warm or cold. Add a scoop of vanilla ice cream, if you like, to cool you like a fresh ocean spray.

For the crumb topping:

½ cup firmly packed light brown sugar
⅓ cup all-purpose flour
¼ teaspoon ground cayenne pepper
½ teaspoon ground cinnamon
¼ teaspoon ground nutmeg
4 tablespoons (½ stick) butter, cut into 4 pieces

For the peaches:

1 fresh habanero pepper, stemmed and seeded
Two 16-ounce cans sliced peaches in light syrup,
    drained, liquid reserved
½ cup honey
2 tablespoons cornstarch
¼ teaspoon ground cinnamon
¼ teaspoon ground nutmeg
1½ teaspoons fresh lemon juice

continued

For the biscuit topping:

1 cup all-purpose flour
½ teaspoon salt
1 tablespoon sugar
1½ teaspoons baking powder
3 tablespoons butter
½ cup whole milk

If preparing the crumb topping by hand, in a medium-size mixing bowl, combine the brown sugar, flour, cayenne pepper, cinnamon, and nutmeg. Whisk together with a wire whisk for 30 seconds to thoroughly mix the dry ingredients. Add the pieces of butter and cut together with two knives or a dough cutter until the butter is completely cut into the flour and the mixture has a granular texture. Set aside.

If preparing the crumb topping using a food processor, combine the brown sugar, flour, cayenne pepper, cinnamon, and nutmeg in the workbowl of the processor equipped with a chopping blade. Pulse 2 or 3 times to mix completely. Add the butter, arranging the pieces evenly around the workbowl. Process until the butter is cut into the flour, creating a granular texture, 1 to 2 minutes. Set aside.

To prepare the peaches, in a small saucepot, combine the habanero pepper, reserved peach syrup, honey, cornstarch, cinnamon, nutmeg, and lemon juice. Stir well, place over medium-high heat, and bring to a boil. Boil for 2 minutes, stirring constantly, until the sauce begins to thicken. Remove the saucepot from the heat. Remove and discard the habanero pepper.

Preheat the oven to 400°F.

If you are preparing the biscuit topping by hand, in a medium-size mixing bowl, combine the flour, salt, sugar, and baking powder. Whisk together for 30 seconds to thoroughly mix the dry ingredients. Add the pieces of butter and cut together with two knives or a dough cutter until the butter is completely cut into the flour and the mixture has a granular texture. Form a well in the center of the flour and pour in the milk and stir until a dough forms.

If you are preparing the biscuit topping using a food processor, combine the flour, salt, sugar, and baking powder in the workbowl of the processor equipped with a chopping blade. Pulse 2 or 3 times to mix completely. Add the butter, arranging the pieces evenly around the workbowl. Process until the butter is cut into the flour, creating a granular texture, 1 to 2 minutes. While the blades are spinning, pour in the milk and process until a dough forms and begins to move around the bowl as a ball, approximately 1 minute.

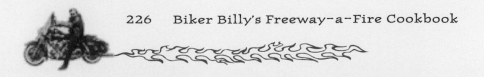

To assemble, place the sliced peaches in an 8-inch square baking pan. Pour the sauce over the peaches and stir to coat the peaches evenly with the sauce. Spoon the biscuit batter on top of the peaches (you want to distribute the biscuit batter evenly, but not to form a crust or completely cover the peaches). Sprinkle on the crumb topping. Bake until the top is golden brown, 30 to 35 minutes. Allow to cool for 10 minutes before serving.

MAKES ABOUT 8 SERVINGS

An early take on "Help me, I've fallen and I can't get up": an unidentified rider clowning around for the camera, from the Tramontin family photo album.

Bub Tramontin hands the keys to a new Lambretta scooter to the Passaic County Park Police, circa the 1960s.

Spare Parts Kit:
Miscellaneous Recipes

Spare parts are something that an experienced long-distance rider never travels without. If you know your machine well, you are familiar with the little things that always fail on the road. Those little things often have a habit of surprising you a few hundred miles from the nearest dealer or bike shop. The road has taught me also to carry a few universal goodies that are useful during unscheduled roadside motorcycle-maintenance sessions. Over time, this collection of bike-specific parts has grown to include items that are generally useful or that improve comfort while on the road, even when everything is running perfectly.

The following collection of recipes is this cookbook's equivalent of a spare parts kit. In it, you will find some recipes that are great at fixing up dull food, like Pulsating Pepper Puree or Firecracker Salsa, which will breathe life into any meal. Under the category of generally useful but just-didn't-fit-anywhere-else-in-the-book, there are three sauces: a barbecue sauce, a chipotle sauce, and a tasty herb sauce. With theses sauces you will be able to add some fire to many otherwise misfiring dishes. I hope you enjoy these spare parts.

Pulsating Pepper Puree

This combination of dried peppers is one of my favorites. The blend of flavors is wonderfully complex and the fire is equally so. This mixture of hot peppers adds a great depth of taste and fire to almost any dish. The only drawback is that when you want to cook a small quantity of something, the punch of using four different peppers is often more than most people may enjoy. You can prepare this puree using only what you need, saving the rest for another recipe. Just don't be surprised if, after a while, you find yourself saying, "I can't believe I used the whole thing!" The fire will grow on you.

> 1 dried habanero pepper, stemmed
> 1 chipotle pepper, stemmed
> 1 ancho pepper, stemmed, seeded, and torn into
>   small pieces
> 1 pasilla pepper, stemmed, seeded, and torn into
>   small pieces
> ½ cup boiling water (see page 15)

Place the habanero, chipotle, ancho, and pasilla peppers in a small bowl and cover with the boiling water. Allow to cool to room temperature.

In a blender or a food processor equipped with a chopping blade, puree the rehydrated peppers and the soaking water until no large pieces of pepper remains, 1 minute.

Use as desired or divide and freeze (see page 17) for later use.

MAKES ABOUT ½ CUP

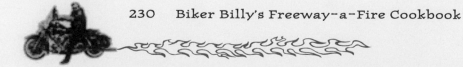

Smoky Chipotle Sauce

This recipe gives a whole new meaning to the term "special sauce." Pour it on burgers or smother hot dogs with this sauce. Look out.

> 2 chipotle peppers, stemmed
> ¼ cup boiling water (see page 15)
> 1 tablespoon olive oil
> 1 medium-size onion, diced
> 2 tablespoons chopped garlic
> 1 cup canned pureed tomatoes
> 1 teaspoon salt
> 1 teaspoon ground black pepper
> 1 tablespoon Liquid Smoke
> 2 tablespoons cool water

Place the chipotle peppers in a small bowl and cover with the boiling water. Allow to cool to room temperature.

In a blender or a food processor equipped with a chopping blade, puree the rehydrated peppers and the soaking water until no large pieces of chipotle remain, 1 minute. Do not clean the blender or food processor.

Heat the olive oil in a small sauté pan over medium heat. Add the onion and sauté until the onions begins to brown, 3 to 5 minutes. Add the garlic and cook until it begins to brown. Reduce the heat to low and add the pepper puree, tomatoes, salt, and black pepper and simmer for 10 minutes.

Transfer the mixture back to the blender or food processor. Add the Liquid Smoke and cool water and puree until smooth, 1 minute. Return to the sauté pan and simmer on low for 2 minutes. Serve hot or at room temperature.

MAKES ABOUT 2 CUPS

Firecracker Salsa

Over the past several years, I have traveled around the country doing cooking shows for every imaginable type of event. At those events, I have made thousands of batches of salsa. I have never measured ingredients when making those salsas, and I never make salsas exactly the same way twice; I just know what to add by sight and experience. Everyone is always asking me if I sell the salsa. Well, someday I will, but until then, here is a recipe that is representative of what I have been preparing lately at the events.

Here, I use the new Biker Billy jalapeño pepper that W. Atlee Burpee has developed. This pepper adds a surprising punch and a fresh garden flavor. I also like to make this salsa using a blend of hot peppers (see note), giving it an earthy and complex flavor. Add as much of the blend as you like so the fire is just right for you.

The key to really great salsa is to use quality ingredients and to adjust the fire and spices to fit your taste. Experiment—salsa is what you make it. Canned tomatoes are easy and are always in season, but you can use fresh tomatoes (I do when my garden is producing tomatoes). Salsa adds a lot of flavor to almost any meal. It is also good to munch on with corn chips while watching *Biker Billy Cooks with Fire*—alright!

1 Biker Billy jalapeño pepper, or more to taste (see
  Note), stemmed and minced
2 medium-size onions, coarsely chopped
1 orange bell pepper, cored, seeded, and minced
2 tablespoons chopped garlic
1 teaspoon ground cumin
1½ teaspoons dried cilantro
1 tablespoon dried parsley
1 teaspoon Liquid Smoke
1½ teaspoons golden molasses
1 teaspoon salt
1 teaspoon ground black pepper
1 28-ounce can whole plum tomatoes, coarsely
  chopped with their juice

If you are preparing the salsa by hand, in a large mixing bowl, combine the Biker Billy jalapeño, onions, bell pepper, garlic, cumin, cilantro, parsley, Liquid Smoke, molasses, salt, black pepper, and tomatoes with their juice. Stir well. Refrigerate for 1 hour before serving (this allows the flavors of the spices to blossom).

If you are preparing the salsa using a food processor, prechopping the ingredients is not necessary, as this method is fast and blends the flavors more quickly. Coarsely chop the Biker Billy jalapeño in the workbowl of the processor equipped with a chopping blade. Add the garlic, cumin, cilantro, parsley, Liquid Smoke, molasses, salt, black pepper, and the juice from the tomatoes. Process for 1 to 2 minutes. Add the onions and pulse 2 to 3 times, or until coarsely chopped. Add the bell pepper and pulse 2 to 3 times, or until coarsely chopped. Add the tomatoes and pulse 2 to 3 times, or until coarsely chopped. (Use care to avoid overprocessing once you start adding the onions, bell pepper, and tomatoes, or you will lose the desired chunkiness.) Refrigerate for 30 minutes before serving (this allows the flavors of the spices to blossom).

MAKES ABOUT 4 CUPS

NOTE: Start with 1 Biker Billy jalapeño (you can add more later, but it will take too many of the other ingredients to reduce the fire). While you are waiting for your Biker Billy jalapeños to grow, try using ¼ cup or more of the Pulsating Pepper Puree (page 230) instead.

Jennifer and Pete Tremblay's Barbecue Sauce

This is a Viewer Recipe Contest Winner that I modified a little. Jennifer and Pete use it on chicken, but I found that it works well on vegetable kabobs and bean curd, too. The combination of orange and tomato juices and mustard blends well with the fresh bite of jalapeños. The molasses adds a hint of sweetness and helps the sauce to cling. For a change of pace from ketchup-style barbecue sauces, give this sauce a try the next time you fire up the grill. For some extra burn, use Biker Billy jalapeños.

2 to 4 jalapeño peppers (to your taste), stemmed
1 tablespoon chopped garlic
Juice of 2 oranges
Juice of 1 tomato (see Note)
2 tablespoons prepared mustard
2 tablespoons golden molasses
¼ teaspoon salt
¼ teaspoon ground white pepper

In a blender or a food processor equipped with a cutting blade, combine the jalapeño peppers, garlic, and the orange and tomato juices and puree until no large pieces of jalapeño remain, 1 minute. Add the mustard, molasses, salt, and white pepper and puree until smooth, 1 minute. Refrigerate for 30 minutes before serving.

MAKES ABOUT 1½ CUPS

NOTE: To juice the tomato, you can use a hand juicer, or just cut up the tomato and press it through a fine strainer and discard the solids.

Creamy Herb Fire Sauce

Here is a mouthwatering sauce laced with fine herbs and a warming blast of cayenne pepper. You can serve this over almost anything that calls for a cream or cheese sauce. The combination of warming fire with the gentle herbs will surprise even the most jaded biker gourmet. Try this on the Snappy Stir-Fried Vegetables (page 195) for a surefire side dish. Who says only French gourmets can create elegant sauces?

> 2 tablespoons butter
> 2 tablespoons all-purpose flour
> ¼ teaspoon dried thyme
> ¼ teaspoon dried basil
> ½ teaspoon ground sage
> ½ teaspoon ground savory
> 1 tablespoon dried parsley
> ½ teaspoon salt
> ⅛ teaspoon ground cayenne pepper
> ½ teaspoon ground white pepper
> 1¼ cups whole milk

In a small saucepot, melt the butter over low heat. Add the flour and stir well. Continue to stir until the flour is a very light brown, 2 to 3 minutes.

Add the thyme, basil, sage, savory, parsley, salt, cayenne pepper, and white pepper and stir well. While stirring slowly with a wire whisk, add the milk. Simmer, stirring often, over low heat until the sauce thickens, about 5 minutes.

MAKES ABOUT 1½ CUPS

Breakfast Burritos

When I get a hankering for a hearty breakfast that will burn the sleep from my eyes and fuel me up for a long day in the saddle, there is one thing that I always go back to—Breakfast Burritos. Now, this recipe has a little history to it. See, I never really thought that this was a recipe that other people would be interested in. It was just how I liked to cook my eggs. Then one year, while I was doing some cooking at Vanson Leather's Fall Open House, we all wanted something for breakfast before the crowds arrived. So I just multiplied my breakfast eggs. Well, the crowd got there sooner than we expected, but everyone loved the Breakfast Burritos. Since then, these babies have become a must-do recipe at Vanson Leather's Fall Open House.

> 4 tablespoons (½ stick) butter
>
> 2 medium-size onions, minced
>
> 3 tablespoons chopped garlic
>
> ¼ cup Pulsating Pepper Puree (page 230), or more to taste
>
> 1 red bell pepper, cored, seeded, and diced
>
> 1 teaspoon ground cumin
>
> 2 teaspoons dried cilantro
>
> 1 tablespoon dried parsley
>
> 1½ teaspoons salt
>
> 1 teaspoon ground black pepper
>
> 2 teaspoons Liquid Smoke
>
> 6 jumbo eggs
>
> 2 cups shredded mild cheddar cheese
>
> Eight 10-inch flour tortillas, warmed

In a large frying pan, melt 2 tablespoons of the butter over medium heat. Add the onions and cook until the onions begin to brown, 5 to 7 minutes. Add the garlic, pepper puree, bell pepper, cumin, cilantro, parsley, salt, and black pepper. Cook until the bell pepper is just tender, 5 to 7 minutes. In a small bowl, combine the Liquid Smoke and eggs, and with a wire whisk, beat until smooth and frothy. Melt the remaining 2 tablespoons of butter in the frying pan and add the beaten-egg mixture. Cook, stirring often, until the

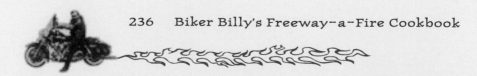

eggs are solid and begin to brown, 5 to 7 minutes. Reduce the heat to low. Cover with the cheese and cook until the cheese is melted. Stir well and remove from the heat.

To assemble the burritos, put a warm tortilla on a plate. Place several tablespoons of the egg and cheese mixture on the lower third of the tortilla, forming a line from the left edge extending to 2 inches from the right edge. Fold the near end of the tortilla over the filling. Then fold the right end over the filling (this creates the bottom of the burrito) and roll up the tortilla away from you. Repeat with the remaining tortillas. Serve hot with Firecracker Salsa (page 232) on the side.

MAKES 8 BURRITOS

Ernest "Red" Tramontin inside the first Tramontin Harley-Davidson dealership in Clifton, New Jersey, circa 1924.

Moo Shu for You

I like to think of these as Chinese-style burritos. They have a cross-cultural flair, thanks to the influence of the ancho peppers, while still maintaining their strong Chinese character. The fresh pancakes are especially appetizing wrapped around the crispy vegetables. The black bean sauce possesses all the exotic flavors of Asia and a moderate kick from the ancho peppers. You can shift the fire level to high gear by adding some de árbol or cayenne peppers. These make fun party food if you let your guests roll their own.

For the sauce:

2 ancho peppers, stemmed, seeded, and torn into
   small pieces
¼ cup boiling water (see page 15)
2 tablespoons sesame oil
¼ cup peeled and minced fresh ginger
¼ cup chopped garlic
6 scallions, trimmed and cut into ½-inch-thick
   slices
One 16-ounce can black beans, drained, liquid
   reserved
¼ cup light teriyaki sauce
1 teaspoon coarsely ground black pepper

For the pancakes:

2½ cups all-purpose flour
1 tablespoon light teriyaki sauce
1 cup boiling water, minus 1 tablespoon (see Note)
2 tablespoons sesame oil
2 tablespoons peanut oil

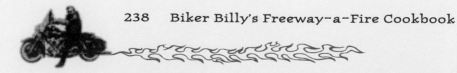

For the filling:

1 cup sliced water chestnuts

1 head bok choy, trimmed and cut into ½-inch-thick slices

1 cup sliced mushrooms

6 scallions, trimmed and cut into ½-inch-thick slices

1 orange bell pepper, cored, seeded, and julienned

1 bunch broccoli, florets only, cut into bite-size pieces

To prepare the sauce, place the ancho peppers in a small bowl and cover with the boiling water. Allow to cool to room temperature.

Heat the sesame oil in a large wok over high heat. Add the ginger, garlic, and scallions and toss well to coat with oil. Stir-fry until the scallions are tender, 2 to 3 minutes. Add the rehydrated ancho peppers, soaking water, and the black beans and stir-fry until the scallions begin to brown, 3 to 5 minutes. Remove from the heat and allow to cool to a comfortable handling temperature. Transfer to a food processor equipped with a chopping blade. Add the reserved bean liquid, teriyaki sauce, and black pepper and puree until it forms a sauce, 1 to 2 minutes. The sauce should be slightly on the chunky side.

Fill the bottom half of a double boiler (not quite halfway) with boiling water and place over medium heat (you don't want the top part of the double boiler to be in direct contact with the water). Every so often, check the water level to ensure that the pot does not boil dry. Keep another pot of water boiling on the stove so you can add water if necessary. Transfer the sauce to the top of the double boiler to keep warm, stirring often while you prepare the pancakes and filling.

To prepare the pancakes, place the flour in a large bowl, forming a well in the center. Pour the water and teriyaki sauce into the well. Cut the liquid into the flour using a dough cutter or two knives. When a dough has formed, remove it from the bowl and knead it in your hands for 2 or 3 minutes, exercising care, as the dough will be hot. (This dough should not need additional flour during the kneading process.) Return the dough to the mixing bowl and allow to rest, covered, for 10 minutes.

Preheat the oven to 200°F. In a small bowl, combine the sesame and peanut oils. Take small pieces of the dough, enough to form balls about 1 inch in diameter, and flatten each piece into a pancake shape between your palms. Dip the pieces of dough into the oil mixture to lightly coat both sides. Place on an unfloured surface and, using an unfloured rolling pin, roll them into a pancake shape, about ⅛ inch thick or less. Turn them over once or twice during the rolling process to prevent sticking.

Lightly coat a large wok with some of the oil mixture and place over high heat. Lay a pancake into the wok and fry for 30 to 60 seconds on each side, or until lightly browned. Transfer to a covered baking dish and keep warm in the oven. Repeat until all the pancakes are fried. (It should not be necessary to add additional oil to the wok, as each pancake is preoiled in the rolling process.)

To prepare the vegetable filling, heat the remaining sesame-peanut oil blend in a large wok over high heat. Add the water chestnuts and bok choy, tossing well to coat with oil, and cook for 2 minutes. Add the mushrooms, scallions, bell pepper, and broccoli florets and cook until the broccoli begins to turn dark green, 3 to 5 minutes. Remove from the heat.

To assemble the pancakes, put a pancake on a plate. Place several table-spoons of the vegetables on the lower third of the pancake, forming a line from the left edge extending to 2 inches from the right edge. Cover generously with the black bean sauce. Fold the near end of the pancake over the filling. Then fold the right end over the filling (this creates the bottom of the Chinese-style burrito) and roll up the pancake away from you. Repeat with the remaining pancakes. Serve hot with extra sauce on the side.

MAKES 12 TO 18 PANCAKES

NOTE: You want a total of 1 cup of liquid, comprising the combined light teriyaki sauce and water. The easiest way to do this is first to put 1 table-spoon of light teriyaki sauce into a measuring cup, then add the boiling water to make 1 full cup.

SOURCES

Biker Billy Cooks with Fire
P.O. Box 124
Florham Park, NJ 07932
Toll free: (800) BIKER BILLY
Web: www.bikerbilly.com
BikerBilly@BikerBilly.com
E-mail: bikerbilly@bikerbilly.com
Newsletter, Biker Billy products, and
fiery stuff

Bold Ventures Company
P.O. Box 572110
Tarzana, CA 91357-2110
Web: www.boldweb.com
Fiery foods and products

Burpee
300 Park Avenue
Warminster, PA 18974
Toll free: (800) 888-1447
Web: www.burpee.com
Hot pepper seeds and garden products.
Source of the Biker Billy jalapeño
pepper!

Chile Pepper Magazine
Avenue Chile Pepper, LLC
River Plaza
1701 River Run, Suite 702

Fort Worth, TX 76107
Toll free: (888) 774-2946
(817) 877-1048
Fax: (817) 877-8870
Web: www.chilepepperzine.com
A magazine of spicy world cuisine

Fiery Foods Magazine
National Fiery Foods Show
Sunbelt Shows, Inc.
P.O. Box 4980
Albuquerque, NM 87196
(505) 298-3835
Fax: (505) 298-3826
Web: www.fiery-foods.com
A magazine for the fiery foods industry

The Hot Shop
P.O. Box 7917
North Augusta, SC 29861-7917
Toll free: (888) 850-HOTT (4688)
(803) 202-0395
Fax: (803) 202-0489
Web: www.hotstuff4u.com
Fiery foods and products

Kalustyan's
123 Lexington Avenue
New York, NY 10016

(212) 685-3888
Fax: (212) 683-8458
Web: www.kalustyan.com
Indian and Middle Eastern spices and
foods

Lazy Acres Natural Way
9911 Bexar Road
Somerset, TX 78069-3106
(830) 429-3768
Fax: (830) 429-3768
Web: www.hot-peppers.com
Organically grown, hand-picked hot or
sweet peppers

Los Chileros de Nuevo Mexico
Gourmet New Mexican Foods
P.O. Box 6215
Santa Fe, NM 87502
(505) 471-6967
Fax: (505) 473-7306
Web: www.hotchilepepper.com
Fiery foods and products

Lots of Hots & Fiery Foods
P.O. Box 293
Fairport, NY 14450
Toll free: (800) 836-1677
Fiery foods and products

Mo Hotta-Mo Betta
P.O. Box 4136
San Luis Obispo, CA 93403
Toll free: (800) 462-3220
(805) 544-4051
Fax: (800) 618-4454 or (805) 545-8389
Web: www.mohotta.com
Fiery foods and products

New Cherry Hot Shots, Inc.
215 North Mill Road
Vineland, NJ 08360
Toll free: (888) 609-5956
(609) 507-9119
Fax: (609) 696-8524
Web: www.newcherryhotshots.com
Fiery foods and products

Passion for Peppers
8620 Wagner Drive
Richmond, B.C., Canada V7A 4N9
(604) 271-7944
Fax: (604) 596-2181
Web: www.apassionforpeppers.com
Fiery foods and products

Pendery's
1221 Manufacturing Street
Dallas, TX 75207
Toll free: (800) 533-1870
(214) 741-1870
Fax: (214) 761-1966
Web: www.penderys.com
Fiery foods and products

Peppers
Rehoboth Outlets #3
1815 Ocean Outlets
Rehoboth Beach, DE 19971
(302) 227-4608
Fax: (302) 227-4603
Web: www.peppers.com
Fiery foods and products

Peppers & Pasta
8 First Street East
Kalispell, MT 59901
(406) 257-4478
Web: www.cyberport.net
Fiery foods and products

Shepherd's Garden Seeds
30 Irene Street
Torrington, CT 06790
(860) 482-3638
Web: www.shepherdseeds.com
Hot pepper seeds

Superbly Southwestern
2400 Rio Grande Boulevard NW
Box 1-171
Albuquerque, NM 87104-3222
Toll free: (800) 467-4HOT
(505) 766-9598
Web: www.hotchile.com
Fiery foods and products

Terra Time & Tide
590 E. 59th Street
Jacksonville, FL 32208
(904) 764-0376
Web: www.pepperhot.com
Seeds

Tomato Growers Supply Company
P.O. Box 2237
Fort Myers, FL 33902
Toll free: (888) 478-7333
(813) 768-1119
Toll free fax: (888) 768-3476
Web: www.tomatogrowers.com
Hot pepper seeds

Outside the Italian-American Co-op Hall on Parker Avenue in Clifton, New Jersey, at the Passaic Valley Motorcycle Club's Annual Barn Dance, circa the 1950s.

AMERICAN MOTORCYCLIST ASSOCIATION

The American Motorcyclist Association (AMA) is a 234,000-member organization with an unparalleled seventy-six-year history of pursuing, protecting, and promoting the interests of the world's largest and most dedicated group of motorcycle enthusiasts. Founded in 1924, the AMA exists to further the interests of American motorcyclists, while serving the needs of its members.

The AMA is the premier defender of motorcyclists' rights in the United States. The work of the AMA Government Relations Department extends beyond AMA members to all motorcyclists. Staff members ferret out bad laws and anti-motorcycling discrimination at the local, state, federal, and corporate levels. When critical issues and problems arise, education, common sense, political clout, and, when necessary, compromise are used to make changes beneficial to all riders—even those who aren't AMA members.

The AMA is also the world's largest motor-sports sanctioning body. Its AMA Pro Racing Division oversees more than eighty national-level racing events all over the United States, from the high banks of Daytona and the high jumps of Supercross to the shoulder-to-shoulder combat of dirt-track racing and the explosive action of hillclimbs. The AMA's Member Events and Entertainment Department coordinates thousands of amateur races with dozens of competition classes for everyone from grade-school kids to senior riders.

In addition, the AMA is the sole American affiliate of the Federation Internationale Motocycliste (FIM), the international governing body for motorcycle sport and touring activity.

Since its founding, the AMA has relied on its chartered clubs and promoters to help advance the goals and protect the interests of motorcyclists. Today, there are more than 1,200 chartered clubs and promoters organizing over 3,700 road-riding and competition events each year.

245

The AMA also publishes *American Motorcyclist* magazine, covering every facet of motorcycling. In addition to the people, places, and events that make up the American motorcycling experience, the magazine offers in-depth stories on the legislative issues that affect everyone who rides.

The AMA's headquarters in Pickerington, Ohio, is also home to the Motorcycle Hall of Fame Museum, where visitors can see a collection of vintage bikes and informative displays showcasing the beautiful designs and remarkable technologies that have placed motorcycles at the leading edge of the transportation industry.

If it's motorcycling, the AMA is very likely involved in it.

American Motorcyclist Association
13515 Yarmouth Drive
Pickerington, Ohio 43147
Toll free: (800) AMA-JOIN
(614) 856-1900
Fax: (614) 856-1920
Web: http://www.ama-cycle.org

MOTORCYCLE RIDERS FOUNDATION

The Motorcycle Riders Foundation (MRF) is a Washington, DC–based Motorcycle Rights Organization (MRO). It maintains a full-time office in Washington, DC, and works nationwide with motorcyclists and MROs to ensure that when motorcycle-related legislation comes up in the U.S. Congress, the motorcyclist's voice is heard.

The MRF is a grass-roots organization, not financially tied to any motorcycle industry interests or legal firms. The MRF was started in 1988 by motorcyclists, and continues to be run by motorcyclists. All financial support for the organization is generated from membership dues, donations from state motorcyclists' rights organizations, and motorcyclists' rights seminars.

The MRF was involved in the 1998 repeal of the national helmet law mandate upon the states. It assisted in the repeal of the national speed limit. It was instrumental in having language inserted in the 1996 Health Care Reform Bill that ensures that you will not be dropped from your health care coverage simply because you ride a motorcycle.

But the job is not over. As you read this, there are those in Washington who are trying to reverse all that has been accomplished in motorcyclists' rights, and without your help they just might succeed. You can help by joining the MRF (and your local state MRO) and help protect your rights in Washington, DC.

Motorcycle Riders Foundation
P.O. Box 1808
Washington, DC 20013-1808
(202) 546-0983
Fax: (202) 546-0986
Web: http://www.mrf.org

Bobby Tramontin on his first customized motorcycle at the Union Valley TT Race Track in New Foundland, New Jersey, circa the late 1940s.

THE MOTORCYCLE SAFETY FOUNDATION

The Motorcycle Safety Foundation (MSF) is a national, not-for-profit organization promoting the safety of motorcyclists with programs in rider training, operator licensing, and public information. Since its inception in 1973, the foundation has supported state and independent programs in training over one million students to ride more safely. The MSF is sponsored by the U.S. distributors of BMW, Ducati, Harley Davidson, Honda, Kawasaki, Suzuki, and Yamaha motorcycles.

To find the MSF RiderCourse nearest you, call (800) 446-9227. Several states now consider that successfully completing an approved MSF Rider-Course is equivalent to passing a motorcycle operator licensing road test. For more information, check with your state motor vehicle department.

Always wear protective gear:

- helmet
- over-the-ankle boots
- gloves
- goggles/face shield
- long pants
- long-sleeved shirt/jacket

Read your owner's manual and prepare your vehicle.

Know your limitations:

- personal
- vehicle
- environment

Know the state and local laws.

Ride aware—avoid accidents and injury.

Don't drink and ride.

The Motorcycle Safety Foundation
2 Jenner Street
Suite 150
Irvine, CA 92618-3806
(949) 727-3227
Web: http://www.msf-usa.org

INDEX

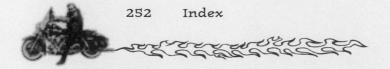

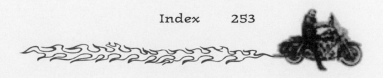

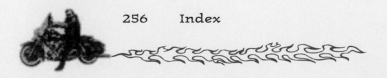